Chance A Fine Thing

By
Kate Draper

ISBN: 978-1-916820-03-6

Chapter Index:

PART ONE

PART TWO.

PART THREE

PART FOUR

PART FIVE

circa1938

Nana, Kate Draper,

(1888-1980)

The person who taught me the importance of stories

PART ONE

OPENING WINDOWS

CHAPTER ONE

For all want or reason, a book is essentially, a logical portrayal of a story set out in an anticipated order; namely, a beginning, followed by a middle, and perhaps, most importantly an end. Enter the *Character* procured to narrate or become the story, effectively helping the reader to link themselves to the plot, by describing each new scene and so providing the story with a recognisable placement – thus ultimately binding each section of the tale together.

Narrative and dialogue combine as ingredients to enhance the integrity of this verbal soup which is effectively being served. Too much and the story becomes over-salty, too little and it begins to lack the essence which the pallet desires. I begin with an undefined character, for that is surely what you would prefer? - a person left to the imagination. For if I were to exaggerate their description, you might be deprived of utilising your own thoughts and ideas. Now finally, a descriptive setting needs to follow allowing you an introduction to the first scene within the book. Your imagination will be enhanced and all being well, you will be able to superimpose my character onto this imagery before both of you finally become acquainted. A private immersion.

Just a word of guidance, when you meet my character, they will be in a crowd; at present they have no name and of course no recognisable features. But remember you don't want to be underestimated in your ability to form your own explicit images. You are intelligent; you have a spirited mind. Your keenness to use your internal processing and your lateral thinking, stand you in good stead. There is good reason to believe that you will recognise this person instantly, the moment that you begin to take up the space of their shadow.

You will hopefully remain in good company, for remember that other readers will be embarking with you too on this word-full journey, through numerous and various temperate settings, where, undoubtedly, before long I will be able to assuage your appetite for the unknown character and allow you to feel the fulfilment of having embraced the hidden one, who seemingly knows all.

Remember they see you and I have already acquainted them with you. They wanted to be told unlike yourself - you wanted the mystery, intrigue; the suspense and thrill, because it is your human nature, and so, that is indeed what I have conveniently ordered for your delight and pleasure.

Place your napkin, unfolded upon your lap, for I am about to serve you a feast of words. But please if your realisation and imagination are starved at any point, promise that you will close my book straight away and never tell another soul the secret that you may already know. For every story lies within our imaginations and that is, perhaps, ultimately where it should remain!

If, however, you should prefer to continue through all adversity and therefore reach the end, we will no doubt, eventually come to share a mutual ingredient within our pools of knowledge. We may feel an intense telepathy between our paths of thinking, or we may continue as opposing magnetic points - never journeying mindfully together but nevertheless, appreciating the forces that exist between our plains of thought.

However, I trust that you will use your manners and etiquette in order to consume this story as you would a culinary delight. For it is indeed rude to begin the first set course without the intention of eventually reaching the seventh or even the eighth, maybe! Would you please sit up straight and hold your elbows in, while you inhale and capture the odours that ride surreptitiously on the air that surrounds you. Hold your body still and let your enhanced senses transcend you to a welcoming scene, though you are far from home, I hope that you will soon warm to the essence of charm that envelops you, right now. Stay alert to this state of mind, accept its calmness without discourse, trust me that this is status quo personified, for when individuals question minds and the pendulum begins to swing, this feeling is the embodiment of compos mentis.

Your hors d'oeuvres is now served …a warm atmosphere of tempting delights attract the olfactory nerve - Moroccan cuisine, maybe? Egyptian tobacco - expensive, certainly not your everyday Camel brand. Feel the shimmer of a tropical evening's breeze upon your shoulders, *Ladies,* and across the nape of your necks, *Gentleman,* that sensuous area, that when enticed, never fails to induce the raising of a hair or two; surrounding palm trees react similarly their leaves twitching nervously.

Hear the music, imitating the snake charmer's flute. The cadences echoed by the slurred quavers, dancing around the convulsive candlelight. Like the artist's brush they display colourful images of an emotional scene that nestles deep within your memory. Occasionally the images link in harmony with the translucent notes and you feel a tear emerge from the corner of your right eye, - the eye that always cries first.

A woven seat lies beneath you. Uncomfortable but welcome. A cushion of sweat settles between your clothing; you shift your body slightly, but discretely so that your movement will not be mistaken for a sudden restlessness. This evening holds vibrant bewitching illusions that you feel are not to be missed. The kind of evening that epitomises, the spell of Africa. Let no one become misguided by your bodily reactions and their correlated affects.

Please remove your elbows from the table. Your first course is approaching - you are served with a delicate crisp white wine that you intriguingly sample. The welcome juice touches your lips, a virginal kiss, sensual and new. Your calm hand connects to the cool stem of the fluted vessel as if engaged in an endearing handshake. Enjoy each course, meeting rich and welcoming tastes. Wash away each, with various fermentation of the vineyard's offspring. With your napkin wipe away the signs of debris from your languid lips. Not so easy to cancel, are the hot spicy remnants, which are now tracing along the serpent-like channels to your salivary glands. Your mouth is ablaze, as are your senses and your mind. In differing ways receptors are awakened, and at this moment, every part of you is conscious.

You cherish this evening for its naturalness and empowerment and ultimately you are stimulated by its mood. Regard your surroundings. You have now reached your fifth course and glass. Your vision is becoming a little distorted. Don't be put off for you are still in full control. Nothing has slipped from your grasp not physically or mentally. And your spoken word is still coherent to those around you. These are your Friends, and no one is looking to fault you or catch you out. Your un-reserve is now slowly colliding with your inhibitions and the combined forces relieved, to provide an explosion of free talk and comical innuendo. Laughter erupts from around the table, though it feels that this laughter is attached in some way to the musical notes that surround you from all the corners of the courtyard. A tumultuous laughter, that resounds in a pounding rhythm of fever and excitement.

You open your heart to these sounds, and raising your face to the darkened skies, the Arabian night opens like a box of jewels before your eyes. Each bracelet of stars, blazing and perfect set out in nature's Cartier box. The beguiling backdrop of the night's drawn curtain adding to the perfection of this fascinating window display. Feel encapsulated by these charms, for these are the moments that remain as memories. The memories that remain when all else is gone. Hold this moment carefully in the hands of your mind. Grasp its beauty fast and secure. Clench it without remittance before all is forgotten; for memory and emotion are closely linked and when all else is gone, you will hear this music and remember this night.

I will whisper in your ear, for I am still here. Listen to me as I perform my last task as your author. For I have begun your story and set you a scene. Your character will be with you shortly. But please we have so far omitted dialogue and you must feel permitted to speak whenever you wish, for to feel part of the story is supposedly what every reader craves.

My notes tell me that too much dialogue will ruin my story; too little and you will feel detached. So please be kind to me. Do not ask too many questions, and do not acquaint with too many strangers, or my words will become distorted, unreal and most of all, undeniably, confusing. Ultimately, if you follow this course, my book will be rejected. Please! I have reached the publishers' desk; do not spoil this chance for us. I know you can work this for me. So, will you do that which is wisest? Take my story from me, and place it in the folds of your pocket, and when you feel that it is right, move with it so that it moves with you. Keep a tight hold of its contents when you are troubled and listen carefully if you should hear this quiet whisper in your ear. Now, ask your first question, to the gentleman across the table to your right.

You see him, don't you? The one whose glass-stem is greased from his constant grasp. Yes, that's him! the dark featured one whose eyes have been shaded from your vision by the brim of his wide chapeau. The kind faced one, whose profile has been on view to you, throughout the evening, whilst his attentions have been sworn towards the young female sat immediately to his right. You have been watching her all night, her slender arms conducting the orchestration of the stars as she gesticulates in time to her words. Her voice has been difficult to hear and her conversation a little hard to follow. But her fingers have carved letters upon the night sky and in some unknown and uncertain way you feel that you have understood, in the way only the fluent linguist could. Yet the words of a creature this beautiful are merely secondary to the language of the body from which those words are expressed. Her torso wrapped in midnight blue satin, would be of envy to the night if the night too had emotion and the virtue of awareness. Those thinly strapped shoulders have borne themselves to the airless conditions without response. No glimmer of sweat, or a shiver. Her body abandoned by the effects of physiological reproach. Her breasts have lain comfortably hidden beneath that loose fitting garment; veiled in a secretly enticing guise. More subtle, perhaps, than the cleavage which she could have exposed. Your eyes travel down the slender ravines of the cloth that tenderly holds such close intercourse with her body. Her shoes remain hidden beneath the linen of the tablecloth. You wonder for a second, if these are the only necessities of clothing that this woman wears, for the heat is oppressing. As your thoughts wander, you feel the sweat of your own physiology responding, and arousal rolls through your body like the waves responding to the lunar pull.

Bring yourself to attention if you would. For I have further things to say. Remember that it may be dangerous to let your mind wander so far in anticipation of what is real and what is duly unreal. Set yourself on an even keel, for it is the unprepared human who is thrown from their balance in circumstances such as these. Don't let these minor distractions turn you away from the sound of my voice. It is important that you listen when you hear my whispers and reflect carefully upon my words. For the saner mind, is without doubt, the one, that knows its closeness to madness.

Now remember you have that question to pose. I doubt the gentleman will be surprised, a question or two from your cautious lips will only help to seal a newfound friendship. You have already engaged in small talk a while, and he has seemingly shown a liking for your conversation. Perhaps, a similarity of interests between you both has already been discovered. It's quite possible even in this short space of time, that your body chemistries have linked ethereal hands.

But now we must recreate the mood. First look up and place yourself back under that amazing sky. See those stars…and you will surely feel it soon, that warm breeze approaching again; silently stirring through the otherwise stillness of the night. Its whisper will be as my voice, a guiding force between the unseen and the unknown, calling to you softly. Listen carefully and follow its persuasion.

Oh, wait a moment, please, for there is just one thing more I have to say. My notes tell me that I must have a 'hook', something to capture your attention, that, which will keep you gripped to the moment - an object to focus on, perhaps? - something that will forcibly turn the page for you. I'm trying hard to think of one, but I feel I am too slow. For already I feel you slipping away from me, your mind is wandering, searching for something to lure you. - you have read so many other books and have been fascinated too many times before. This is becoming hard for me. Your mind is working faster than mine. You just want more detail…more impression…. More reality!

Well, I have tried. The rest now, is up to you. For he who plays with fire, may well relish the pangs and passions, which it procures. I hand control to you, for you seem the wiser, whereas I am merely and shall remain, but a whisper. And so, I whisper -

'Ask your question!'

CHAPTER TWO

"Which part of England, do you come from?"

He averts his gaze from the woman beside him. And slowly turns his face towards you, regarding you through a pair of striking azure eyes. The slight hint of a struggled smile lifts the corners of his taut lips as he begins to raise his left hand towards that hat. With a delicate, but clumpy hand he grasps the top of the article and lifts it clear from his tousled hair. Placing the hat down upon the table, he takes pains to cock it at such an angle, so as to display the absence of its once attached label. Possibly Armani or maybe Gautier? What reverse Psychology would prefer him not to allure you to his expensive tastes, or advertise the merchandise, which he prefers to afford?

He notices you in the fashion of a man who seemingly knows everyone, a person who has mastered their homework; someone who has a clear realisation of the thoughts, beliefs and ambitions of those present - and therefore - the Charming Intimidator. One who could make you feel weak and uneasy if you didn't have the presence of mind to own up to having confidence too. Weaklings suffer in the wake of such a gentleman, but of course he is the man to be seen with and everybody wants to make his acquaintance, even if only with his shadow. You have won a moment of his undivided attention; many would beg for this occasion. Some have waited a lifetime already, You, however, fulfil a momentary adage. - being that you are in the right place at just the right time.

His austere gaze remains with you, and you exempt yourself mentally from accepting too rapidly, the assumed smile that you see in front of you. You have seen it on the face of too many others before. That perpetuating illusiveness that makes you feel that you have to obey, without being allowed to give credibility to your own persuasion. Maturity has made you less gullible; you continue to think rationally, despite the wine. This man creates an illusion of tremendous power by means of his stare and his charisma; yet underneath his designer haute couture, he is nothing but a mere mortal, another simple human like you yourself. Besides you have seen poorer paid men dress themselves, in just the same manner to impress. Many owing several months' worth of wages in order to accommodate their purchases. Despite the smell of profound wealth, no man has ever harmed you with their fortune. Let this not be the first!

He begins to answer your seemingly mundane question. It was a question that perhaps you hadn't needed to ask. But somehow you just felt intent on making small talk, for the sake of it. Besides, the table had begun to quieten, noticeably. Maybe tiredness had caused conversation to reach a lull. These moments of impending silence are always uncomfortable on such occasions, and you were only trying to prevent an unfashionable occurrence. You know you have done well, as your answer is delivered.

"Twickenham…. That is originally, Twickenham!" He smiles, as if the thought of his origins provides him with a sense of comfort and equable strength.

"Yes, that's where I was born, but I only lived there for a short period of my life. My parents moved when I was four."

The pattern of his face now changes, as he begins to remember the earlier years of his childhood. Memories of these times, often receive a more evocative appraisal, following the consumption of wines and spirits. You can see that his inhibitions are becoming spontaneously rebuked as he begins to link his thoughts to the past. Like yourself, you wonder if the persuasion of the music has connected him more emotionally to these times. But this is a strong man - surely, he cannot be influenced so easily by such means? Is there not a thicker skin encasing this man's soul, than one that seems so easily torn by sentimentality? Surely, he should not display this weaker side so readily.

You wonder if others have seen this too, surely you can't be the only one to have opened this man's heart. So many questions… Yet, no answers! Except the personification of the man in front of you - who now continues…..

"I remember my childhood well. Well, I remember snippets, that is. Odd little things that happened that seem to have remained in my memory. Some of the pictures that I recall are far more vivid sometimes than recent happenings. I find that peculiar. Don't you?"

Remaining silent you sense that some questions are not asked in order to be answered. He therefore continues without your interjection of agreement and appears to look increasingly more intent, as he poses his first direct question to you. He faces you, like the opponent, who is just about to serve a clean ace into your court; and knows it. That wicked, unhallowed, determined look, trained to withhold all recrimination. You hold your breath slightly and suddenly begin to wonder why you set out to engage in this conversation in the first place. Your opening question was obviously a good one. Though you never imagined that it would be so effective in gaining the attention of someone, normally so allusive to such simple *dit passé*. Neither did you believe that this conversation would have gained ground so fast in such a brief capsule of time. Suddenly the slowness of the evening's tempo seems to have awakened itself to a livelier movement. The rhythm of your heart and voice now seems to have gained momentum with the surrounding accompaniment of the entertaining orchestra. You no longer feel detached in any way from all that surrounds you; people and atmosphere being at one with you.

Others party on, as he now asks you. "And where is it that you are from?"

"London, Kensington to be precise." You elaborate on the exact location, before you realise that you are adding unnecessary detail to your homes' whereabouts. Suddenly you feel that you have given a more than sufficient answer to this enquiring question. You may be thousands of miles away at present, from your country of origin, but the world is but a small place. Paths cross, coincidental situations occur every day. Tomorrow this man could be back in London with you, continuing this conversation on your personal home ground. In your favourite near-by club. On your own front doorstep. By your………Who knows? Yet comfortingly, you feel there is an undercurrent of charm displayed in his voice… theatrical perhaps? It certainly seems more enforced than just the acquirement of a public-school boy's dulcet tones, a contrived linguistic portal. And as he continues you feel more certain that this is definitely a man playing to an audience. You listen to his crisp tones as he answers.

"Oh - How lucky!"

Is he patronising you? You continue to wonder.

"Such a lovely area Kensington, I tried to find property there myself many years ago. But free hold is so hard to come by and I would have hated to have had to rent. In fact, I wouldn't have even given it consideration."

Gratefully you let him skate over this area of interest. Hopefully he will not enquire as to how you acquired your own property. You may have to be a little stingy with the truth if he does. You wait to see, as he continues with his repartee.

"I have always felt so at home in the city. Not just London, funnily enough, Paris, New York, even here in Haifa. The closeness of people around me makes me feel protected. I love the hustle and bustle, the movement, the noise and the excitement. Whenever I am away from this existence my life seems so empty and, in some ways, frightening, for suddenly I feel that I have nothing to hold on to. Does that sound strange and ridiculous to you?"

You hesitate to answer, but this time you feel that there is perhaps a need for a reply. You know that you have understood and can relate, to some extent, to what has been said, but your understanding comes from a different experience of city life. One you have had to learn to cope with. Spontaneity and naturalness have never come to you in the same way as an opportune moment has delivered them to your curious interloper.

"I have differing views to yours, though, yes, I do feel that I understand. The city behaves like a mother figure to me in some respects. It provides me with all the nourishment I need for survival, but sometimes when it is harsh and procuring, I also find it to be a little threatening too. I don't suppose you would understand what I mean by that. It even sounds a little peculiar to me now that I have said it."

"You explain yourself well and I think you have a remarkable perception of what you know and what you don't. There is an old philosopher who would have considered you very wise."

"Really?"

"Oh yes, definitely." He stretches his arms a little as he searches for the quote in mind. "Yes, I remember now, something to the effect of, - 'Wisest is the man who knows what he does not know.' Ha, Ha, A good one that, don't you think? … Can't quite remember who said it now, perhaps it was Socrates. Oh well. Maybe it will come back to me, you never know. I have a head full of quotes, but do you think I can ever remember who said them? Don't suppose that it matters really. I could spend my entire life worrying about their origins, instead of learning to understand the philosophy, which is by far the more important thing."

"Where does your interest in the subject, come from?"

"Heavens, I have no idea. I've never thought about that." He again laughs to himself as he ponders in his reply. "I don't think that it matters really. There doesn't have to be an answer to everything, after all. Does there?"

This time it is your turn to ponder, before proceeding.

"Not unless you feel that it is absolutely necessary to have one."

"Then I think you are in agreement with me." He pauses momentarily. "Not many people ever are. This must be a first. Do you know I seem to spend so much of my time in heated discussion that I almost forget how it feels to actually find someone who agrees with me? I think I could get to like it! - Did you do it purposefully, to avoid confrontation or was it spontaneous?"

He sounds rather interested in what your reply will be. He has obviously not encountered too many genuine people before in his life. He seems so desperate to understand you. Let him continue believing you, after all you are doing well in your actor's role.

"Perhaps I answer questions according to how I feel at the time. Sometimes I feel that there is more need to be confrontational than others. Tonight, I feel mellow and at ease, and so therefore I have no necessity to engage in an argument. Don't you feel that way yourself, sometimes?"

"I suppose I'd like to think that way. To be honest, I was unaware that I could. It's not something that you give thought to, too often, but now that I am, perhaps you're making me wonder about myself. How extraordinary! I don't think anyone has ever had this effect on me before. Mind you. It's probably the alcohol, making me feel…. What did you say earlier? -Mellow, yes that's it Mellow. What an American expression! You're not American, are you?"

"No I'm not. But I have watched a lot of American films and serials. Things like NYPD Blues, Homicide - that sort of thing. I think sometimes, I extract words that I hear and use them occasionally when I get bored with the English language. I don't suppose there's any harm in it. Maybe it's a bit out of character, but then sometimes it's a good thing to be different. Who wants a predictable person around them all the time?"

"Perhaps someone, who's a bit nervous and doesn't like surprise. Somebody, who likes everything on an even keel, maybe?"

"Really - I don't think I know many people like that. Or maybe I just don't know the people around me too well."

"You should always watch your back. Never assume that you know everyone just by one encounter. Be cautious. Ask questions. Pretend you are interested in the person. Your charm and intrigue will always flatter, even the coldest of characters."

"But I actually think I use those tools quite frequently."

"Ah - but not tonight! For, so far, you have asked no intriguing questions of me. Yet we have been talking for some minutes now. In fact, you have not even asked my name. You are obviously interested in me as you have been drawn to watching me, on and off throughout the evening. Yet you have not asked who I am. Is that, perhaps because you already know? Anyway, I must put my own mind at rest, and ask you your name, that is if you have one!"

You feel the breeze pick up around you. The floral leaves present in the table display begin to flutter and a petal or two become dislodged from the parent flower. You watch as nature is moved by the small command of mother natures' voice. But is it her that calls? For listen…Listen carefully, is it not my voice you hear?

-Choose whether you give a fictitious name, the decision is yours. This is in your control. He'll probably believe whatever you tell him now. You seem to have won him over. But stay on your guard. This man is smart!

"*Didi*, that's the name I'm known by. My surnames' Davidson you see. Sometimes I prefix it with my initials. M.R. It's confusing when I announce myself on the phone to people. They think they hear me say Mister, and of course other ears, hear me say Emma. It keeps them guessing - I like to do that to people, though it might be a nuisance for those who prefer an 'even keel', as you mentioned earlier. I must take those folk into consideration in future. Isn't it amazing how sometimes you just have preconceived ideas of what others do and how they think. I must frustrate an awful lot of people by my strange habits. Never mind it wouldn't do if we were all the same. Oh! I'm sorry! I'm frustrating you with all this nonsense?"

"No, not at all." He smiles affectionately in your direction, "On the contrary, I find what you say very intriguing."

He begins to re-light his cigar, as he searches to regain the string of the conversation. …You notice that his cigar has failed to respond to the kiss of his lighter and has subsequently remained extinguished. He appears not to notice. His mind seems too intent on furthering the conversation.

"Well. How do you do DiDi! You have already stolen a question from me, by explaining the origin of your name. But it is intriguing all the same."

He begins to draw on his cigar, responding to its lack of activity, by retrieving his lighter from his breast pocket.

"Now that you have let me share your secret, I must introduce myself or you will think me impolite. My name is also a secret, for most people know me as Professor Burlington, but to my true friends I introduce myself, as Wayne." His hand shoots out in your direction.

"Pleased to meet you Professor Wayne!" Your voice transforms to a charming but emphatic persuasion. Applying the informal to the formal, is where you feel at your most comfortable.

"The pleasure is all mine. But there is still one thing that intrigues me. What is it that you do? And what brings you here to the conference?"

"I am a philosopher, Professor Wayne."

"Intriguing! Where do you study?"

"On the street"

"The street? DiDi what do you mean, I have never encountered a 'Street' Philosopher before. Is this a new branch of study that I have never heard of? Or is it perhaps something that you are setting up for your thesis? Please tell me more."

"I have no qualifications Professor Wayne."

"Really? - How unusual!"

"My philosophy works on the principle that to have common sense and the constant access to is far beyond the worth of a few letters on a piece of paper."

"Well, well, Didi. If I didn't know you better, I would feel a little insulted by your remark as indeed would many other scholars."

"But Professor Wayne incredible though it may seem to you a lot of philosophers like myself feel quite insulted that, because people like you have worthy letters to attach to their names, they see those that haven't as being unimaginably barren."

"If that is truly how you feel. Why are you here tonight? Surely you must feel revulsion towards the company that surrounds you this evening."

"No! No! Not at all. That really isn't true, Professor Wayne. My friend Rachel Rosenway, who was lecturing at the conference earlier today, invited me along. Her family is from Haifa, and she wanted to combine this business trip with a long-awaited family reunion. Unfortunately…"

"Oh Rachel! Yes, I have met with her at several meetings, recently. I noticed that she left hurriedly a little while ago. Was she alright?"

"Well, that was what I was just about to say. She unfortunately felt unwell at the start of the meal. I think it may be the aftermath of having been so nervous before the talk. She's been worrying about it for days."

"She needn't have been. Her subject was extremely intriguing. No one was looking to catch her out for being nervous we were only looking to be enlightened!"

"I know. I tried to explain that to her myself. Anyway, she was keen for me to stay on here, this evening, even though I knew nobody else. She felt I wouldn't want to miss the chance of talking with some of the other guests."

"I see…" He slowly begins to frown as he questions you further. "So, you have no real interest in the confederation as such?"

"Professor Wayne you are making me feel like an intruder. and I don't feel that I am, for I have many interests in your concerns. That is why Rachel encouraged me to come along. She felt that I believed in a lot of the ideas, which have been discussed today."

"Why the interest Didi? What do you really know about all this?"

"A lot more than those that don't know, Professor… A lot more."

CHAPTER THREE

The imprint of the evening is slowly beginning to fade. Recollecting many conversations that took place, your mind connects intently on the words that passed between you and the professor. It has created such awareness within you that you want to relive it word by word until you are certain that you too, have made an equal impression, in his eyes. You feel that you may have done so. The suggestion of accompanying Professor Wayne and the rest of his party on a tour of Jerusalem tomorrow makes you feel very worthy. He really didn't feel he'd spoken enough to you, yet you must have chatted for an hour or so at least, last evening. You couldn't find the means to refuse the invitation when it came last night. Besides you would have been letting Rachel down, had you not accepted - She's relying on you remember!

Looking out across the harbour, you lean casually against the railings of Rachel's balcony. Her family home stands high on the hills leading out of Haifa and boasts a most spectacular view. The midday sun has stolen the shadows that earlier lay across the building. You adjust your scarf over your head, though it does little to protect you from the intense heat of this Israeli afternoon. You appreciate why the trip to Jerusalem has been effectively planned for tomorrow. You doubt that many of last night's guests have risen any sooner than you this morning - or afternoon as it happens to be now. You are sure that you heard the midday strike; a faint voice from a muezzin in his minaret, his far away call, summoning the faithful to prayer.

Well, those drinks are certainly lying heavy upon you. You still feel a little dizzy. Though, thank goodness the nausea has at last parted company with you. The strong heat, to which you are unaccustomed, intensifies around you, and bears you little of the air, which you are so desperately in need of. Yet you remain at this vantage-point, surveying this holy land which lies framed before you, and you examine, contrast and keenly extract from it, all its wonder, impression and energy. You stand contained in this wonderment, as if perhaps you were Moses himself surveying the Promised land.

Far below the tiny ships and boats, penetrate the waves, leaving faint trails etched on the water, as they pass in and out of the harbour. The sun glistening on their backs, disguises them, creating the illusion of small garden creatures sliding this way and that, for the purpose of moving seemingly to nowhere, then back again. The picture last evening had been so different. Each ship had been encompassed by the darkness, and the light that it had thrown around itself had betrothed it to the night sky. The two had then become mirrored together, sea and sky, so that no horizon had been distinguishable, until the sun had revisited at the morning's dawn.

It reminds you of your own fate some years ago, when you too felt contained within that sheet of blackness. Your mind covered over by the nights' intrigue. Picturing the signs of what lay beyond. Little specks of light at the end of the tunnel. Encouraging but not assuring enough. No hint of a familiar dawn, approaching - that ever constant dawn. It's existence so important; in order to strike a balance between mind and soul. Without that reassurance would the scenes of beauty and intensity bestowed upon us by the night, be made quite so beautiful? For the mind when darkened becomes an immortal place to exist.

You continue now, to follow the ships through the darkened lenses of your sun spectacles. Impressive movements have been made since your thoughts began to wander a few moments ago. New boats have suddenly appeared as if earlier boats have been recapitulated upon the scene. But when was that precise moment that they first came into view? -Why is it that we so seldom see the moment of change? These saccades of nature continue to mystify us and by the time we recognise them another change has already occurred.

Your eyes follow the bold line of the coast. Then placing your gaze upon the countryside beneath you, you start to trace out familiar features. You watch as in the distance a moving object winds its way along an invisible path. A small train only just distinguishable - it moves in the guise of a hungry caterpillar searching intensely for its next meal. Slowly it continues unremittingly, in search of its sanctuary and reward. As its path leads behind a mass of trees and green, you wonder where its outcome will be. Your attention is not sufficient enough to provide an answer to your curiosity. Already you have begun to remember those times in the past; those times when you felt like that hungry caterpillar. Tearing along different paths both mindfully and physically, believing that there was something beyond. – something, somewhere that would satisfy you; yet your guidance came from nowhere only in the form of faith and belief.

Those moments of cruel anxiety that used to encompass you. Those times when you felt that the routes of your rational thoughts had been barricaded. No human can exist that way. Yet what else could you do, but sit, wait and endure?

Your present freedom lies before you, personified in where you stand now, in the presence of an historic land, which although it has altered little in its physical appearance through the passage of time, has nevertheless grown in strength, maturity, and learning; and has never failed to hold importance to those who embrace its existence.

Hear me now, for I am with you again. I have no current or breath of air to travel on at present. This atmosphere in which you find yourself has denied me much source of energy, to reach you, but I hope I have your attention enough to connect with you. I have been watching whilst you have been wondering and I feel the emotion and spirit with which you attach yourself to the past. You are wise to segregate yourself from dwelling too hard and long on these curiosities, of thought. To remember is not to forget, but forgiveness is by far the harder persuasion. It is this that you must learn to do. Forgive yourself each day for what happened then, for it was only your innocence and naivety that caused you such pain. With understanding comes control, and that is ultimately what you strive for. You have done well! I say that not to patronise you, but to make you aware and ever mindful of the fact that you have come through many battles, and because of this, a war has been fought and won.

Stay a while with your thinking and your philosophy and continue to lead your mind onward and forward. Your strength has in it a property for teaching and healing the bent and twisted minds of other mortals. I leave you now to your thoughts.

As you stand and admire the gallery of scenes before you, your thoughts rest for a moment on the noises in the narrow streets below. A humid air of putrid smells engulfs your nasal senses, but still, you make no attempt to leave your lookout. Swarms of young children bustle around a maze of avenues, their swarthy complexions standing out against the Jerusalem stone that decorates each building. In tiny corners where the sun's rays cannot seep through, only the children's voices are visible their tiny bodies lost within those rare shadows.

You smile to yourself. These were the games that your childhood presented to you….Those incredible days of fun! - Days when the sun was always shining, and even the clouds and rain danced with a powerful hidden energy that transferred itself to you, in a handshake of chemical exchanges. Those were the days when everything was real. Nothing held a hidden meaning and there was a literal translation to everything that you saw and did. Apart from an ordered list of prayers, which you carried out joyously every night; each part of the day was spontaneous. Every child has a need to feel in control of their space in the world. Your need, in order to carry out this task, was to say your prayers each night; in order to pray for the souls of departed relatives; to pray for the sick and the suffering and to pray for others around you whom you loved. At the age of two, this had taken, but a few minutes, by the tender age of seven, it had amounted to half an hour! But the important fact was that you felt totally in control, and that the world could deal you no harm, because you had tended to your prayers.

You realise how selfish you have been over the years, for many of those prayers have been said for yourself, and no one else. You have been well favoured, for most of those prayers have since been answered but not in the fashion that you would have necessarily intended. It is obvious to you now that most prayers are often answered in this stranger way.

How effective are the prayers, you wonder, of those that fail to pray at all? Perhaps they just wish, maybe that's easier. For surely a wish can only be answered or ignored.

Yes! Perhaps wishing would have been easier. Things always make themselves seem so much simpler when considered in hindsight, what a wonderful virtue it is.

CHAPTER FOUR

The new day begins with a glorious sunrise. Stretching out across the skies in streaks of fiery coloured ribbons etched on a glorious background of blue; painted by the dawns' finest brush the lack of texture giving rise to a quality unlike any other. This natural masterpiece stands before you and held to its centre, the sun stretches her arms, yawns and casts her morning's breath over the land, calling the resting world from its sleep.

You sit on the old bus as it trundles along through the streets of the newer town. Then leaving Haifa your route takes you along a modern open road, where high banks of wasteland align the route, with unremitting repetition; interspersed with a few Jewish settlements, marking themselves with the sudden appearance of little two-storey buildings huddled together. Then as quickly as they are sighted, they are out of view. Your attention is duly drawn away from this panorama, by the tour-guide, as he cordially welcomes you and your fellow passengers aboard the bus. First the driver is introduced.

"This is Gideon, who is your driver today. Please join me in wishing him a good morning in the normal customary way – Say, 'Salaam' to Gideon."

You join a chorus of Salaams, which pass down the bus.

"Salaam" Gideon replies and that is all he is heard to say for the rest of the journey, as Joseph, your guide proceeds to take centre stage. Having introduced himself he then, with considerable affirmation begins to recite the history of the Jewish plight, allowing you to travel back many centuries in order to appreciate the hardships that his race have had to face throughout the passage of time.

"We have become known as swindlers and cheats." He adds. "But when we first returned to our homeland after the wars, our homeland had been taken. Because we did not worship as Christians, we were not allowed to make a living easily, we could not take on a trade or reputable job. We could only work the best way we knew how by handling money. That is why many of us became moneylenders, and were able to make fast money, we had the gift or so it seemed to others." He smiles dubiously, to collect the reactions of the passengers before proceeding with his patter.

"A Christian man once asked a Jew how it was that he made money so quickly. Is it a gift from God? He had asked. And the Jew had replied."

'I know a Jewish friend who sells headless tuna fish for ten shillings. They have become so fashionable that he sells hundreds every day.'

'Really!' Replied the Christian. 'But down the road there is a market where Tuna fish are sold with their heads still on, for eight shillings.'

'Ah!' Replied the Jew. 'How quickly you catch on!'

…You sit listening quietly to the continuous repartee of this enigmatic character. Occasionally he switches to Swedish in order to extend his knowledge and entertaining jokes to a small party of students from Stockholm, invited on board earlier, in order to fill a few empty seats on the vehicle. Your ears close off at the sound of this foreign tongue and you begin again, capturing the scenery, from your viewpoint on the left-hand side of the bus. Your feeling of nausea has been alleviated a little, by sitting in this position, as Rachel had said it would. You haven't resorted to placing copper pennies in the palms of your hands to enhance the same affect. You thought you would hold that one in reserve in case the journey became more bumpy or windy.

As you pass through the centre of Tel Aviv, Joseph switches his conversation between his favoured two languages: explaining more history whilst pointing out several places of interest. As you leave the city, he disconnects his microphone and for the next hour continues a pleasant exchange of Yiddish, with Gideon.

The tall modern buildings of the city now left behind, your view changes, to simple farmland, which pushes out to the boundaries of your vision and beyond.

"Enjoying it so far?" Rachel's voice ejects you from your gaze and your reveries. Its commanding tone begs for an answer in the affirmative.

"Yes, indeed I am. I'm a so lucky to have been given this opportunity. Thank you for everything."

"Don't thank me - thank yourself! You were obviously the one that won over the Prof. the other night." She grins infectiously. "I don't know what it was you said or did, but I've never known him react in such a positive manner before. I don't really know the man that well, but from the rumours that I hear; he is never one to give graciously. Always works behind a hidden agenda. Always sees conditions attached to everything that he says and does - seems that you've cracked his outer shell." Rachel now turns to face you, with an even larger grin across her wide but narrow lips. "Well, are you going to tell me what happened, Didi?"

"I would if I knew the answer. I may have come across as a little assertive, but I only asked him some simple questions and answered a few of his."

"Do you think you know him, or understand him?"

"That's hard to say. He doesn't give much away." -You pause, thinking carefully. "Mind you there was a point where he started talking about his childhood that seemed to humanise him a little."

"Goodness me Didi, I never thought the man had a childhood. You're making him seem like a human being.

Don't you just think of some characters as being android like? As if they were just placed on this earth at say - age twenty-five, then just programmed to work?"

"Well, I think Professor Wayne is a little older than twenty-five, Rachel!"

"Oh, I know! Maybe I just think of him as having been an android for the last twenty years!" She gives a very feminine sigh, as if doing her best to defend the civil rights, and beliefs of all other women on the planet. How grateful they might be if they only knew! You realise how men could easily be tarred by the same brush as Professor Wayne, if every woman was as vehemently opposed to their ways as Rachel's demonstrative realism frequently suggested.

Realising, suddenly, that your conversation is taking place in earshot of some of the other members of the party, you suddenly recoil, and try to lower your head behind the headrest of the seat in front. Rachel often loses her decorum in public; in fact, she is quite renowned for it, but you can't afford to upset anyone being that you are effectively the 'uninvited guest'.

Rachel notices you are becoming a little edgy.

"Not feeling so good Didi?"

"No, I'm fine, honest! - I was just trying to listen to what Joseph was saying, I think he mentioned something about the Mount of Olives?"

"Oh, there it is! See that mountain over there?" Rachel points between the passengers on the other side of the bus. "Can you See, Didi?"

Turning your head to the right, your eyes train your vision to follow the mountain along its length. Its flattened top appearing like a table waiting to be laid.

You make no attempt to answer Rachel's question; hoping that your faint nod will be sufficient. You attach your mind to the scenery and charisma of the land that you are passing through. With awe and wonderment, you take a mental photograph of yet another scene from the past.

Open road beckons again. No visual stimulation except the bare and arid land that surrounds you on both sides. Some hours later after a lengthy journey, you finally arrive in the city of Jerusalem. Both mentally and physically you take another photograph; one to place in your memory and one for your album.

Well done! You have advanced a little further upon your journey, but this is indeed a mindful, pursuit, as well as a physical one. Please don't think that all your routes will be as easily pursued, as this one.

CHAPTER FIVE

Disembarking from the bus, you follow the other passengers and conveniently huddle beside the great wall that continues to encompass this biblical city; waiting for Joseph to organise himself for this his 'piece de resistance' – *The tour*! He begins by announcing - how easy it is to lose yourself in the city! Then he continues to reassure you by confirming that the bus will leave without you if you are not back at the set-down point, in time for its departure. His only means of not losing you are contained in the shape of a long stick, which he has produced seemingly from nowhere. On the end of this stick are two items a colourful scarf and a hideously fashioned artificial flower. Joseph is not mocking neither is he laughing. These two items are your only link with escape from the city. You're only lifeline. Later you realise their importance and their ability to stand out not only in the huge crowds, which you later encounter, but also how effectively they display themselves from a distance; for you soon discover the speed with which Joseph is intending to conduct his tour.

On entering through the old gates of the city, you allow yourself to be searched, as is the law, by the patrolling armed Israeli police. Everything is a little daunting, but somehow the sight of Joseph's gregarious rose and silken scarf held at least two foot above the tallest head in the prevailing crowds, provides you and others with some degree of comfort and security. It beckons you and you feel yourself drawn, as you move hastily forwards.

Finding yourself in a large expanse of open space, the crowd having dispersed to left and right, you see immediately ahead of you the 'Wailing Wall'. You realise that the crowds have not dispersed entirely but have amalgamated at the foot of the wall. The abundance of religious noise seeps through between the tightly packed praying pilgrims. Through tear filled eyes they seek the tinniest crack in the rock before them, in which they can tuck their notes of small prayers and messages. You do not feel a need to join in with this ritual, but nevertheless you are amazed at its effect on the people around you. You compromise by touching the wall with your outstretched hand. You feel emotional, but you are not entirely sure why.

Rachel is no longer beside you; you had felt her touching your arm as you first approached the wall, but somehow you became parted in the wake of the people around you. You know that she will not be far, and you take comfort in knowing too, that somewhere behind you, and not too far you hope, Joseph will be holding his totem high. You cope quietly with this situation, and remind yourself how for many years, such occurrences would have been beyond your control and endurance.

You have come far. Yet still waters run deep. When the surface appears to have quelled the undercurrent, beware the strength of the current should it return! As you stand here now commanded and strengthened by the spirit of those around you, try and hold on to this presence of mind. It is there, yet its body is like a greasy surface, where there is little to hold on to when turmoil and chaos rush in. No one wants a status quo that provides a staleness to life and no change at all. But beware the energy, which you constantly search for and energise yourself with. For too much will be extremely hard to bear!

You have listened to me well despite the noise of prayer, which settles on every particle of air about you. It has somehow embodied the pathway of my voice and brought me nearer to you. We are almost one at this time. Your strength is building rapidly, but it is important to secure a firm foundation to build up this fusion between us. We cannot allow slippery surfaces to separate us.

Your thoughts lean back to the present. Suddenly you are swept by a wave of retreating people, as you move backwards away from the wall. There is seemingly no room in which to turn your body completely round, and so you compromise by edging your way sideways like a tiny hermit crab, looking for new shelter before it is preyed upon. You bombard with an opposing wake of others just arriving. Between struggling movements casting you this way and that, you retain your sideways stance. There seems no organisation to this magnificent conglomeration of nations. Yet finally you find yourself once again free enough to spread your arms about you and breathe an air which is alive - once again fresh and fragrant.

"Didi!" A voice seems to call you from nowhere. "Over here!"

You search in the direction of the voice, but you see no one. It is hard to know who the voice belongs to as its sound is not recognisable to you. Then it comes again.

"Didi!" This time it is attached to the caller. You simultaneously hear the call and see……

"Professor Wayne?! I didn't recognise your voice."

"Perhaps it is a little parched from this heat, Didi. It needs a hasty drink. Whilst we were waiting for you, Joseph was suggesting that we all have a break. Give us some time to collect our thoughts. There's a refreshment hut just over there." He points to a small, green-roofed building, beyond the edge of the square. "We were starting to get worried." He continues.

"Worried...Why?"

"Well, you were gone for ages."

"But I was only over at the wall with Rachel."

"Yes!" He looks quizzically at you. "That's what Rachel said. But she met up with the rest of the group half an hour ago, and Joseph did suggest we allow ourselves only fifteen minutes to see the wall." He coughs, further indicating his need for a drink. "This is turning into a bit of a lightening tour, isn't it? I think Joseph is going to have me on my knees by the end of the day and I don't mean praying!"

"Oh, - I think there's worse to come." You recall a conversation earlier this morning, where Rachel had described the narrow-cobbled streets of old Jerusalem built on the steep gradient of mount Zion, its Biblical host. But you remain silently uninformative for fear of upsetting the Professor further. He meanwhile continues…..

"What were you doing at that wall then, Didi? - Were you praying?" His smile vaguely resembles the consistency of one of those smiles which he sold to you the other evening - A mocking smile - a discerning smile. A smile that looks at you in such a way as if to say - 'I know all there is to know about you but do let me know more!'

"I was not praying as such, Professor Wayne. But I did feel quite overwhelmed by the experience, I have to say."

"Are you always overwhelmed so easily? ... And for so long?"

"In answer to your first question … Yes! But I am not sure how to answer the second part of your question at all, for I really was totally unaware how I had been bled so easily by the vortex of that crowd." You pause before continuing, unsure whether you should be sharing too much with this man or in fact whether it is of any relevance to you or him. Sometimes you are guilty of analysing things far deeper than is necessary; could this be yet another of those occasions?

"Sometimes my mind takes to wandering or perhaps I should say wondering, there isn't much difference between the two, at times, surely? … Anyway, I think that's probably what I was doing earlier. I'd lost myself in my own little world for a while and had become oblivious to everything around me. Strange though in some ways I actually felt that my surroundings became more intensified for a while." You begin to hesitate. "Oh, I'm so sorry, I'm boring you again, and I really should have learnt my lesson the other evening. Please forgive me. I mustn't let it happen again!"

"No. Please Didi, don't trouble yourself, there is nothing wrong with what you have been saying - It sounds like a perfectly normal experience to me."

"Perhaps you're only saying that, because you are a Psychologist, Professor Wayne! All Psychologists must like to think that way. Surely even if they don't profess to, knowing all the answers, then at least they must like to think that they understand the reasons!"

"Now who's mocking? - Didi, I may find myself at times expressing myself very impersonally to people. I know that it doesn't go unnoticed by those around me. Unfortunately, it's just the way I am – we all have our faults. But I can assure you Didi; I am not patronising you in any way at all. I find what you say interesting and intriguing. Studying people's *'Thoughts'* is what I do best. What frustrates me, a lot of the time is that some people just don't seem to have any thoughts in their heads; and I don't mean that unkindly. And if they do have any at all, they certainly don't make any attempt to divulge them or share them. To find someone like yourself who openly admits to what they are thinking and shares their thoughts in such a generous way, is a person rarely encountered, and a person truly priceless to humanity."

A few minutes ago, whilst still absorbed in your conversation, you had noticed Rachel and a couple of other members of the group approach from across the square. They had not interrupted your flow of conversation and had kept a small distance from you whilst they too, had indulged in a lengthy exchange. It was this knowledge of presence that you so often appreciated in your friendship with Rachel. No words passed between you and yet the telepathy was enough to allow you both the security and knowledge of each other's company. Rachel would have been worried about you as had the Professor, but as a friend and psychologist she perhaps knows you better than most. At one time you had been sure that she knew you better than even you knew yourself, but that certainly was no longer the case.

In the process of your chatting, the thirsty members of the party have hastened their way towards the watering hole; and are already sat around the small tables adorned with blue and white chequered tablecloths. Somehow the building appears less attractive at close range, but nevertheless still as welcoming. A carafe of water standing sentry-like in the centre of each table, offers adequate thirst quenching for those seated around. However, for a few, a cool, appetising beer is further required to fully satisfy the needs of their parched lips. You join the drinking party. Extra chairs are found for you and the professor, in a free moment of the waiter's time. No doubt he is hoping that his speed will influence you in the expense and range of your order. Unfortunately, he will never know for just as you taste your first sip from the cool complimentary glass of water set out on the table, Joseph's stern opera begins from across the way. His solitary rose, still clasped to his wooden stick, waves feverishly to and throw, in time to the rhythm of his words, not unlike the conductor's baton; only this conductor is not standing still, and his musicians are at this moment frantically organising themselves and hurriedly trying to catch up with the beat - Joseph is away! No moderato to this mans' performance. Everything that he does seems to conduct itself with a farcical fortissimo manner. Yet you can see that below the surface this man has a calm and emotional belief in the world. His family are his entrance and exit to life; all else is superfluous. Except right at this moment nothing else matters to him apart from this tour and the party of people who are to follow him like the pied piper of Hamelin through, those yet undiscovered streets, of old Jerusalem.

"Looks like we're off again already folks!" The Professors' observation is seconds too late, for most of the party have already gathered up their belongings and have advanced themselves in the direction of the persistent semaphore that expels from Joseph's guiding stick. The patterns of the silken scarf as it drifts slowly backwards and forwards give the appearance of a flame licking the air, lighting your way. Guiding you as the shepherd guides his sheep.

"My God," A hand rapidly clasps to her mouth, as the exclaimer realises her place. "Does this man ever stop for breath?" She disposes of her curtness this time, in order to defuse, a little, the intonation of her first statement.

Looking across to the origin of the cry, you make out the distinct features of the woman; the one who the other night had been the wearer of the satin blue dress. People always look different with clothes on. You momentarily reminisce to the occasion of the dinner, when you had quietly studied this person, collecting ideas about her, which have suddenly been destroyed. Perhaps a little older against the spotlight of the sun, the moonlight had done her justice, as had her satin dress. Her hair now worn loose across her face seems to accentuate her high cheekbones and somewhat gaunt appearance. No longer swaddled in the silks of the evening her attire now leans towards the more clinical aspect of fashion - stern navy-coloured trousers, a plain linen shirt, kissed at the neck by a pastel patterned scarf; she now appears noisily conservative, a member of status out for a walk. The sensualness that had lain under her dress the other evening does not appear to sing from beneath this less fashionable cliché of clothes. No aspect of her body sings of woman. The curves of her breasts have vanished as if some mental mastectomy had taken place, and the paleness now of her lips, having been robbed of their Helena Rubenstein paint, sit naked upon her face; a bare canvas waiting to be expressed. But somehow even behind the mask of her plain clothes there echoes the hidden signs of a ghostly secret. The silent hint maybe, of a flamboyant and colourful life that has settled upon quieter times. Perhaps it is your imagination.

-Who is she? You wonder …. Just, who is she?

No one answers your question and neither do they answer the questioning outburst of the mystery lady. Everyone has already hurled themselves into fourth gear without the opportunity to de-clutch. Hurriedly they anticipate Joseph's next move as they file past street traders in the gloomy shadowed alleyways. The trader's cries for attention go unheeded as your momentum continues to increase. Some struggle to keep up with you for a while trailing the wares straddled across the length of their arm's. Beautiful jewellery. Holy artefacts. Cheap leathers. You could have haggled and saved yourself many pounds in just those few minutes, but .….alas there is no 'Halas'. Your journey moves upwards and onwards, nearing the church of the 'Holy Sepulchre'. The church which historians proclaim marks the site of Christ's crucifixion. At this moment your mind excels in all sorts of blasphemous thoughts, connected to your present journey, and that of Christ with cross in tow. For the sake of those around you and any ever-present angels who must exist in these parts, you refrain from offending, and think yourself gallant for doing so. From the far reaches of the crowd behind you a voice decries the situation with elaborate ease.

"God Almighty! Are we nearly there?"

You confess you hoped it might have been another voice, but you feel sure it came from that woman - the owner of the late blue satin dress!

Didi! Don't dwell! Remember what I said before. The mind must keep its thoughts elsewhere. To all intense and purpose this woman has no reason to know you, or you to know her. Why do you watch her so? What do you hope to learn? Such worries are fickle.

Cast all irrelevant thoughts aside. And if you must dwell - dwell on life itself for there lies your safety net. ....

CHAPTER SIX

You sit in an airy corner of the reception area, behind a couple of ornate pillars that extend majestically towards the ceiling. It was not your intention to sit here discretely in order to eaves drop, but after a while you begin to notice the familiar tones of two voices in conversation close by. Beyond the pillars, and towards a little recess to be precise. Apart from the low whirring of the fans above you there is no other sound available to distract you from listening to the ensuing conversation. And despite knowing that listeners hear no good of themselves, your knowledge is immediately outweighed by your human curiosity. Discovering that if you shuffle your body forwards you can angle yourself against a mirror on the adjacent wall, you intermittently adopt this pose in order to gain a periodic view of the two conversers.

"I have to confess. I didn't notice anything particularly strange about her behaviour, Wayne… May I call you Wayne? You did introduce yourself to me at another meeting last year, and you were very keen that I use your Christian name. I was just a little hesitant, as it had been a while ago."

"Oh… No Rachel. Please go ahead. I remember you very well from that occasion. I think formalities are unnecessary at times such as this. You just carry on calling me Wayne! And if I don't see you for another year, just keep remembering what I just said. Is that Okay?!"

"Yes of course that's fine…. Wayne. Now may I ask you a question? -Why are you so concerned about Didi?"

"It's not concern, so much as intrigue, Rachel, that makes me feel so puzzled. It's very rare that I feel uncomfortable with a person when I meet them for the first time, but somehow with Didi, although I feel this unease, Didi also makes me feel extremely humanised. Haven't you noticed that yourself Rachel? You're obviously very close to Didi as a friend? Do you ever sense that kind of feeling, when you're together?"

"Wayne. Didi has been through an awful lot of trauma in the past. Reactions that you see today are all forms of coping with that trauma and trying to deal with it rather than pushing it to the wayside. You know this already, surely? We are both psychologists here Wayne. If I explain things to you anymore, I will feel that I am being discerning of your status. Surely you understand what I am trying to say…Don't you?"

"Yes! Of course, I do, but there is something deep and meaningful about this person and I think you may have some answers that you're not disclosing Rachel."

"What sort of answers Wayne? I can't go on discussing my case histories in public, you should know that!"

"Case histories? But I thought, Rachel, that Didi was your friend. A philosopher. Isn't that, right?"

"'Well yes, but anyone can be a philosopher… anyone who thinks therefore they are. By definition!"

"Yes! Yes! Rachel, I know that. But are you saying that it is true what Didi told me?"

"Wayne, I know I may seem rather evasive in answering your questions. But what exactly was it that Didi told you?"

"That philosophy was down to logic mainly and…*um* …a basic understanding of the world. Yes I think that's right!"

"Do you disagree Wayne?"

"Certainly not. Well… Not exactly Rachel."

"Where does your difficulty lie with this, Wayne?"

"'I'm not entirely sure. But exactly 'what' qualifies Didi to be here at this conference without any credentials?"

"Didi has 'lived'! Wayne, and from experience, knows and understands an awful lot of what this conference is all about."

"Yes, I believe that was pointed out to me the other evening, at the dinner, and I think it was hinted at a few times earlier today in Jerusalem. What is so important about this person's 'case history', to you Rachel?"..... Wayne stretches his hands behind the back of his head and links his fingers together in what is seemingly his favourite pose; the pose that helps to say, 'I'm in control of this matter'. In this instance it is used as a decoy... "And what allows you the right to invite this patient of yours to our conference, in the role of a guest? I'm surprised that the board allowed it, not to mention security. There is so much confidential material being discussed here, Rachel. This could put your career in jeopardy."

"As a matter of fact, I had no trouble clearing this with anyone. I was just honest from the start, and explained everything as best I could."

"Explained what Rachel?"

"Didi's case history of course!"

"I see!" Repositioning his hands, Wayne now leans forward in order to make his conversation more private and asks…. "Rachel, Ought I to know this history that you keep mentioning?"

"Oh, you will Wayne. You will!"

"Wonderful! Any clues as to when that will be?"

"Yes! Tomorrow afternoon at the Tel Aviv lecture"

"Oh no, Rachel! Surely, you're not inviting Didi along to that. It will be far too academic for a lay person to……"

"Wayne, Didi's not coming as an audience to this lecture. Didi will be talking to us."

"Jesus Christ! Rachel. Is that wise?" Wayne begins to redden at the sound of his own outburst; hoping that he has not offended this officious Jew, who nevertheless seems unperturbed.

"Didi will be the best person to instruct and inform us, of what it is like to suffer from these conditions."

"But OCD that's going to be difficult. It's a deep subject."

"Nobody knows that better than Didi, Wayne, I can assure you. Trust me this will work I'm certain of it!" Rachel's normally haunting features have taken on the appearance of a more radiant complexity. Her sallow cheeks and deep-set beady eyes suddenly seem less shadowed by the rest of her face, as if a spotlight has been lit. So transfigured by her immediate excitement is she, that Wayne looks on for a moment as if he is talking to a complete stranger.

"This is having a profound effect on you, Rachel. I don't think that I have ever seen anyone quite so excited by their own ideas. Are you really sure about what you're doing?"

"Oh absolutely. No one can stop me now Wayne. This is the start of a new beginning; Lifting the facade off mental illness, and hopefully throwing away the stigma attached. It's so important. This is something that the world has been waiting for since the time Freud first came onto the scene. Freud gave us the backbone to this science now after a century of trying one way and another a new revelation is taking place, and the funniest thing is that the cure is plain, simple logic; just as Didi will explain to everyone tomorrow."

"Aren't you jumping the gun a bit, Rachel? What are you preaching here? …That you have discovered some new revolutionary cure for mental illness. You've experimented with something in your backroom, and it's worked for one individual, so now you think you know all the answers?"

"Stop a moment Wayne, you're jumping to conclusions and being so facetious doesn't help. It is just the kind of attitude that puts the problem where it has lain for so long - unsolved. No one is prepared to acknowledge new changes in psychiatry in case the mechanics are found to be unsuitable or unworkable. They are frightened that a disapproving finger will be pointed at them if things go wrong. But Wayne there are no worries with this and incidentally I'm not the procurer of this treatment. All I have to go by is the end product."

"That being?"

"Didi, of course!"

"And I suppose I don't get to see any of this magic until tomorrow?"

"That's right Wayne! So until then you'll have to be patient."

"I can't wait… I just can't wait!" He continues to eye Rachel with trepidation. Then his voice softens to a more patient tone. "Somehow, I can't help feeling that I should be, trusting you on this. My sixth sense keeps telling me that you have done your research here. Let's just say that I hope I can back you on this idea, whatever it is!"

Bringing the conversation to an abrupt halt, he stands and thrusting his hands deep into his linen trouser pockets, he wishes Rachel a hearty good evening and makes his way hastily towards the lift, at the other end of the hotel lounge. Turning he watches as Rachel collects together some literature, which she appears to have found on the coffee table, in front of her. Women's Magazines perhaps? Wayne's face shows signs of amusement. Obviously realising his forgetfulness, he returns to pick up his daily newspaper from the same table, and whilst doing so he shares a little thought with Rachel-

"Just when 'She' is certain 'She' knows everything about herself, she picks up yet another magazine and tries to find out more!" Rachel's face remains unchanged. Chuckling to himself at this little quirk, he then returns to the now waiting lift and enters alone.

You stand and then lean forward between the pillars, resting your head against the pillar to your left, you watch the lift doors close and your eyes follow the ascending lights situated above the solid silver doors.

CHAPTER SEVEN

The air is warm, but the atmosphere feels cold around you as the eerie presence of a hundred silent black faces, focus their hidden eyes upon you. Have you performed before? You can't remember. Maybe! In a nursery play… a school drama…a musical ensemble? Yes, perhaps you've had some practice, that always helps...well it helps a little anyway!

Above the hidden audience the dim theatre lights signal their presence; carefully positioned at random intervals though in sufficient quantity as to provide the suggestion of a reoccurring pattern. Your eyes are transfixed for a moment on this intriguing illumination and then the focus of your senses altars as you notice the faint hint of a murmur. Is the audience impatient for you to begin? Surely not! This is a noise, distant yet so close; a voice calm yet persuasive, un-seen yet with character, body-less yet tangible.

Listen for it is only I, once again. Hold fast to your reason and knowledge. Believe in yourself, and all that you stand for. Extend your thoughts to the minds of others, so that they may begin to understand. You are no guru, but from a small seed....

"Ladies and gentlemen, I present to you a case history with a happy ending; an enduring middle; a tragic beginning and an impetuous flurry of morals, which all in all, could be a great lesson to all of us!" Rachel glances momentarily at her notes laid out on the lectern in front of her. Then clearing her throat, she continues. "I could have conducted this case history myself, as is more usual, perhaps? But I somehow felt that to hear this lesson first hand from the mouth that could best speak on the subject, that is the one adjoining the mind of a recovered OCD sufferer, would be a revelation to our ears. Hopefully it might execute the epiphany of a new approach, to our understanding and subsequent treatment of this illness.

Obsessional Compulsive Disorder has been well documented, researched, studied and pondered over for many decades, if not centuries. Accounts show that OCD has been recognised by many in lay fields too, especially the literary world, Shakespeare's portrayal of lady Macbeth being a prime example. There are of course others. As well as fictitious characters many well-known figures have been diagnosed with the illness, but seldom do we hear more than the initial shock-coverage in the press headlines. The media are quick to label people, but seldom as keen to follow up their stories. Their naïve perception of the population persuades them to think that their readers are keen to read the headlines but not necessarily as interested in reading the small print. Many lay people are of the understanding that they know OCD because they know what the letters stand for. Public awareness of this illness is so minute and we as a professional body find it so difficult to attribute our knowledge to a wider audience, because ironically, it is usually only the sufferers who actually want to read our books, in the first place! -But seriously. -If three million people were discovered to have a medical illness, then an epidemic would be acknowledged, yet it is estimated that at least three per cent of our current population may suffer from OCD, and yet no cries of alarm are being heard. There would be public outcry if this was occurring in any other part of the health practice. We therefore owe it to ourselves to further our findings, and if this can be done by effectively using our success stories then let us do it now for there is no time like the present. Ladies and gentlemen, I give you, ... Didi!"

The small lights that you have been concentrating on suddenly appear to be showing an intrigue in your presence as they begin to brighten. Slowly the auditorium begins to transform from night to day, in the fashion of an eastern dawn. Like the memorable scene in an epic movie, you wait for the blast of musical sound, which normally presents the occasion with a dynamic introduction. Alas there is no musical accompaniment to your entry, but this, of course, is no fictitious occurrence, this fundamentally is reality. No acting or façade is required now; all this audience wants is the bare, nakedness of your story. And any introduction that you hear is only the crescendo of courteous applause, as the audience awaits the beginning of your mental striptease.

You remember those moments spent in front of mirrors in your childhood, searching longingly for the hidden person within you. You parody the monkey searching behind the mirror to locate the other image which naively seems not to be its own. Without meeting the image, the flat mirrored face bears no life or justification. That face which you saw was the same; a hidden face that you were unable to touch or relate to; a shy face that bore no resemblance to the 'you' inside. Sometimes you thought you saw it grinning back at you - Mocking you by way of a sympathetic smile that you could almost have mistaken for genuine concern.

Momentarily mesmerised by the lights and your thoughts, you begin slowly to return to the present. Like those lapses into 'unrealness' that would affect you during your school days. You would feel flat, and your 3-D vision would collapse into two-dimensions, as if a giant foot had pressed itself down on your world. You would hear and see everything from a distance and yet you felt near at the same time. You never told anyone because 'it didn't matter' it was only happening to you, and you didn't think that anybody else would know or understand what to do. School was terrifying. Although this feeling would happen elsewhere, school seemed to be that metaphoric foot. It was painful! Being trodden on was more painful than being physically kicked because you had no means of defence. OCD was a bully that could not be brought to justice in the eyes of others because it was always hidden. Even in your own mind it bore no face or recognisable voice. It was just a being that spread itself systemically into all the folds of your brain - Your hidden enemy who you tried to hold hands with; for sometimes that was the safest way. 'Know your enemies, for better the devil you know!' Powered by this philosophy, naivety and ignorance, you continued in this framed mindset for over twenty years.

The imagination was the scariest thing. It was like an ongoing horror movie where you were constantly on guard, waiting for something to make you 'Jump', it was like an endless roller-coaster ride with no time to get your breath back. Never allowing you that reprieve to let your body settle itself back to normal and put the adrenaline rush on hold.

You remember checking and repeating actions, recycling endless lists within your mind; washing repeatedly all hours of the day and night; missing appointments, being late for work. Being frightened to touch the ground; then becoming frightened of associated things, shoes, slippers, cases, bags, wheels...Absurd? …Yes! But now who's the fool, for surely the world is a little slow... read the logic here - they all touch the ground, don't they?!

You saw rationality in this illness, for you were able to explain the workings of the mind in linking these articles to the one foreseen fear that was ultimately 'Contamination' There! You were not such a fool after all, and because you knew you were slightly mad, it seemed to place you closer to the realms of sanity. Comforted by these thoughts and many similar ones, you put up with the deal that life had dealt you albeit a poor one. A strange existence - where you feared the touch of objects, and even other humans.

You had felt so ungrateful for materially you had so much. So much that there was little you wanted for. Opportunities seemed to fall your way and you acknowledged them when you saw fit. But for all the things you had, there was one thing you hadn't got - there just didn't seem to be a shop in town which could sell you a clear mind. Just a day's reprise from the constant bombardment of intrusive thoughts, obsessional needs and compulsive actions that was all you required. It just didn't seem possible and as each year passed the day of deliverance just seemed an extra day away. Holding on to belief and hope, you kept going, to this day you don't know how. Sometimes it was almost impossible to bear. Like your worst nightmare wrapped up with pictures from a horror movie. Every horrid detail over emphasised and misrepresented in an overt and cruel fashion, the torment and fear almost indescribable. No reprieve ever gained through moments of sleep, as weird and bizarre patterns of thoughts would arrange themselves into your dreams. Creating situations where you were control-less, to the point where you would wake up in the morning and wash everything around you in case it really had become contaminated as had been suggested by the dream. You didn't run in search of this illness; it just seemed to constantly find you and there seemed no way of turning it off or shutting the door in its face. Rationalisation was taking a nosedive at this point and to all intents and purposes you were just waiting for the crash!

Your world around you were becoming such a fearful place, that it was easier to retreat and avoid, rather than willingly place yourself into situations that caused such anguish and peril. So, for many months you were little more than a recluse. No job, few friends, little social contact, your world was being squeezed into a sardine tin, the original barrel-sized version having been discarded.

Doctors had tried to help in the best ways they knew how; Drugs, Freudian therapy - which allowed them to search the past for clues, Behavioural therapy, which you weren't quite ready for. You didn't feel able to cope with this medicine; all too disgusting and equally too large to swallow. You were more or less told that you would have to put up with this illness for the rest of your life. It would always be apparent the psychiatrists had told you, to a greater or lesser degree, depending on other stress factors that your life might incur.

Not very reassuring or encouraging! What happens next when there is no hope for the patient because he will not take his medicine? What a sad state of affairs! Surely it would be so easy to just 'TAKE' the medicine? If only it had been. But you couldn't, and there seemed no alternative. They didn't even want to institutionalise you. God! How bad did you have to be to get a recommendation?

It was obvious! You had acted out your life so well trying to conceal this illness, that even the psychiatrists were unaware of the severity of your condition. Inside you were burning to tell them but on the outside, you were frightened of blowing your cover. Such a difficult dilemma, it was so frustrating and tiring. Part of you desperately wanted to keep trying - to keep living if that's what it could be called? The other half of you just wanted to lie down quietly, fall asleep and dream beautiful dreams forever and ever.

You knew you could choose either of these alternatives, for once in your life you had a choice in controlling the matter. But ultimately it was a very difficult choice. Perhaps, one of the hardest choices that any human being might have to face in their lifetime. Choosing to save another person's life is hard but to choose whether to save your own is harder, especially when that body needs all its strength and is perhaps already weakened by its plight. In the words of the martyrs - you soldiered on! - despite feeling totally unworthy.

Your road to victory had been the narrowest, uneven road imaginable. It had felt as if you were making that journey barefoot and in clothes not befitting the vileness, of the elements. All weathers poured their worst upon you, and it was seldom possible to catch a moment's breath. Without a guiding figure, you were very much in the dark. Every method that you tried was an experiment. Everything that you did became a potential danger to you, as it evoked the fear response. You applied common sense and logic because fundamentally that was all you had left. You flushed away your pills because you wanted a clear head. You utilised hours of your time each day pushing and persuading yourself to try again, to do the things that you wanted to do. Although they caused you so much pain. What right had this illness to tell you what you could or could not do?

It had hurt, really hurt. Facing crowds; stepping on buses; touching lamp posts and park benches. To touch them and then not wash that was the test. Sometimes it worked. Often it didn't! You hadn't needed a person behind you though, shadowing you in effect. That to your mind would have been too hard to bear. You could only manage it your way, using your methods, because that way you didn't feel so threatened. You had needed that degree of control.

It had proved right in the end, although it had taken many years longer than perhaps it could have done or should have done. Fortunately, you had met up with a self-help group in more recent years, and their teachings and advice had been similar if not the same as your own means of success. However, because they followed a more structured programme and encouraged listing the problems in order of severity, working at one small problem at a time, the level and speed of recovery proved triumphant, over all your own feeble attempts. You had spent only two sessions at this group and had felt radically improved, and from then on the effects of the illness had continued to gradually subside until the present day. Nothing now, seemed beyond your capabilities. Your confidence had been empowered as well as your mind. Charged up ready for the rest of your life!

CHAPTER EIGHT

The coffee clutched in your hand feels cold. You slowly sip another quenching drop, whilst the conversation slips across to your questioner, yet another member of the conference party, eager to share a quick word with an intriguing, unqualified lecturer. They look at you in a way that people might study someone who has travelled on a miraculous journey... the North Pole... the top of Everest - Somewhere beyond their own means or capabilities. They almost want to touch you in order to share some of that experience. Yet they stand away from you a little too, as if you are no mere mortal. They do not see you as resuscitated, so much as a resurrection personified.

"What made you think the way you did, was it your imagination?" The tall fair-headed gentleman did give you his name, a moment ago but unfortunately you have heard so many names this evening that they have all fused themselves into a blur of sounds within your memory. He looks very seriously into your eyes as he passes his question over to you. Maybe he is trying to read your mind before you answer, just to see if he can!

"Oh no! - Believe me! No one could imagine those things. They were worse than any nightmare!"

"But where do you believe those ideas and strange thoughts came from?"

"They had a deep origin somewhere within the depths of my mind, no doubt. But if I told you that they were caused by strange voices talking to me then I would definitely be lying. It is so hard to explain, but if there was a voice it was my own voice speaking through my conscience. If I had been a schizophrenic I would have believed in the voice, but although I followed the persuasion of the compulsions, I battled with them all the time. There was certainly no belief on my part that what I was doing was ordinary. From the onset I felt that I had an insight into the strangeness and peculiarity, of my obsessions but somehow, I found it so difficult to let them go. But they certainly were not alien voices, although that would make a nice story, wouldn't it?"

"Didi, I'm a psychologist here not a journalist, I am interested in the truth whatever it may be. I know that truth is sometimes less fascinating than fiction, but in your case I think there is a slight over-lap! - You certainly are a remarkable specimen!"

"Thank you I feel flattered! Though I'm not sure I ought to be, having been granted such a title!"

"Well, I didn't mean……."

"Oh Jo, … Hi! I've been searching for you."

Your conversation is prematurely halted by the interruption of a familiar figure, namely the woman 'de la robe bleu' in yet another guise - her appearance taking on yet another transition, this time wearing a Channel suit of cream linen, a classic substitute to any flounce or starkness shared previously. It provides her with an air of dignity further denoting that coolness of quality in both, style and mood. Behind her fashionable rectangular spectacles, she eyes you up and down in the manner that a scientist might scrutinise an ordinary specimen. Perhaps that's really all you are to these people, but they didn't have to make it so obvious, surely? Was there no dignity or decorum among these people? As you wonder, the gentleman who has been talking to you acknowledges the interruption.

"Well, Hello Colette, come and meet our hero!"

"Well, I think I prefer that title to the one you applied earlier!" You turn your gaze towards Colette as she approaches and extend your hand. She acknowledges your gesture simultaneously.

"So, you are Didi? May I use that title, I have not heard you referred to by any other name, though, Didi is a little strange?"

"Didi is fine. There are other names on my birth certificate, but Didi is the one that I prefer."

"Quite. It seems that most things about you are a little extraordinary. So why not your name too? I have little to follow that unfortunately. I am simply Colette - How do you do?"

"I'm pleased to meet you, Colette. I have seen you many times over the last few days, but it is difficult to say hello to a complete stranger, without first being introduced."

"I don't know Didi, from what you have been telling us in your talk; I dare say you wouldn't have had any problem at all."

"Well, there are some exceptions, Colette!"

"Indeed!"

"In fact, until this afternoon I hadn't had the opportunity to speak to hardly anybody else from the conference party."

"You certainly seem to have made up for that now, Didi! And I have noticed you talking with my brother a few times."

"Your brother.... You must mean Wayne?"

"Yes, Didi that's right!"

"Goodness Two psychologists in one family, that's quite an achievement, surely?"

"No more than having two Obsessive Compulsives in one family, I wouldn't have thought Didi?!"

"How did you know that? Did your brother tell you?"

"No 'Didi, you did, just now in the lecture hall. You said your own brother suffered with a similar form of the disorder."

"My goodness. I don't remember saying that, but then I said so many things. I must admit I amazed myself that I had spoken for so long. I'm sure I must have repeated things and confused people at times. I just hope that I didn't bore anybody."

"Well, you didn't bore me I can assure you of that, Didi!"

"Thank you, that makes it all worthwhile. And now if you'll both excuse me, I think it's time for me to slip away, and have an early night!" You smile at Jo who has remained silent for the past few minutes and exchange a friendly handshake with each of your intrepid listeners; whilst beginning to edge away from the corner of the room where you have been huddled for the past hour.

Suddenly Rachel sees you from across the foyer. Your eyes meet momentarily - you were hoping to have escaped the party unnoticed. You place your jacket over your shoulders, knowing that the walk across the forecourt to the hotel apartment will be a little chilly as it is late into the evening. Glancing at your watch you realise that already the chances of an early night have slowly started to fade. All that lengthy talking has stolen a considerably amount of time and it is now already eleven - fifteen. The hands on your Tissot watch have never been wrong in the ten years or so that you have owned it; an heirloom it remains reliable, providing you remember to wind it up!

This is the first night that you have not spent at Rachel's family home. The confederation was happy to put up all the listed guests from the conference and house them for the night at this rather luxurious hotel. It makes for a welcome change. A little space – quiet time. Everyone needs to unwind occasionally. And it would have been an exhausting task to have made that journey back to Haifa at so late an hour.

Your chances of an early night are fading even more rapidly now as Rachel calls to attract your attention further. She hastily crosses the room as best she can, though restricted by the tight-fitting skirt that adorns her lower body. She looks brighter in her complexion than usual. Perhaps the foyer lights are providing a justice for her. Or maybe the table wine has already accepted that pleasure. Her pace now slows as she approaches you. You see by the opaqueness of her eyes that whilst perhaps tired, she may also have been crying.

"Hello there!" You hope that your look of surprise will cancel any suspicions she had that you might have already glimpsed her earlier and chosen to ignore her. "I was just creeping away silently into the night, before anybody saw me. But of course, I forgot what sharp eyes you have. - By the way is everything all right? You look a little concerned."

"Oh Didi, I feel awful. I don't know whether I did the right thing bringing you here. I had to speak to you, and make sure that you weren't feeling the same way. It's been such an exhausting day. I've been thinking about this lecture for weeks, and now it's finally happened I just feel so deflated and empty."

"I don't think you need to worry. Please don't think that you are going to hurt my feelings. I'm just enjoying the terrific holiday, everything else is a bonus, believe me!"

"I don't want you to feel humiliated and used, Didi."

"Why should I Rachel? Everyone has been so kind to me today. It has been a wonderful experience. I really don't feel at all humiliated in fact I feel rather special. I can't believe that I spent so long performing on a stage without the need for a rehearsal!"

"From what I understand you have been rehearsing all your life, Didi. What you do each day is a performance in itself. All I wanted was for other people to see that too. I just hope that we did this right."

"Well, if the response of everyone is anything to go by; I would say that a majority of people present today, found my revelations, helpful and informative."

"Did they say that?"

"Most of them, yes!"

"Well, that's a consolation. It seems like you've stolen all my limelight here Didi. Everybody's giving you the credit - you're famous!"

"That's a matter of opinion!"

"Well, I feel better now that you have shared that with me Didi. I hope you didn't mind me keeping you from your early night?"

"Don't worry. I think I missed out on that a long while ago!" You slowly start to edge out into the courtyard avoiding a potted palm in the way of the entrance. Why, when so blessed with palm trees across its land, did this country, insist on bringing them indoors too?! You move towards the open gate, which leads into a small garden surrounding the hotel apartments. The well-lit path lights up the garden, creating an artistry of colours that transform each flower into a magical display of numerous shades like those on an artist's palette. You imagine the delight of the artist whose job it would be to create an image, from these unimaginable colours. Reaching the open gate, you stop and bid Rachel 'Good night'. Continuing along the path you make your way through the flower garden. The security light is beginning to dim after initially lighting up on your approach. The flowers are now retreating into the shadows and only their soft scents remain, casting their essence into the sky like invisible fireworks. The day has been long and only an ample sleep will clear your mind from the intrinsic pictures that the last twenty-four hours have created. Your thoughts as well as your body require, putting to bed!

At last, in your small apartment, you lie heavily on top of your cotton sheet, and begin to recast the images of this eventful day. You remember standing beside Rachel at that lectern and feeling totally in control. You had watched her unsteady hand shuffling her notes and sensed the uncertainty in her voice as she introduced you, although she spoke so confidently about you. You had, had no script. No quiver had interrupted your movements, your voice had spoken evenly, in a way that you would previously have thought impossible and yet you had done it all so calmly, almost as if another voice had spoken from inside you, although you know that is not true.

You are speaking from the heart. Trust in yourself that's all that it ever takes. Don't judge from response and reactions, do what you do because you believe in yourself, and others will believe in you too!

Before you sleep your mind rests on the conversation that you overheard taking place in the courtyard behind you, as you had made your way through the garden's shadows.

The conversation returns to you almost verbatim, and you imagine how the conversation played out: -

"Evening Rachel, everything okay? You seemed a little glum earlier. Looks like Didi just cheered you up!"

Rachel jumps at the sound of the unexpected voice. "Oh, Yes, she has Wayne thank you. I was feeling a little bit uncertain about how events had gone today. But Didi says she has been inundated with questions and comments about her presentation and they are all apparently very positive, which of course was encouraging to hear."

"That's good. I suppose you feel that you are playing second fiddle to all this now?"

"Yes, I am just a little." She laughs hesitantly.

Wayne draws on a large king Edward cigar which he is evidently making slow progress with. "Let's face it, what would have been the worst scenario, Rachel? - A question that maybe Didi would have found difficult? …… Now what might that have been.....? Let's see – it's hard Rachel, because Didi seems to have an answer to everything. - Ah yes, I know, what if somebody had asked her whether she thought the illness might return. That would probably have been the hardest question for her, wouldn't it? - How do you think she would have reacted to that Rachel …...? Could she have coped with a question like that, do you think?"

Rachel ponders quietly for a few moments. Then an encouraging smile spreads itself across her narrow mouth;

before she answers "Wayne, your question is hypothetical and so my answer will be too, but I would like to think, that knowing Didi as I do, her initial reply would perhaps have been something like – 'Chance would be a fine thing'!

"Exactly!" Wayne's smile mimics that of Rachel's as they then retrace their steps in the direction of the ensuing party; drawn and enticed by the potent warmth of noisy echoes and excitement escaping from the depths of the courtyard.

CHAPTER NINE

The airport lounge buzzes with the sounds of intercoms and conversation. The hum of noise drifts up away from its origins and up towards the ceiling as it slowly embroiders itself around the tobacco smoke creating a heavy canvas above the heads of waiting passengers. In certain positions the artificial lights capture this illusion, as it floats like a huge Aladdin's carpet across the room.

You sit quietly with a few other members from the party who are also returning home to England, tonight. Rachel has decided to stay on with her family for a week or two and perhaps visit some old school friends, who she hasn't seen for a few years. There were not many she had told you, for most of the younger generation of Jews, preferred to accept any opportunity to work abroad for a few years even if they eventually decided to return to their homeland. But homeland has perhaps not been a very apt word to use here, although this description typified Rachel's directness; for most of the troubles that expressed themselves in this land seem to stem from the Jewish belief that this was their land, both 'Holy' and 'Wholly'! Your thoughts take on a political air for a while, as you ponder over the controversies of this land where you are presently placed. Everything seems so peaceful, and as you gaze around, you wonder in disbelief, for these Arabs that sit peacefully about you now, could just as easily be fighting one another in the streets tomorrow. Your mind continues to wonder further, the political flavour of your thoughts beginning to attach themselves to a more clinical speculation and you question whether any of these people sat here with you now are suffering from OCD - What a strange thought...But wasn't it true? ...that when other more life-threatening situations occur, like a war, the primeval urge to survive kicks in and all other strange worries and concerns are trivialised.

Suddenly you are alerted from your daydreaming by a loud voice transmitting itself through the tannoy system.

'Attention please, attention please, would Mr Didi, that is Mr Didi, passenger on British Airways Flight BA164 to Heathrow. Please proceed to passport control immediately.'

Quickly gathering up your hand baggage, you hastily obey the announcement; wondering amusingly what this could be about. Turning this way and that to find a helpful sign, the unfamiliar surroundings create a confusing maze, the simple rule of keep left does not apply here; your only satellite is a sign hung high from the rafters below the normal ceiling level, which clearly displays the words: -

PASSPORT CONTROL

The Arabic equivalent of this sign, you conveniently ignore.

Following these directions, your movements are conveniently assisted by the combination of several hundred passengers who are all heading in the same direction. The current of their movements creates a respite of air that is welcoming to you, inside the oppressive airport building. You pass over a small walkway, lined by yet more palms, which are housed in large ceramic pots, each uniquely painted in a display of ethnic colour and design. Looking ahead, you see a line, of, what appear to be checkout counters. Behind each counter sits a uniformed guard, you quickly calculate a total of five. All display poker faced expressions as they examine in turn the documents of each passenger who passes through their individual gate. As you approach the area, a clear sign 'Passports' above your head confirms that you have reached the countries Exit point. A formal queue of passengers, await the attention of each attendant, and you see no immediate means of making someone aware of your presence. A second announcement is made identical to the previous one. Someone obviously wants to speak to you urgently, but where on earth should you go?

A policeman passes you as you stand still, anticipating your next move.

"Excuse me, I am M.R. Didi. I have been told to come to Passport control."

He turns and looks at you suspiciously. Perhaps it is the way all Police are taught to look when first confronted by a passer-by; a means of giving themselves a more sustained air of authority. Meanwhile there is no hint of understanding or recognition, in response to the information you have just shared with this man. Perhaps he does not understand English. You decide to repeat your sentence. This time you speak slowly, as is unique to speaking to someone who you are certain has difficulty understanding your native tongue.

"My na-me is Di-di. I have come to passport con-trol. I was called on the tan-noy?"

Immediately some kind of appreciation lights up his face and in beautiful English he replies.

"This is passport control you have come to the right place. You are not British passport?" Following his own deduction, he begins to assist you along the side of one of the queues waiting in front of the counter marked overseas passports. You refrain from arguing your nationality with him at this precise moment. For at least it seems you are about to get some assistance.

Placed in front of the desk, you make yourself known to the attendant behind it. His deadpan expression does not alter but his reactions do. He quickly picks up a small telephone receiver, dials a couple of numbers, hastily transmits a message in Arabic, and replaces the receiver with a gesture similar to the appearance of his face, cold and without demur.

Within seconds two security police appear from nowhere. Their guns and handcuffs strung across their belt buckles give a picture of little tolerance and little patience. Immediately the soft feel of a whimsical smile that had previously adorned your face has been wiped clean away by the sudden introduction of facial terror and anguish. For a moment a passing thought lifts itself through your mind. The flight is due to leave in three-quarters of an hour.

In synchronisation to this thought the tannoy system pipes out yet another announcement.

"Attention please. The departure of British Airways Flight BA164 to Heathrow has been delayed."

An immediate sense of relief passes through you, on hearing this news, then just as suddenly it dissipates as your attention returns to the present. In a dreamlike way, a mark of shock no doubt, you continue to make your way across the airport concourse in full view of other passengers with a policeman guarding you on either side. You wish that you could humour yourself in this present situation, but your humour is slow in coming.

You sit in the white-walled room feeling already like a prisoner, guilty of an unknown crime. You remember all those Police programmes that you have watched in the past. You had always wondered to yourself as to what it would feel like in those situations, where the suspect was being interrogated, now you were about to find out first hand. And in a country less favoured for its patience and tolerance than your own.

Uncertainty and agonising frustration wait with you as you pray for whatever is about to happen next, to happen. Three policemen are standing in the doorway, one shouts a protest at what appears to be another's suggestion. The other two shake their heads impatiently. Although they speak their own language you notice that your name interrupts their foreign sentences periodically and is probably the main cause of their concern. You sit silently, while they continue their discourse for another few minutes. Shaking their heads and gesticulating to the space around them. Finally, one man looks up, raises his eyebrow and walks across in your direction. Unsure whether to stand in his presence you begin to move, immediately he flinches, and you return your bottom abruptly to the seat.

Beginning his questioning, he resolves to give you a hard stare that is milked by a slight look of hesitancy and confusion.

"You are M. R. Didi?"

"That is correct."

"And you hold a non-British passport?"

"No! I have a British passport."

"I see...And you are travelling to London today?"

"That is my intention."

"Good. We hope to have you on board the aircraft very soon, but, if you could just bear with us for another few moments." He adjusts his tie as he speaks, obviously feeling the effects of the heat, you notice him unbutton the collar of his shirt, seeking some relief from the stifling conditions. There is evidently air conditioning, but it is lost within the small confines of the room. And the whitewashed walls add to the heaviness of the atmosphere. Your head begins to throb.

The questioner now returns to his fellow police officers, who have remained in the doorway to the room. No one has attempted to close the door, and you welcome this small relief from the oppressive atmosphere. With a guarded tentativeness, you reach for a small handkerchief, tucked in your pocket and wipe the faint trickles of sweat that have formed on the back of your neck. From the far side of the room there is a moment of further discussion resulting in more gesticulation and verbal interaction. Finally ending abruptly with three stern police faces all looking in your direction in what appears to be a most intimidating and perplexed manner. There seems to be no obvious clue as to what all this is about, and it seems to be the intention of everyone in the room, not to disclose the answer to you at this present moment in time. You remain puzzled wondering what it is that is causing such an amazing amount of confusion.

With still no answers apparent, you are led politely by the shortest of the three police officers, who escorts you from the confines of the stifling office across a large lounge to the departure area. Escorting you onto the aircraft, the police officer hands you over to one of the awaiting stewardesses. It is still not obvious to you if you are free to go. Everyone seems determined to keep you in suspense, if they possibly can. Then the kindly voice of a cabin steward acknowledges your entrance, welcoming you on board and requesting that you occupy a seat in first class, presumably an appeasement for your recent inconvenience. With some degree of relief and surprise you readily accept.

Your luggage has still not been returned to you, since it was requested in the interrogation room. You had at no stage, had the presence of mind, nor the inclination to ask anybody, as to where it had been taken. With some relief you notice it now in the hands of the steward as he guides you through to the front of the aircraft, following you, assuredly.

"Here we are." He catches up alongside you as the sound of his voice halts you. He gestures with his hand, beyond a thin spiral staircase, which winds up to the next floor of the aircraft. The décor and atmosphere have changed in a matter of seconds. And it is like walking into the foyer of Claridges or the Ritz. The smell of upholstery intertwined with strong tobacco, once again and the striking hints of various pungent perfumes.

You are shown to your window seat, a glass of champagne sits on the small table adjacent to your seat. A small packet of St Moritz and another of Dunhill compliment the wine along with a plate of canapés. Thanking the steward, you obligingly place yourself in the seat and taking a glimpse through the porthole window, you take your last mental photograph of the country you are about to leave behind. It is a very striking picture, for this has been a very poignant visit. You have to adjust your thoughts momentarily to remind yourself of all that has happened here in the last week, as the events of the last hour or so have taken precedence over all else that has previously passed.

You listen, as the engines of the aircraft become noisier. The high pitched 'ping' of the safety signs repeatedly draws upon your attention, as their intermittent flashing requests you to 'fasten your seat belt and extinguish your cigarette.' A 'Sky life' magazine placed in a rack beside you catches your eye, reaching across; you pull it free unfolding the front page. A list of interesting articles, display themselves across the cover. You consequently make a list of those that you may later be interested in reading, though, for the time being you are happy just to browse through the vast duty-free list duly whetting your appetite. Wines, spirits, cigarettes, you follow the endless list of countless choices, reminding yourself that there are a lot of gifts already in your suitcase and that maybe it will not be necessary for you to buy too many more.

Glancing out of the porthole window beside you, you glimpse the lights of another aircraft departing ahead and so you prepare yourself for your flight home. You continue to watch as the other aircraft lines itself up on the runway, and slowly picking up speed, lifts its weightless body from the ground, further and further into the sky. Its red tail lights marking a pathway across the night sky until suddenly it is no longer visible.

"Good evening!"

"Good evening" You reply, before completely turning your gaze around to the passenger who has just spoken. An elderly lady who is just beginning to seat herself beside you gives you an enormous grin with the accompaniment of her mischievous blue eyes. "Looks like you've got me for company for a little while!" She seats herself with what appears to be some relief then continues. "My goodness - what a to-do! Apparently, someone was holding the flight up. A passenger had some problem with their passport, I think. Probably some stowaway! Can't trust anybody abroad these days! I feel so much safer in England. I always think that the British are the only people that you can really trust!"

"Yes perhaps!" You make no attempt to say any more at this moment, for you have become somewhat alarmed at the prospect of being the cause of this delay. How strange that rumours get about so quick and become so easily distorted. You wonder for a moment how this is. You look again at the innocent old lady sat beside you and manage a small harmless smile. You decide to keep her guessing, not wanting to deprive her of any further incriminating thoughts that she may have on the subject. Besides you don't really know any more than she does. Everything that happened earlier is still a complete mystery, but ideally not worth agonising over any longer.

You both adjust your position and in a gruff tone your neighbour continues.

"I shall be glad to get home. This heat has been unbearable for me!"

You sympathise, as the weather has been exceptionally hot and the heat almost inescapable as not everywhere has been air-conditioned. Your mind thinks quickly back to the little whitewashed room where you were sitting not so long ago. And then again with some relief, it flashes back to the present.

"Where is home ... near London?" You ask your question politely, feeling that the lady is obviously inviting conversation. Her lengthy reply suggests you are correct.

"Home used to be in London, but now I live in a small village near Walton-on-Thames. Marvellous place, set up for oldies like me who've got nowhere else to go. No one wants you really, once you get to my age." Looking closely at the ladies face you judge her to be in her sixties, maybe closer to seventy. What does it matter you wonder, you're as young as you feel at the end of the day, and it's not really that important. Having your faculties about you is probably something that is far better considered. You remember back to your past; days in your twenties - when you felt about ninety. That's what a course of depression does for you. Covers your face and surrounds your mind with wrinkles.

"I hope what you say is not true, there must be family who care about you?"

"Oh! They drifted away; all I wanted was to have them near me. I didn't think it was much to ask. Perhaps I loved them too much, I suppose that's possible?"

"Well sometimes it's not always possible to have things exactly as you'd prefer them. Sometimes you just have to make the most of things the way they are!"

"Gracious, what are you - Some kind of philosopher?"

Without answering, you quietly find another smile painting itself across your lips.

The situation begins to relax, and your travelling companion seems to have become content to sit quietly. The inevitable take-off of the aircraft has seemingly put her into a trance-like state as she prepares to be hurtled thirty-five thousand feet into the air as part of the contents of a thin metal tube.

Once airborne you are spared from much further
conversation with this lady, as she chooses to remain in
slumber for the rest of your six-hour flight.

69

CHAPTER TEN

The aircraft circles London, the early signs of dawn are just apparent. Thin ribbons of colour begin to paint themselves against the blackened skies. A mist sits below the cloud, breaking periodically to allow you a peep over the map below. Familiar sites stand out evident between the curves of the Thames. Then quickly they disappear, hidden once again by nature's hazy curtain of cloud.

The engines begin to throttle back, and the heavy dull thud is felt as the undercarriage drops ready for landing. A sudden turn as the right-wing dips, then lining herself up again the aircraft makes ready for her final approach; the runway rolled out ahead, beckoning.

Just seconds later you touch down on British soil, those sudden feelings of relief and achievement nudge you in the solar plexus. A gratifying sensation of returning home, again; misplaced by a more urgent need to satisfy yet another urge for adventure. A peculiar mixture of feelings, requiring a careful balance in their interpretation.

As the aircraft reaches its dock, passengers immediately begin to fumble for their effects. Those holding seats alongside you in first class appear no less inclined to fumble than the rest. The calmness that these people have exhibited for the last six hours during the flight is now rapidly dissolving into waves of diverse behaviour; common to large numbers of human beings desperately trying to re-orientate themselves, after travelling through a period of the night in a semi-restless slumber.

You gather your luggage and prepare to leave the aircraft. Checking that your passport is where you placed it earlier in the side pocket of your flight bag, you suddenly become aware that the document was never stamped when you left Tel Aviv; somehow the impromptu goings on had put paid to the usual stringent checking and confirmation of these affairs. For a moment your mind toys with all the possible reasons that could lie behind the confusion, but only oblique answers present themselves to you. Strangely it seems that once you were discovered not to be the person, whom you were thought to be, you automatically became a trustworthy passenger who needed no confirmation of identity at all. Perhaps having an honest looking face had paid off after all!

"Don't suppose we'll ever meet again, but nice to have met you." Your fellow passenger extends a welcoming hand out towards you, and with a diplomatic farewell you shake her feeble hand. It feels cold and spindly as it grasps, you're own, delicate and easily crushable. The vulnerability of this ladies body clearly does not match the toughness of her mind.

"Feelings mutual." Such a cold reply, but on the spur of the moment you can't think of a more original retort. Your tiredness is beginning to overwhelm you. As you make your way past the circular staircase, your limbs feel as if they are stuffed with kapok, and as you advance forward your feet step but do not feel the firm surface beneath them. You fear falling but somehow like the spaceman trying to keep his body in an identifiable field or plane of balance you endure the walk from the aircraft through the long airport corridors to the arrivals area.

As you approach the luggage collection bay, a firm hand grabs you from your right- hand side. You immediately flinch, your tired mind frightening you, and when you turn round you expect to see that Arab policeman standing over you, handcuffs at the ready! You refuse your mind the continuation of any further gory thoughts as your vision begins to focus on the surprised and concerned face of Professor Wayne.

"Everything OK Didi?" He fails to pause long enough for you to attempt an answer. Presumably your current appearance has given him enough evidence to answer the question himself. "We were all a little concerned to say the least with all that confusion before the flight. Colette said she had thought she saw you being escorted away in handcuffs."

"Well not quite!" You speak with a confident air but you are not sure what has inspired it.

"We didn't know what to say or think."

"Well, I gathered you hadn't tried to bail me out. I wasn't expecting too much assistance. It's always best to think that way then whatever happens is a bonus!"

"Now Didi, you're sounding cynical. So this obviously hasn't knocked you for six like it would have done some people. Please don't tell me that you are used to these kinds of things happening to you?"

"Certainly not!"

"Then, what was it all about? Do you know?"

"No idea, absolutely no idea at all, I'm afraid it's as much as a mystery to me as it is to you."

"So why did they put you in first class?"

"As an apology, for all the inconvenience!"

"But what did they question you about, when they led you off. Surely their questions hinted something to you?"

"That's just it, there were no questions. They only seemed interested in my nationality. Once they knew I had a British passport they didn't seem too concerned with any other matter. Although there did seem to be something about me that they were puzzling over."

"That doesn't surprise me Didi?"

"Professor Wayne you are not taking this seriously I fear!" You watch him with a tentative smirk on your face, and he replies with a similar gesture.

"Ah well, Didi. We'll just have to try and forget the whole incident, if that's possible. It won't do us any good to ponder too long on this one."

"No indeed!"

After a few minutes the baggage conveyer-belt begins to rotate and after a short pause, cases from the flight begin to appear, emerging through a flap adjoining the belt. Eventually you retrieve your complete set of luggage: the sum of two suitcases. Modest by most people's standards. Others around you are struggling with enormous amounts of baggage, and you wonder curiously what can be held inside all these cases. Surely no one required such a vast amount of clothing in the warm climate you have just left behind. Perhaps some of these cases, like your own, are heavily laden with gifts and wares from a faraway land. Trinkets and ornaments from Jerusalem, maybe? How you wished that you had not missed out on that rare opportunity, to haggle with those traders who had seemed so desperate for your participation. Such beautiful rugs their materials injected with addictive colour. Leather handbags and shoes so delicately finished. Pottery and glass with designs so eye catching. Not to mention those hundreds of wooden ornaments and carvings the product of strong and patient hands. You remembered the tunnel of shops that spread along those narrow streets creating a kaleidoscope of shapes and patterns all around you; many merchants displaying their goods by stringing them across the street's way above your head. Yes, this was certainly one of the most striking images that had arrived home with you; already your mental camera appears to be developing its film of pictures. With all this beguiling richness you could have probably filled another five cases at least, if you had had a chance to part with your money.

Professor Wayne extracts you from your daydreaming as you push your luggage trolley across the concourse towards the Arrivals entrance; having already passed uneventfully through passport control.

"Well, Didi, looks like it's finally, time to say Goodbye." He extends a hand towards you at the same time displaying a gold cufflink hanging loosely from its starched cuff. Once again, signing himself off in his classy self-confident way. "Glad we had this opportunity to meet up, Colette and I are both keen to have you as our guest one evening, maybe an evening meal, a dinner out somewhere, perhaps. Colette has a flat in Hampstead so I'm sure she could suggest a few decent restaurants that end of town. If you're interested that is?"

"A great suggestion, I'd love to do that!" You quickly retrieve a pen and diary from that convenient side-pocket of your travellers' bag. Tearing a blank page from the back of the book, you quickly write down your phone number and scribble your name above it. "There we are that should be all you need. I look forward to hearing from you both soon. I hope this won't be a business dinner?" Your final quip sounds amusingly serious.

"Only if you think that talking philosophy is not pleasurable!" With that Professor Wayne having found his sister among the hurrying throng of people, takes her by the arm and leads her out of the terminal building towards a waiting taxi.

You pause for a few moments whilst you continue to clutch the warm pen that you used to write your number. You flick the end a few times in a careless way, and focussing on the golden nib, you think carefully how many times in the past, you yourself, have been the recipient of numbers written down on flimsy pieces of paper, placed them in your pocket and never given them a call. You will have to wait to find out if Professor Wayne and his sister execute the same kind of dismissive behaviour over your note. You feel certain that this last gesture or request was just their courteous way of signing off. What if they hadn't caught up with you a few minutes ago at the baggage carousel? You would probably have never seen them again, although, if they had chosen to, they could have always rung Rachel and made contact that way. But you really don't feel that they were the kind of people that would put themselves out quite so much for the sake of one insignificant human being, like yourself. Oh well, once again, only time would tell. But you certainly are not going to hold your breath while you are waiting for their call!

Eventually you retract the pen placing both it and the diary, back in your bag. Hailing a taxi you wait as a few engaged cabs drive past, then finally a cabby leans out of his window.

"Where to?"

"South Kensington!"

"The city! …..Great - Jump in quick!" He leaps out, snatching your luggage from your hand, and opening the rear door for you before he runs round to the back of the cab. Taking heed of his command you hastily seat yourself against the cold leather upholstery and close the door beside you. A light drizzle has just caught the edge of your sleeve. You feel the bump behind you as your cases are placed inside the boot. The cab is stuffy, and an unripe smell seems to linger around you. As you slowly open the window to allow some of the pungent air to escape, you notice a sudden smell of fresh rain waft in; a new rain; a rain that lifts the odours of nature and re-kindles freshness to the atmosphere. A rejuvenating rain, that often appears after a long dry spell.

"Has it not rained for a while?" The cabby throws himself into the driving seat as the deluge intensifies.

"Yer-Wat?" Comes his reply as he reaches to turn down the volume on the radio. "Yer bin away fer a while, did yer say?"

"Yes, I have." Not attempting to repeat your initial question. You decide to stick to simple, easy conversation.

"Wher yer bin, den, some-wher nice?"

"Israel"

"'Blimey! Bit of a nasty place ain't it? Smelly! Bit ov a war der not long ago. Ain't dat right?"

"Well, it all seemed quite peaceful, last week. I think things have been calm for a while."

"Never know though do yer? Could all start again t'morrow!"

You remain silent for a moment as your driver continues.

"So, wat der yer wanna go der for? Bit ov-a funny place fer a holiday ain't it?"

Not wishing to disclose too much about yourself, you explain that you have been staying with a friend. Your reply seems to suffice, and the subject matter immediately changes.

"Erd der latest news?"

"No, what's that?"

"Governments still trying to get us all in ter dis blumin foren money lark. Wan us t'ave der same money as der Frogs and der Gerries! It'll never aspen! It can't! Can it? Me Dad would shoot der bleedin government for suggestin it if he were alive t'day."

You hold back in prescribing a comment here; not really wishing to disclose your political persuasion in front of such a vehement politician, especially as he has a hand on the wheel which is driving you towards London at a good eighty miles an hour.

The weather again centres its. grip on your attentions, as you watch the drizzle of rain on the windows of the cab. Slowly it increases to a more rapid and persistent pelting and instead of staying put these patterns of moisture now trail their way down the window beside you, like the small torrents that combine to work a river into flood.

Suddenly Bert starts up again. Mentally you named him Bert, some while ago actually; perhaps it was the moment you first saw him, back at the taxi stand. Somehow when you meet somebody who is unlikely to introduce him or herself, you often sense the desire to give them a name. This one suits him. Some names just do that, and you don't really know why. You wonder if has sought to do likewise, with you; the stranger sat in the back of his cab.

"Where-bouts in Kensington are we go-in then?"

"Just before we get to Kensington Gardens, there are a few small roads off to the right. I'll point out the one as we approach. Sunday shouldn't be too busy traffic wise, so you'll be able to slow down a little, otherwise it might be hard to spot the turning."

"Blink an I'll miss it, that what yer mean?" Bert chuckles to himself in response to his witty reply. You smile too as if you have never heard that particular anecdote at least a thousand times before.

"Something, like that!"

"Nice place Kensington, ain't it? Not like where I come from down Kilburn high Road."

"I know it well. My mother was born there!"

"Suppose der's a chance fer the likes of me yet den! Who knows?"

"Indeed, who knows?" Somehow Bert wouldn't look right anywhere else than behind the wheel of a cab. You imagine that he wouldn't give up his job no matter how many millions he won in the lottery. He is another of life's philosophers on a less daunting plain. His life lies well within the boundaries of simplicity and for that you almost envy him. For him, his blissful ignorance of other major concerns in life, provide him with a degree of detachment that is probably healthier to him than the worries and cares that others agonise over each day. Perhaps he is the wiser man for sitting back and allowing the Politicians to do all the hard work!

"Blinkin Heck!" Bert suddenly draws the cab to a forceful halt. Jolting his whole-body forwards in an attempt to apply further pressure to the brake pedal.

You are thrown forward with such a force that you knock your head hard against the padded door beside you as you rebound.

"Did yer see that bleedin fool pull out?!"

In your momentary daze you have to confess that you didn't.

"Give a bloke a Mercedes and he finks he owns der flippin road. You alright there in der back?" He turns his gaze away from the scene of the potential accident and takes a glimpse at you over his left shoulder.

Your reply is hesitant "I think so. Just give me a moment or two."

Amidst the confusion you happen to glance out of the cab window to your right, only to realise as your vision begins to refocus, that you have passed your road and are heading on into Knightsbridge.

"Bert, you've missed the turning!" Realising your blunder you hold your hands quickly to your mouth, but the words have already escaped.

"What's dat. We missed it ave we?" He doesn't seem to have reacted to the use of his fictitious name. Maybe it's his real one. That would be strange.

"Must ave blinked, mustn't I?!" His humour restored after the earlier scare he begins to look for a place to turn his vehicle round. "Here we are - This'll do it! He pulls over to the left and swings the cab into a complete U-turn outside Harrods department store. Returning in the direction he has just come; he retraces his steps back to Kensington. You notice that his clock is still ticking away the journey time, but that will be a small price to pay against returning safely home in one piece.

"That's it there!" Your right hand singles out a finger as you point in the direction of the sign stating-

'Abingdon Road W8'

"Ere is it!?" Bert puts the indicator on and turns into the narrow road. "Crikey this is the road that that mad maniac in the Mercedes pulled out of just now. Ope he weren't one of yer neighbours, pardon me if I was rude or anythin."

"Don't worry; I don't think he could have been. Now how much do I owe you for the journey?"

Bert mumbles some extortionate amount, and you quickly wonder whether he is charging you extra for the entertainment value. You feel too tired to question or complain. Settling up politely you step out of the cab and wait whilst your luggage is retrieved from the boot.

"Cheerio then! Thanks for the tip." Bert smiles and disappears back into his cab and immediately drives off.

Was he being sarcastic for you weren't aware that you had provided him with any addition to the bill or did you perhaps mishear his initial quote? Oh well, some things in life are set to remain a mystery.

Under the shelter of your porch, you stand for a moment close to the edge of the steps which have brought you down from the pavement and you observe above you the tranquil street in which you live. The busy and sometimes noisy pub on the corner is at the moment without trade. Its Sunday customers will no doubt be arriving soon, but they will do little to evoke many disturbances, not like the Friday and Saturday night players. You turn your thoughts round, and turning your body round simultaneously you glance up at the window box which sits on the sill of your bedroom window above. The rains have provided a natural watering can for your geraniums and they appear to be flourishing. They would never have been your idea, not being a keen gardener. But Mrs Brooks the previous owner had already planted and nurtured them for you, leaving only the watering to you. So far in the last three years you had seemed to cope admirably with this task. There seemed no reason for their survival not to continue, providing that you obliged with an occasional rain dance or two if required.

Apart from these living geraniums, another important muse is your Siamese cat – Xindi, who will need fetching from the cattery, presently. One day you hope to share your home with another human being, but there is no rush, at present. As you place your key in the door, you feel comforted that for now you have time to yourself.

CHAPTER ELEVEN

Quietly you sit in your favourite seat, the one by the window at the shadier end of the lounge. From your sitting position you peer through the window, taking in the view over the small garden. Its seclusion guarded by the surrounding high wall covered in trailing ivy. The recent rain has battered down the more fragile stems in the flowerbed. Small daisies and other early flowering plants have been fooled into thinking that the spring had kissed the garden farewell, and the weathers of summer were about to cloak the garden in their warm and favourable embrace. Birds sit in the tall firs growing huddled in the far shadowy corner, darkened by the angle of the wall against the suns' rays as she now tries to penetrate through the diffusing clouds. The glistening of the raindrops spotlighted by the sun, glisten like tiny diamonds among the grass. The song of a wood pigeon startles the picture into a live frame. This freshness and beauty draw you to focus on this creation as its newness breathes a warm exhaled air on to the new day. You shut your eyes listening more intently to the music that plays on the radio. A slow piece by Liszt, the enchanting 'O Lieb', it lures your mind into a deep altered state. Your body has not slept properly for many hours and the music seems to pull you away from all that is around you, transporting you away from your senses and thoughts and into a dreamlike existence. The rise and fall of the notes dance with the slow murmur of your pulse, and there is a unique link between these melodic sounds and your bodies' orchestration. Peace and tranquillity fall upon your soul and mind and without reluctance or fight your mind drifts off into a tender sleep. Your body feels as if waves are persistently massaging your back, and your mind spirals with thoughts that supply you with picturesque dreams. For the next few hours, you sleep peacefully and alone. Memories from an Arabian evening lie close to your arrested consciousness; suspended in the paradigms of time itself.

Lying beside you the Sunday paper lays untouched, it's hidden headlines as yet unread. A small clock, ticks peacefully on the mantelpiece, recently wound, it's time corrected from the hour at which it stopped. It now holds both hands to the twelve, and conveniently displays another midday in the concept of time. A moth passes through a small open window and dances in front of the hearth mirror. The strong reflection of light confusing it, it impacts repeatedly without relief. And far away a church bell is ringing, the wind carrying its chime, supplying it to your ear, but you do not hear the sound. Only the music from the radio stays with you and its sound elopes with the air as it encircles you and escorts you through your dreams. In the next room the soft purr of the telephone rings to itself for a few minutes and then with a despairing and impatient final ring it stops; the inert object paying no attention to its own sound remains stationary and transfixed. Around the room everything stands still and patient as each composed object waits for you to return from your period of slumber and oblivion.

I speak to you now from the realms of your sleep, yet I am no dreamer's voice that you hear. My lips only part with words of truth and wisdom, never those of fruitless and unimaginable disorder as often are the words heard in dreams. I create pictures for you that are true and real. Pictures that show you a direction ahead, and never a faded path that whispers away into the distance and the future; not allowing you to see its end.

My words though not always explicit, nevertheless, are not supposed to hold hidden meaning. There is reason behind my methods and sometimes what appears to be my madness. To think and understand is far better than to be taught and not question. The scholar is not always right, he can be as human as the next person in making his mistakes, but for his experience he should not be underestimated. I act merely as a guide and a fundamental prompt in your life, I have travelled your path. I am to you a prophet, in the present day, allowing you a means of sharing my knowledge which I trust I can impart on you, although I do not see into the future and can only foretell, those things that I myself have already experienced.

Do not be humbled by my words, for they do not create me into a supreme or influential being, on the contrary I am as humble indeed as you and from your own experiences you may too, become me, if indeed you only repeat my words. For that is how the process of life is formulated, by the scholar encompassing the pupil, passing on his knowledge and thus allowing the pupil to become the scholar.

You were asked to search for my leading character, and I wonder if you have found them yet. although there is no gender portrayed, I think you will agree that there is no need. Think on for you are so close. Your mind has almost established a link, and at that moment of recognition I think you will agree there will be no doubt, whom it is I have concealed!

You murmur softly as you slowly stir. Your limbs are stiff from the awkward position in which you have lain within the chair. Placing one foot down upon the cool floorboards, you stretch out and plantar flex your foot allowing it to slowly come back to life. Simultaneously reaching your arms up above your head you allow yourself to inhale a deep breath of air, which exerts itself immediately into a yawn. Your first conscious sound becomes the ticking of the clock, which you now search out.

Focussing your eyes slowly, you read the time - half-past three. In the background, behind the sound of the ticking clock, you slowly pick up and recognise the slow movement of a favourite Mozart piece. As the music begins to resonate more clearly to you, your eyes quietly begin to take in your surroundings. And a dawning awakens your mind as you suddenly realise that you are home!

You gaze silently for a moment, into thin air and then training your sights upon the framed Renoir print above the fireplace, you curiously trace the outlines of the figures within the painting. 'Luncheon of the boating party' - One of your favourites! A beautiful depiction of freedom, beauty and harmony all bound up and presented in one favourable scene. You can't help but feel enraptured by this painting's naturalness. Like the feeling a lover feels when beholding beauty in its most undisguised form. Slowly the figures within the picture begin to look down at you, as if they are welcoming you to the scene. For a moment you are no longer alone, and you can almost feel the presence of their shadows within the room. You imagine the eclectic Charles Ephrussi doffing his top hat to you; purposefully made to stand out of place against the two other posing men in singlets. You admire Renoir's ability to capture a fish out of water - Would you be that fish in another artist's painting?

Suddenly, you are alerted away from your musings, as the telephone once again begins to purr in the adjacent room. You bound out of your comfortable seat, and clutch its arm with a quick involuntary grasp, as your body suddenly registers the lack of feeling within its extremities. Continuing to hobble you reach the phone just at the moment that it decides to stop ringing. At least it has summonsed you to your feet. You decide to put the kettle on, but not before glancing cautiously at the answering machine; at least sixteen messages have been left over the course of the last week. You decide to wait until later to listen to them all. At this precise moment all you want to hear is the sound of the boiling kettle and to sample the taste of a long-awaited cup of tea. Becoming suddenly aware of Xindi's absence you remind yourself that you must ring the Cattery and let them know you're back; but that can wait a while too. Catching up on the last few hours is of more immediate importance to you.

You walk downstairs to the kitchen, situated in the basement area of the house. The window at the front end beckons you to look out, and as you flick the switch on the kettle, your eyes wander up to the pavement level of the street outside, your eyes following the sound of passing footsteps. Behind the street railings, you glimpse a pair of elegant court shoes as they pass by, accompanied by a pair of black brogues. They walk in step, harmonising with one another. Perhaps they are the feet of lovers. You watch as they disappear from view and once, they have vanished, your ears continue to follow the disappearing trail of their diminished tapping as they slowly advance further along the pavement, in the direction of the street corner...

The hissing of the kettle awakens your attention, and you return your thoughts to 'making tea'. The phone once again beckons you with its persistent bell, reaching it before it becomes silent; you lift the receiver to your ear. A hush ensues.

"Didi?"

"Yes!" another hush.

"Welcome home!"

The voice is not recognisable to you. Certainly, none of your close friends would edit a call on such a truncated number of words. Nor would they hold their identity from you, not intentionally, of course, they would automatically think you recognised their voice. Most would probably be disappointed if you didn't. This is definitely someone you don't believe you know and yet there is a rather familiar tone to their words. It is mysterious and confusing to you. You ask as nonchalantly as possible.

"Who's speaking?"Yet another hush then there is a murmur as if someone is about to speak. The faint hiss of sound which suddenly dissolves into nothing; a sound that holds the potential to the start of a word.

The line goes dead.

The incident does not puzzle you. Why should it? Perhaps it is some old acquaintance, merely cut off in their prime. It was a boyish voice that is about all you can confirm. The rest remains a mystery.

But you have other concerns on your mind right now. Like - feeding yourself some supper, perhaps. The meal on the aircraft this morning had been nothing more than a glorified breakfast. And your stomach is now feeling empty and confused as to what meal it should anticipate, A light salad? - If only you had a fresh lettuce and prawns. Maybe a take-away would suffice, you hesitate on ringing to order a pizza, or perhaps a curry, just as your thoughts are on the subject you open the door of the freezer. A welcoming TV meal, waves to you from within. Without further hesitation you make an instant decision to take the easy option. Popping the convenient tray into the microwave, you switch on and wait.

Another set of footsteps immediately draws your attention once again to the front window. The steps are heavy and more intolerant than the passive steps that normally pass by. You hear a man's voice call out. A questioning voice as if the man wants to know something urgently. A second calmer voice replies. Presumably from the other side of the street as it is slightly fainter. Immediately the intimidator requests the answer to another question. This time his voice is seemingly more impatient and sterner. There seems no dignity or diplomacy to his angle of questioning. You wonder what this is all about. As the voices become increasingly more coherent you realise that you are listening to the exchanging voices of an ensuing argument.

Suddenly there is the sound of breaking glass. Without a moment's hesitation you run up the small steps from the kitchen which allows you access, via the first small landing, to the next flight of stairs leading up to the lounge. Rushing over towards the window you peer through the net curtains, allowing yourself full view of the street beyond. With silent deliberation you watch and listen further.

A tall man with dark hair and a swarthy complexion is standing beside a blue Mercedes, parked on the opposite side of the street. He is undoubtedly the defendant in the situation. You notice that it was his wing mirror that had provided the sound of breaking glass, and which now lays shattered at his feet. The man stood beyond your front door seems to be the one making all the fuss, his violent temper does not appear to be exhausted by his small act of violence indeed the incident seems to have provided him with more momentum, with his temper enraged still further, he continues -

"Well, if it said No Parking, then why the bloody hell did you park there?"

"Because it's Sunday, and no one ever worries about parking on a Sunday!" The man on the opposite side of the street stands with one hand in his jean pocket the other hand scratching his head in disbelief, as he continues. "Well! - no one except the likes of you it would seem."

"Well, you're wrong there see, because no one in this street wants their spaces taken up. We stick up for one another here, we have to, otherwise little twerps like you take advantage, and we can't afford to have that happen, can we?"

Like two gladiators they stand apart wary of each other's strength, not wanting to come too close. Aware of each other's potential capability, they wrestle with their angers at a distance. The road between them, which has become their coliseum, remains empty and event-less.

At this point the defendant is already beginning to sound his retreat. Stepping back into his car, he slowly surveys the damage to his wing mirror. You notice him shake his head a couple of times, but amazingly he remains calm and winding his window down he has the last word with the perpetrator before driving off at top speed towards the main road junction.

As soon as he has disappeared, you cast your eyes back towards the aggressor, now standing with a contented smile on his face. This man appears to confront the world with the menacing touch of someone, who likes to have his own way. You eye him closely but despite having heard him defending his neighbours during the quarrel, you do not recognise him. And in a way you are not at all surprised when he climbs into another Mercedes double-parked further up the street and drives off, in hot pursuit of the previous vehicle. You did, however, notice that hung around his neck was a rather large camera, large in respect of the telescopic lens that was protruding out from its normal sized casing. Like some kind of phallic symbol, suggesting the sorcery of manhood; the secret behind the cloth. You pay him one last thought before turning away. If not a congenial neighbour, certainly no ordinary visitor either.

As you begin to step away from the bay window, there is a sudden screech of tyres from behind you in the street. You hear once again the sound of fracturing glass, but this time the sound is much more intense. The noise continues for what appears to be the antipathy of an endless silence. Then like the final explosion of a massive firework, spluttering golden sequins for an eternity, the display of sound is complete as it signs itself off with an almighty bang.

You do not rush back to the window this time; instead, you hastily run down the narrow hallway follow down the narrow staircase and fumbling with the security lock you free yourself through the front doorway. Racing out, you trip on the first step whilst in slippered feet you do your best to run up the ascending steps to street level.

Running in this way, your latent physical strength is easily depicted; you always knew you had mental strength, but now you are suddenly aware of the urgency and determination with which your body manages to carry itself.

CHAPTER TWELVE

The child lays still. Boy? Girl? you cannot tell - denim jeans are never a good give away. The child's limbs are contorted in strange and confused directions. From the twisted remnants of the wrists, it is hard to distinguish whether they are right or left hands. The child's torso does not move to breathe. The thick woollen jacket does it's best to disguise someone sleeping, but you know the body is not breathing. In the hundredth of a second that it takes to think before speaking you crouch beside the child and your medical knowledge springs into action as you slowly begin to turn the child's head and body gently into a supine position.

Your mind rushes to organise your thought ..... Breathing, Bleeding, Breaks and Burns!

It is some twenty years since you were taught these rules - the order in which to treat multiple injuries - easier at this moment to memorise than to actually put into practice.

You process eliminate. It's always the easiest way in these circumstances. No burns, multiple breaks, multiple bleeding and no breathing, oh and only your one pair of hands!

Where's help when you need it most?

Staring into the child's open eyes you picture the last registered image that reached their brain. The moment of the impact must have recorded itself somewhere within this still and detached mind. The images now lying there must be those that rerun through the nerve pathways at the moment of life's termination. Pictures of the past, images of loved ones but for this young child there will not be a lengthy farewell for these memories will be few. Despite your initial prognosis of the situation, you thump the small chest as lightly as you can, fearing that you feel the free movement of possible fractured ribs beneath your hand, you begin to imagine the internal damage that your actions are causing, but without relinquishing your efforts you begin to perform cardiac massage. Remembering that you must also breathe for the patient, you close off the nasal passage, clasping the nose between your forefingers and thumb. As your fingers pinch against the nasal cartilage you realise that nature is probably performing the task for you, for the nose sits as a limp feature swollen and futile on this helpless and unrecognisable face. As you seal your mouth over the child's cyanosed lips, you hear a cry from somewhere around you.

"I'll call an ambulance I've got a mobile here. Give me a moment then I'll go and check the guy in the car!"

These words link with you and yet they seem mildly distant too. That moment when intensity takes over the mind, eroding the ability to wholly focus on another task or happening, although your sense of awareness is still there.

"Ambulance is on its' way. You seem to know what you're doing there. I'll leave you to it while I take a look at this other guy. He looks in a pretty bad state too!"

You have still not paid this other person a glance, but between you both, you mindfully interact with one another.

As you continue with your determined attempts to resurrect, you are suddenly able to recall the moments leading up to the 'Now'; those intimidating noises that had drawn your initial attention and thrown your adrenaline into a sudden rush; the previous argument, to which you had been a silent witness. Standing the dominoes back up you provide yourself with a picture of events. The aggressive man had charged off in his car without a care or regard for any other human being apart from the man he was pursuing. And now in front of you lies the result of one man's aggression put behind the wheel of a car and allowed to become unleashed.

You remain stooped over the child, moving your right hand down and feeling with your middle and fourth fingers towards the base of the infant's neck, searching for signs of life within the carotid artery. Amazingly, a weak and sluggish pulse is just detectable, very slight but nevertheless evident. Your own heart rate begins to return to a normal pace, and just as you begin to feel the signs of relief you notice a small arterial bleed in one of the lower limbs. A tear in the material covering the limb allows you to view the source of the injury. A small bloody pool surrounds a piece of bone which has stabbed its' way through the skins surface. It sticks up at a forty-five-degree angle through the body tissue, like a small totem and to one side of this alarming standard -blood spurts up like a small water feature the droplets rising and falling in a regular and efficient fountain. Already the torn and rugged leg of the jean is stained and soaked.

Immediately your hand moves down to find the wedge of the right hip, at the top of the effected leg tucking your fingers deep inside the right groin you press hard against the unrelenting tissue. You watch the bleeding point in search of some evidence that your attempts of arresting the bleeding are paying off. Slowly and miraculously, the fountain begins to lower and slowly it reduces to a trickle, running along the creases of jean and disappearing into a channel between two awkwardly placed legs. Nevertheless, it has abated. With sudden relief you begin to calm for the moment but just as you are beginning to feel that the situation is becoming more controllable you realise that you are in fact watching a body and not a being, for the child once more is lifeless and already colour changes in the fingers and around the lips are returning to a deep and agonising blue. Hastily you seal your lips around the tiny unquestioning mouth that lies beneath you and begin again to pass your own breath down inside this hollow body, whose soul seems determined to reach and connect with another existence. Unrelenting you blow and after a few short breaths you pump the chest you know it should be fifteen times, yet you are not sure. You carry on defiantly but gently. Your own mind is becoming a little confused as a mixture of effort, uncertainty and accumulated jet lag, are beginning to take their toll on your own weak system. Not daring now to accept defeat, you continue to battle on relentlessly and without distraction, until your thoughts are suddenly blocked off by a sudden voice, which initially you do not identify as human. It is a mysterious sound like the voice in a dream; you realise that you have become lightheaded and suddenly you come to.

"All right now?" For the first time since you entered onto the scene you are aware of your surroundings. Not fifty feet away two ambulances with flashing lights and the muffled blaring of recently extinguished sirens define the scene of the emergency.

"You've done a great job there well done! - We'll take over from here - give you a rest!" A tall paramedic takes you by the arm as he leads you over to the pavement and with an encouraging but direct nod invites you to sit down on the kerbside. Another arm begins to comfort and support you and from nowhere a blanket suddenly appears around your shoulders. You are not certain who is sat beside you, but you notice the sleeve of a red jumper attached to a kindly hand, and not a dissimilar hand to the one you held and shook on the plane last night. You prefer to keep your eyes closed, somewhat through exhaustion but also through preference. Of course, closing your eyes closes your vision, but unfortunately it seems to enhance your sense of hearing. The sound and noises around you suddenly become more intensified in an almost unbearable but nevertheless audible fashion.

"O.K! That's five hundred mils of O-Negative in situ. Adrenalines' in. I've popped a number one airway down. I'll just fetch the spinal board Ken, and can you check on splints?"

"Sure, Hue!"

You listen as heavy footstep approach and there is a confusion of sound as Hue obviously searches for the necessary equipment, inside the ambulance. After a few seconds the footsteps repeat and their movement this time pass you in the opposite direction.

"How are we doing there? Ken."

"Not too good. I've ballooned both legs and neck brace is in situ, think we'll just get him on the van, don't you?"

"Yeah, that's probably best. We can monitor him better in there. Let's do it! We may not have much time to play with!"

Listening hard a third voice now introduces itself to the conversation.

"Hue, before you go can you just check our man in the Merc. I think we might need some extra help to manoeuvre him out, but I think we're already too late!"

"Sorry Mike, but I can't risk the time; I've got to get this young lad off. Have we called the brigade?"

"Yeah, they should be here pretty soon. - Oh, looks like the coppers have just beaten them to it! OK. Hue we should be able to manage now. See you back at CAS!"

"Sure Mike. Good luck!"

You lift your head just as the first ambulance performs a three-point turn in the narrow street and with sirens and lights flashing heads desperately towards the awaiting casualty department. As your eyes slowly begin to re-accustom themselves to the surrounding light you focus on the red sleeve and the gentle hand that comforts you. Raising your head further you connect with a slim faced woman, probably in her fifties. Her genuine eye contact speaks to you before any words leave her mouth.

Your encounter is interspersed with the arrival of a fire engine and the intermittent deafening whirr of powerful tools.

"Don't worry, I think you did all you could in the circumstances." She pats your hand a little with the gesture that thoughts cannot seem to unite with words. "That must have seemed like a lifetime waiting for the ambulance?"

"Well actually I was too busy concentrating. I wasn't really aware of the time passing."

"The ambulance came very quickly. It must have been close by when it got the call."

"Possibly?"

"Fancy a little something to shock you back into reality? A brandy may be? The pub's still open from lunchtime. - Don't know if that's a sensible suggestion, I just thought it might help."

"Oh yes -it's probably a good idea. I'm sure you're right. Hold on a moment while I get myself co-ordinated here. I must look an awful mess. Had I better go indoors and sort myself out a little?"

"As a matter of fact, you look fine. Don't pretend to be fussy. Let's just go shall we!" There is an air of frivolity in the way the lady speaks, which is both encouraging and defiant. Without further questioning you slowly begin to rise up and straightening your clothes you try to avoid clutching the stranger's arm, carefully adjusting your legs to the laws of gravity, which momentarily they seem to have forgotten. Walking slowly but surely you pass the second ambulance just as its doors are closing. A small gap allows just enough opening for you to catch a momentary glimpse of the sheeted body which lies within.

CHAPTER THIRTEEN

Inside the pub, a few people still linger, probably swept up from the lunchtime crowd. Most look slightly worse for wear, those that have for one reason, or another decided to remain sober, look positively peeved at spending yet more time with their incapable and embarrassing colleagues. Everyone's attention appears to be drawn for a moment at least to your entrance with the older lady. Brushing their judgements and curiosity aside you find a seat to the left of the bar in a sultry corner away from the revellers. A few seconds later a thin but pretty barmaid approaches and takes your orders. You stick with the earlier suggested medicine; a double brandy sounds more than acceptable. To your surprise your companion decides to remain sober. It is not normally your tendency to drink alone, and you feel just a little uncomfortable, but reminding yourself that you are more than worthy of this tipple you accept your solitary participation in the confinement of the occasion.

"You certainly seemed to know what you were doing back there." The lady's eyes fix on you, as she speaks, as if she is searching your face for clues to the questions that she is burning to ask. "Do you think the lad will be alright?"

You look up a little astonished. Did she know the child? She certainly didn't seem to be emotionally involved, for there were no signs about her demeanour or conduct to suggest this, yet she seemed to hold a certain curiosity. Trying not to analyse her too much, you begin to answer her question as best you can.

"It's hard to say whether he'll pull through. I certainly did all I could for him, but he was pretty badly injured. Incidentally I didn't know it was a small boy. I was working so fast and because of the clothes and short hair I really couldn't tell whether…."

"Oh! But I thought it was the little lad that always plays around the streets on a Sunday. I think he must come to visit someone round the corner. I told the ambulance-man earlier. Usually, I see him playing with another lad who's a little older. Hadn't noticed him today; perhaps he wasn't around. I often see them from my bedroom window, it's always such fun to watch little one's playing don't you think? It's so sad that this had to happen. I heard a load of shouting and arguing earlier. Perhaps the lad was drawn to the noise and went to see what was going on - who knows?"

"Oh! You heard the row too? I was watching. It was most strange. It seemed like it was an argument over parking. But I'm sure neither man was from our street. They sped off at top speed, with the argument seemingly unresolved, and I think it must have been the car in pursuit that was involved in the accident. There can't be too many black Mercedes driving up and down the road at that time on a Sunday afternoon."

"Well you're obviously as mystified as I am. I thought you might have had some more clues, being that you were on the scene so quickly?"

"I'm afraid not." You sip the brandy which has just arrived; whilst your companion sips her orange juice. "This is all a complete mystery to me. And it's not the first in the last twenty-four hours either. There has been a kind of surrealism to the things that have been happening, which I'm almost beginning to get used to. I think my body will be starting to get a craving for these adrenaline rushes soon, if I'm not careful!"

"Hmm" Your listener is no longer as determined to pass comment or so it would seem.

"Well, I'm sure all will be revealed one day if it's ever going to be!" You're philosophical summing up, continues to encourage an air of silence.

At this moment, whilst searching for further conversation you begin to home in on the background music circulating into your chosen little nook in the far corner of the pub. Its origin appears to be a duke box operating in the vicinity of the bar; a recognisable piece from the seventies - one of Steve Wonder's greatest hits. You hum the tune silently in your mind and recognise the lyrics, but the title is not at the forefront of your mind. While you search, the music plays on, and you try to remember the title before the chorus restarts. As always, the music collides with your memory, linking you immediately to the discos of your past. The platform shoes, pink tank tops, heavy make-up, flares and the ever-necessary - wide lapels.At the table next to you, a group of attractive people, perhaps in their early twenties, are attired in yet another generation of fashion. The theme not too dissimilar to the styles imprinted on your memory, for yet again, the wheel of fashion turns. It is obvious that they are busy in discussion, presumably over some current issue. In front of one of them, a newspaper is spread out across the table. Their voices are loud but disjointed and though slightly incomprehensible, it is difficult for you not to catch small snippets of the ensuing conversation. You wonder if you haven't done too much 'listening in' over the past few days. Is it maybe a genetic inefficiency that you are incapable of blocking out other people's conversation?

"It's quite incredible really, when you think how heavy they are on security." A young girl is showing tremendous questioning of the situation that is being discussed. Her face and voice show intense emotion and incredulity over the point she has raised, and she is obviously keen to discuss the issue further. "What makes people commit these crimes...? Is it always for monetary gain?"

"No! Of course, not Faye!" A pleasant round-faced young man addresses the girl who sits facing him across the table. "These people do it for public recognition, to make people aware of their cause. The reason is more political than economical."

"Yes Paul. But what of the innocent lives that they put at risk. Surely that must affect them in some way?"

"These people are cold operators. No more. No less. Their thoughts transcend to one idea, one motive. They block out everything else."

"Bit like the Kamikases?"

"Yes, in some ways, I suppose!"

"That's really unimaginable, isn't it? These people live on our earth. Function physiologically like we do and yet inside their minds work so differently. How do they become so wrapped up in their horrendous thoughts and convictions?"

"Because Faye, they are obsessed. And people with obsessions follow their convictions or compulsions if you like, as if nothing else matters. They are not relieved of their thoughts until they have carried out their obsessive actions. And that's basically what it's all about."

Listening quietly, you judge this tentative, though forthright definition with a degree of trepidation. You understand obsession from the point of view of the person who has lived within the obsessive mind. And although you realise that this example is very near the truth. Some degree of further witnessing or understanding has to be given judgement before the true picture can clearly be understood. You are almost on the side of the criminal in this matter, before even having heard his case. If they are defining them as obsessive; can they judge them in the sense that they are fully in control or indeed liable for their actions? You begin to wonder if there could have been a capability in yourself of becoming a criminal too. What if you had ever been pulled by your compulsions into such desperate measures without realising or certainly without the means of desisting?

"I'm so sorry. What is your name? I suddenly realised that we have not introduced ourselves, yet we are sitting here like old friends!" Your drinking companion addresses you in a friendly but contrived manner. You answer in the usual fashion.

"Didi, For short!" You leave your answer there. You are not in the mood for declaring or explaining the origins of this name. It has been a long and arduous day, and the last thing you want to do is spend time explaining to a stranger who you are.

"And I'm Fran. It's short f-o-r...."

You suddenly have a compelling urge to finish this person's sentence – "For Frances?"

"Oh yes dear that's right how clever of you!"

"It was just a guess!"

"Of course - Good one too!"

You begin to realise that this conversation could be the introduction and farewell to a new friendship all in one. Your art of conversing seems to have become stagnant in a second. All those questions that you could ask, seem apparently easy for you to answer yourself; that mental list of ten, the 'One's' that you keep in the back of your mind for emergencies. They would be wasted here - right now, surely.

What were they now?

- Where do you come from? ..... Have you lived here long? ... Do you know many people here? - Well, the answers were obvious really. The sallow tones of an Irish accent immediately answered your first question. The milder accent certified that she had frequented this green and pleasant land probably for some number of years and as to whether she knew many people you really don't feel the need to care.

"Are you feeling tired dear?" Once more she addresses you in the manner of an old schoolteacher addressing a pupil. Not condescending, but incorrigible and in a tone that makes you cringe.

You are tired to the point of exhaustion and right now you just want to get home, eat, drink, bathe and sleep. Preferably in some sort of order but you don't really care.

"Yes, I am tired" You continue to answer politely. "In fact, that brandy has had the opposite effect on me. I don't feel revived at all I'm afraid. In fact, in some ways, I feel worse, but I shouldn't say that it must sound awfully rude. Please accept my gratitude and I hope you won't think me too unsociable if I leave now and get some rest? Oh, by the way, can I pay for the drinks?"

"Oh no dear, that's quite all right! Well, I'll say goodbye Didi. I'm sure we'll meet again!" Slowly she begins to adopt a more serious expression as she continues. "I don't know if it's any relevance to you, but I think there's just something that I ought to tell you. I happened to notice something odd earlier this morning, about seven, it was. - Well this chap in a Mercedes kept driving round the block, must have done it about five times in all. I got suspicious so I pretended I was checking my front gate. From where I was, I noticed him slowing down a number of times just outside your place - Perhaps it was nothing?"

You immediately want to ask Fran how she knows where you live, but some people just give off that scent, and you can already smell it - Fran is one of those people who make it their business to know these things.

Cautiously you try to hide the widening of your eyes as your interest and intrigue, become aroused. You have already felt a number of times today; that cold shiver of realisation, that ice cold tingling which transmits itself through your spinal column cancelling itself out all over your body as it channels itself through your extremities. You are beginning to sense it again now. What are you supposed to read into all this? - All these weird goings on. Are you exhibiting some sort of energy, some sort of electro-magnetism? You remember reading a book on the subject many moons ago, - 'Human forces' - that was the title, but you hadn't really taken it in too much at the time, because it had all seemed so far-fetched. Somehow within the last day reality itself has begun to feel equally as odd.

Keeping an even tone to your voice you begin to answer Fran's last statement in the best way that you can; showing an equal interest in what you have been told without appearing over concerned. "How odd! - You just don't know what people's motives are for doing these things, do you? And perhaps sometimes we really just aren't meant to know either!"

"I suppose you're right dear! Though it does make you wonder if perhaps you have a curious mind like me. I'm sure I probably don't have enough to keep me occupied - nosing into things that don't concern me all the time. But I do have this terrible curiosity. And a sixth sense when something's amiss."

You begin to rise up from your seat, and as you do so, there is a sudden awareness as your eyes avert in the direction of your feet - you are still wearing your slippers! Light brown moccasins to be precise, they could easily pass as a shoe in this dimly lit room but how embarrassing and whatever will people think? Shuffling around the table you become so aware of the absurdity of these slippers that your irrational mind transfers them into a huge pair of ridiculous coloured shoes that everyone around you is immediately aware of and staring at. Continuing to feel deeply self-conscious you once again thank Fran and move away in the direction of the exit; all those hidden eyes - staring at you through the dimness. As you turn to close the door your own eyes glance back towards Fran, just visible from the edge of the alcove. Odd for someone to make their orange juice last so long, maybe she laced it earlier when you weren't looking! She looks like a regular at the bar. -You know that you really should learn not to be so presumptuous with your thoughts, but it is difficult when the obvious is staring in your face.

You are glad to leave the confined and oppressive room. There is no air, or so it seems, and your head feels heavy and dizzy, your hearing and sight are beginning to blur, sounds and images are becoming faint and then obtusely real, as if you are wandering into some kind of semi-consciousness. Your mouth is dry worsened by the Brandy, and as you walk you can feel the muscles in your legs arguing with the reason why they need to be moved so vigorously if at all. Somewhere in your mind there is a faint pounding as if your mind is being beaten by some invisible cane, placed in the hands of a chastiser whose task is unremitting. A feeling of warmth hits the back of your neck followed by a feeling of acute coldness. The body in its state of tiredness has forgotten how to regulate its temperature or so it would seem. Suddenly the force which is urging you to take your tired body to bed is beginning to win you over; and your physical weakness will not allow you to fight against it any longer. Before you have moved completely through the doorway a voice calls. It is only the officiousness of the voice that causes you to turn your head, only when the words are again repeated do you realise that they are directed at you.

"Hello there. How are you …. everything alright?"

You stare at the caller, trying not to appear too rude, for you are unable to recognise the slim, nondescript youth, despite his enthusiasm and the fact that he seems to know you. Your questioning look has already given away your thoughts.

Realising that he seems to have the upper hand, the caller is fuelled by your uncertainty and presses to continue. Obviously pleased at his assertiveness and the sound of his own voice.

"Interesting Article. Well done!"

Suddenly aware that this comment could be pertaining to a whole multitude of various articles and documents that you have been involved in producing recently; you put your sudden fame down to one of these and smile pleasantly. "Thank you." And not wishing to take the conversation any further, you depart; but not before noticing a few other heads turning your way, presumably drawn by the loudness of your follower's intrepid voice.

CHAPTER FOURTEEN

The morning is cold for April. The chill wind had caught you off guard a couple of times already as you make your way from the car park to the office. Each time it has caused you to pull your scarf up further around your collar to shield you from the sharpness of its approach.

The short walk to the office building over, you enter through the security door and quickly climb the small flight of rickety stairs; the carpet that camouflages their awkwardness appears dirtier than usual - probably due to all the recent rain. You'd have to call the cleaners in to sort that out, but of course that would not be priority this morning, there were far too many other things to catch up on. Your three weeks away has been a long break, the longest in five years. It was hard to delegate in your absence, but it had had to be done! Now you would have to face the consequences if there were any and rectify any problems that had resulted. But you are positive that this will hopefully not be necessary. You would prefer a peaceful morning if possible. Your mind does not feel fully in gear yet, and despite a good night's sleep, you feel that you really need another two hours at least in order to fully recover.

Holding your breath and taking a stride forward you pass through the open office door announcing your arrival to your three office colleagues, who have all arrived ahead of you and seem to have the day's work efficiently in full flow.

"Hi everyone - I'm back!"

"Didi, Welcome home!"

"How are you? Did you have a good time?"

"Did you get my Turkish delight?"

"Did you find a lover?"

"How did the conference go?"

In between short burst of answers from you, in the form of '*Yeses*', '*Noes*' and '*Wait* and *Sees*', the questions continue to rain on you from all directions. Some of the staff had wanted to accompany you, but funds had not allowed this. You feel however, that you took them in mind if not in body, and noticing the effects of their enthusiasm, they seem only too grateful to share your stories and adventures, even though they were physically absent from the events which you describe.

Ken, one of your most dedicated workers, seems far keener to hear about the results of your conference rather than your sightseeing trips and you explain in great detail, the event which he shows such profound interest in; whilst Judy your filer, fetcher and carrier, trots off to make a cup of coffee for everyone; seemingly pleased that she has one extra cup to make this morning. Judy never seems to tire of hard work even when asked to do the simplest and tedious of tasks.

Ken listens intently to your stories. Another colleague Michelle joins him, periodically getting up to answer the phone. She seems as interested as Ken to hear all the details.

Watching Ken's tentative gaze, you realise how lucky you have been in the last year, to have had him as part of your team. His was a sad story, but not unfamiliar to the similar stories of countless others, whom the charity has helped over the past few years. You had particularly admired his story; not dissimilar to your own. He had suffered for many years with phobias before finding out about the self-help group, - Triumph Over Phobia (TOP UK). He had been standing in his local library one day waiting to be served when he had noticed the poster on the public information board. He often referred to the poster when recounting his history; remembering especially a pair of small gates, which were drawn above the words on the notice. They signified the path to his freedom; an escape from the terrible isolation and entrapment that he had felt for so many years as a result of his condition. Not being able to socialise, and only leaving the house in order to purchase essential shopping and to collect his dole money. Since coming to the local support group, he had learnt to face up to his problems and confront all those things which he had feared for so long, until eventually he had been able to feel in control of his life again. His only loss, despite all his gains had been his wife, who after three years of marriage had given him up as a lost cause. If only she had waited another few months, she may have been a witness to the amazing progress which Ken had eventually made. But alas you win some and you lose some! That was Ken's mantra. For at least he knew in himself the unimaginable improvement he had made, and how incredibly his life had changed. He had moved on a million miles from those dull miserable days where he had sat at home for hours at a time, smoking himself half to death, wishing and hoping then wishing again.

Since coming to work at the TOP office he had never had reason to look back. He had been attending the TOP group in Hackney for at least eight months, but the group leader had felt that he had made such incredible progress, it was on her suggestion that Ken had volunteered to do some work at the groups Head Office in Baker Street. He had not felt able enough to seek paid employment and had exhausted all his spare time working in the Oxfam shops dotted around the city, helping himself to gain back his confidence in talking and socialising with other people - something he had not done properly for many years. The last shop had been one, situated in the Hampstead area, where he had been lucky enough to acquire two beautiful suits, which he often wore around the office. His attire promoted his self-esteem, and his position was soon promoted to the post of part time employee, which the charities growing donations had managed to secure.

His hard work and efforts, along with his colleague Michelle's helped to organise and implement strategies for increasing funding, publicity and public awareness to help facilitate the growing number of TOP groups situated around the country. Without this pair's tremendous help and support your job would be much harder, and far less fulfilling. Such dedication could only be fuelled by the overwhelming results gained from those attending the groups and the reflection of their successful recoveries.

"Fry's Turkish Delight!" Ken grins at you amusingly as he licks his lips and mimics the tune of the popular advert.

"Of course!" Typical Ken. Not content with the 'yes' earlier when you had been bombarded with questions and had initially answered them all in such quick fashion. Ken is now determined to see the colour of his fruits, having grown keen in the last few months to display his newfound assertiveness. His sense of humour and delight in participating in every day conversation was evident every time he spoke to you. The spontaneity with which he was now able to begin a conversation and actually feel in control, were immediately self-evident, not only to yourself but to many other people too. Michele was especially helpful in encouraging Ken. She had no fears of her own where conversation was concerned. Her essential problem could easily have been described as the reverse. Her ability to talk incessantly was often more a detriment than an asset to her and probably borne through her noticeable nervousness but she was never discouraged when frequently you would ask her politely to finish what she was trying to say a little more quickly! Michelle, like Ken had been a previous sufferer, her problem had been similar to Ken's in that she had experienced terrible irrational fears, mainly with animals. But as her problems had worsened, she had adopted more and more bizarre phobias which had stemmed from the more dominant ones and had seemingly introduced themselves in a mental 'domino' affect. She often recalled how when she had come to her first TOP meeting, the group leader had informed her that she was the first person that they had ever had who was frightened of feathers. "They reassured me at the time" she often recalls. "But I thought they were only trying to be sweet! -I really thought that I was beyond help!" However, Michelle had fully recovered from her phobias in a matter of weeks, by working at her programme of homework systematically for as many hours as she could afford each day. Like Ken her work and efforts had more than paid off. Between them they had proved to be an exceptional and valuable asset to the charity. Both were fully aware of the difficult problems faced by the people who were so desperately in need of help. Their examples were important in encouraging others to win their battles. They often did interviews for local radio stations and a few daytime chat show hosts had shown a keen interest in interviewing them. All this publicity plays an essential part in ensuring the charities healthy profile and also its credibility; helping to place it in a position of effectively assisting even more sufferers. Reaching beyond a 'Name' on the general notice board list in the library or surgery to a place where it might become as freely talked about, one day, as 'The Samaritans'. You hope by educating people about the nature of the illnesses that you help to treat; you will subsequently begin to eradicate the stigma so frequently attached to these problems. One way or another you hope to reach a wider population and hopefully offer support to many more individual who might potentially benefit from the group's help but who as yet might know little or anything about its work.

"Didi, this calls for you!" Michelle stands on the other side of the office, holding the telephone receiver high in the air, presumably to gain your more urgent attention. Realising that you have not entered working mode yet, you take a deep breath run your fingers through your neat fringe as if inviting thought and adjust your mind to the time and place. Not, however before reaching into your leather satchel and retrieving a small hexagonal parcel wrapped in a thin floral paper. Not your choice of wrapping! Placing it on the desk in front of you, you invitingly nod whilst angling the right side of your temple towards the box, gesturing to Ken his long-awaited present. As he reaches across to accept the gift, Judy places down a tray of steaming coffees on the desk beside Ken.

"Brilliant timing Jude!" In her infectious way Judy smiles but does not encourage any further conversation.

Judy was never a 'phobic' nor to your knowledge has she ever suffered from Obsessional Compulsive Disorder. Judy's presence in the office was precipitated by a local advertisement, asking for a full-time office administrator. Judy had been one of many applicants, but you had chosen her above all the others because at the time your sixth sense had told you that she would be just right for the job. Despite her lack of energy and repartee, she got on with the jobs she was asked, did them well and finished them often in record time. There was fastidiousness about her ways that was not present in her appearance. Often, she would arrive at the office with various items of clothing begging for readjustment. You often wondered whether she possessed a mirror, but this was not your concern; you could not question or judge this woman beyond her capabilities. She did her job well and for that reason alone, you had to give her, her dues. These kinds of people are often as hard to find as gold dust and you were more than grateful for her resourcefulness. This morning as Judy stands beside you, you can't help noticing that her clothes are all facing in the right direction and for once she appears to have a little colour on her cheeks. You make no comment as you edge passed her and move across to take the phone from Michelle.

"Thanks!" You cover the receiver tightly as you ask, "Any idea who it is?"

Michelle shakes her head "He wouldn't say. But he asked for you."

"OK" -You watch as Michelle heads in the direction of the coffee tray. Then assertively, you speak into the receiver. "Hello, can I help you?"

"That depends! Hello Didi. You alright?" The familiar voice of Russell expresses itself in ever-friendly tones. One of TOP's leaders from the Sheffield group. Russell is making one of his weekly contacts with the Head Office, 'just to keep in touch' as he always put it.

"Yes! I'm fine!"

Cautiously you begin to wonder, why everyone seems so keen to ask you if you are all right, first the young lad in the bar yesterday and now Russell. There is a certain element of paranoia mixed into your thoughts, as you begin to sense the strangeness in being asked such a question especially in the concerned manner in which it has been delivered on both occasions. Perhaps you ought to reassess the accuracy of your reply. Maybe for some reason these other people don't imagine that you should feel fine at all.

Russell makes no attempt to stretch his questioning further, seeming content for now with your genuine reply.

"Just keeping in touch! Didi. Did you have a good break?"

"Wonderful thanks. A totally unimaginable experience I fell that I have done such a lot in such a short space of time."

"Conference went well?"

"Excellent thanks. I think I made an impact on some of the professionals."

"Let's hope so!"

"Everything all right your end Russell?"

"Yes thanks. Five new members in the group in the last fortnight, and some of our older members are nearly there."

"Good work Russell! Keep it up! Anything else to report?"

"Not at present, but take care in the meantime, I'll catch up with you again soon. Bye for now!"

"Bye Russell. And take care, yourself!" Placing the receiver back in position you start walking back to the office desk where everybody else has congregated around the coffee and Turkish Delights. The combination of the two does nothing for you, so declining Ken's offering up of the half-empty box, you pick up your coffee, thanking Judy at the same time.

Ken is probably the first to notice your inquisitive look, as you sit down in one of the chairs positioned around the desk, in a dinner- table like fashion, for the benefit of the sociable tea break atmosphere. A behaviour which has obviously been adopted whilst you were absent; you'll soon have things back to normal if you have your way! There needs to be just a touch of discipline to keep everyone in order. Pleasant but formal, that's always best! TOP's teachings are disciplined, so by disciplining the team it helps to maintain a discipline in the methods that you teach. 'Start from the top' that's always been your motto - too many cups of tea and too much sympathy spoil's the effect. Inducing your strict regime has never proved too difficult up to now. It is your firm belief that people respond best to strictness and order, whether they will openly admit to it or not.

Another telephone ring startles you out of your silence. Michelle energetically jumps up in order to answer it. Meanwhile Ken swallows the last remnants of one of his sweets and quickly licks his lips to eradicate any last traces of icing sugar. He then proceeds to question you with a statement. .

"You look perplexed?"

Acknowledging the rhetorical aspect of this question you quickly decide to answer with a question of your own. Place the ball back in his court for a while maybe and see if he can come up with any answers.

"Do I?"

"It would appear so. Yes!" Ken eyes you a little more suspiciously, raising his left eyebrow like some detective from a Humphrey Bogart movie, about to see if he can test the criminal without the use of a lie detector. "Anything you care to share Boss?" For a moment he has moved into the driving seat, and you don't like to feel you are the passenger in this situation. Trying to remain in control of the matter, you face Ken and try to avoid focussing on his brow which seems to have become comically locked in what is effectively a rather outdated pose. Your reply remains passive.

"Nothing really, I don't suppose!" You hear the defensiveness in your voice as you continue. "It's probably just the jet lag. My mind playing tricks on me, so to speak."

"What is it Didi?"

"This feeling that I have, like … there are people concerned about me. As if there's something I should know about, but I don't - If you see what I mean? It's most peculiar and I really wonder if it's my imagination or whether they really do know something. The trouble is there have been other things too, but I think that it's all just a coincidence."

"What things Didi?"

"Oh, it seems so silly Ken." You begin to feel your defences weakening. Feel the burning urge to off load. Any other time you might have been able to hold on to it, but today you are too tired. You begin to feel your stomach register hollowness deeper than hunger, as you open up to your thoughts.

"Well, there was the car chase yesterday in the street and then of course there was the episode at the airport on Saturday evening……."

"So, you heard about all that. I wondered whether it was your flight, when I first heard it on the news."

"Heard what Ken?"

"About the Hi Jacking on that Israeli plane." He is reading the shock on your face, as he keenly continues. "You didn't know?"

"No, I didn't!"

"Perhaps they kept it as quiet as they could your end, so that they wouldn't alarm too many other passengers?"

"Perhaps!"

"Maybe that's why your friends were asking after you. They may have been worried for you when they heard the news?"

"Maybe." You notice your increasing number of mono-symbolic replies. It was always your sub-conscious method of coping in the past, to events or news which you were unsure how to respond to. 'Shut up and shut off' That had always been your technique, and here you were, implementing it again.

"Sure, you're OK, Didi?"

Ken's reassuring smile is sufficient enough to revive you and give you back your tongue. "Yes thanks!"

"Guess you haven't had much of a chance to read the papers since you've been back?"

"No! No, you're right I haven't!" You remember noticing yesterdays' paper lying beside your chair, when you ran into the lounge this morning to grab your keys. You hadn't even glanced at the headlines nor switched on the radio to catch the early morning bulletin. Trying hard not to stammer, you sense your heartbeat increasing as you ask your cautious question. "Is the Hi-Jack over, do you know, Ken?"

Ken looks awkward, as if he doesn't particularly want to answer the question directly, as if he wants to cover up or at least not be too liberal with the truth. "I'm not sure! The breakfast news said that there were still negotiations going on and that as yet they could only hope that all the hostages were safe."

You are beginning to relate to this incident as if you are taking part. It seems that you were so close, and yet at the time oblivious to all that was going on. You feel almost guilty, that you were so unaware. Suddenly your list of mindful questions return – "What do the hi-jackers want?"

"They are PLO sympathisers; I think it is pretty obvious what they want. They want their land, and they want the Israelis to keep their hands off it. That's basically what it boils down to."

"But it seems such an extreme measure to hi-jack a plane full of innocent people, to get your point across. If only they could voice their opinions in a more diplomatic fashion, it would make life safer for everyone."

"Unfortunately, these people talk with their guns and their actions, their political diplomacy left the conference table a few decades ago. They are just fanatical about their cause. Obsessed by what they see as their rights. But surely you know all this, already. You question these issues as if you were born yesterday. Didi?"

"Oh absolutely - I understand the reasons but I don't understand the tactics. Can't there be some kind of compromise drawn up, which allows each side a small proportion of land, then the Israelis would at least have some of their Promised land back."

"Wonderful! Passive intervention would ideally be the answer. But if you were an Israeli worshipping by the laws of Judaism, would you want a mosque stuck in the centre of your territory?" Ken doesn't even wait for your reply but finishes by answering his own question. "Of course not, and neither, if you were a Muslim would you want a temple built in your market square."

Listening quietly to Ken you realise that his understanding and thinking are similar to your own. There is an air of passivity to all that he explains. Does your phobia and OCD make you this way? You wonder. For to have felt the turmoil and stress of years of battle within your own body and mind must make you less inclined to go out into life and demonstrate to the point of destruction, after having spent years recreating yourself. For you are sure that ridding the body of these illnesses is almost beyond the idea of resuscitation and more in the realms of reincarnation. For a human being to then want to go out and 'destroy' would surely be nothing more than an act of pure insanity. Thinking on, it becomes apparent to you that fighting for the rights of your nation, simultaneously annihilates you from reaping all the true rewards, for though physically capable to put up a fight, mindfully you may be well passed it. Sadly, the evil of the battle always lays passionately alive within the minds of the future and the history books, any true reasons are often buried deep within the rotting minds of the corpses on the battlefields.

Ken livens you from your reveries as he decides to close the conversation, and you realise that on this bright, but windy and spring-like morning in England; you can do no more to alter the world and its problems than you can make the sun go in, behind the clouds.

Quickly rearranging the chairs back to normal, you apologise to Ken for interrupting his work. A subtle and diplomatic means of requesting that he get back to what he was doing before your arrival. He registers your thoughts immediately and obligingly lifting his seat, he carries it back towards his desk in the corner; apologising to Michelle as he narrowly misses striking her shoulder with one of the chair legs as he proceeds to manoeuvre himself and the article around her. Still intent with her phone call, she hardly notices. Judy has returned to the kitchenette with her washing up.

Sitting at your desk now, you observe the input tray in front of you. There are not as many documents as you perhaps expected - a relief. Not really wanting to delay any further from getting down to business, you try to stretch your mind to concentrating on the first item that comes to hand. But hard as you try, there is a moment's hesitation where you find yourself drawn to look across in the direction of the window, housed on your right.

Concentrating on the weather you notice that there are rain drops running down the darkened pane of glass. Not much, just enough to affirm that you have really arrived back home in England, and you will have to wait a while before any guaranteed days of wholesome sunshine arrive. Then just as if nature is trying to show you that anything is possible, a thin glimmer of the sun's rays penetrates the clouds and secondly through the glass. Facing Southwest, the office is situated in the line of the sun whenever it appears, almost to an astrological fineness. If God had wanted to line up the planets to this sun, he could have used your office window as efficiently as he had guided Aristotle's tools.

A faint shimmer of a rainbow appears against the darkness of the sky, transferring the world into a fantasia like quality, all but briefly; the image spoilt periodically by the invasive double-decker bus, which skim past just above the level of the lower sill. You see out but no one can see in. Everyone on board seems engrossed in newspapers, magazines and conversation. Some hardly notice the rain and some do not even witness the rainbow, which drapes itself transiently above their heads.

CHAPTER FIFTEEN

It is roughly five o'clock; you are wandering along Baker Street in a southerly direction towards Marble Arch. The clouded skies from earlier, have now given themselves up to a pleasant scattering of sunshine, which at this hour of the day, always seems to provide an illuminating freshness that is never as evident at any other time of the day. It provides a welcome pass-over as the transfiguration takes place between the late afternoon and early evening. The hour of the day, when most lucky employees break from their work and return home to their families or various abodes, to begin enjoying their 'free time'.

As you continue along the street the stray puddles left by the earlier rains, cast periodic stepping stones along your path and the odd tree gives off a healthy scent, from it's freshly watered leaves. Everything stands in a revitalised pose, seeming to smile. Your mind views this watery picture, it is like the impressionist's painting, stark in it's colours and shapes but undefined by linear containment. You begin to hum the old Gerry Rafferty favourite, though you cannot quite remember the lyrics. Strangely enough you are not sure whether you ever really did know them -
> Making my way down Baker Street,
> Sun in my eyes and dead on my feet...??

Not wholly inappropriate lines for such an occasion. Though you were only guessing that the street was the same one, as in the song. It had to be!

Dodging the puddles, you liberally tap the point of your umbrella against the pavement pacing out your stride. The sound of metal hitting concrete has a comforting quality about it, you are unsure why. You feel like a child discovering a new sound and wanting to repeat it. To continue on and on; absorbed in the contentment of being in control.

You had decided to leave the office early, leaving Ken to lock up. You will pick the car up from the underground car park later, but first you wanted to buy the Evening Standard, not having properly read a newspaper for so long, you feel an urgent need to catch up with the latest news. As you approach the corner of George Street, you sight an old News - vender at his stand, busy with his sales. You cast your attentions towards his billboard, giving yourself a taster of what the headlines have to offer.

ISRAELI HOSTAGES. NEW NEGOTIATIONS
IN PROGRESS.

Immediately you apply your mind to some quick calculations, working out that these poor hostages have now been captive for forty-eight hours. You try to imagine the thoughts and feelings that must be going through the minds of these people. It is almost unimaginable, almost unbearable. And hear are you FREE, home safely, getting on with life. Feeling a little tired maybe, but for heavens' sake, what have you to grumble about in comparison? Looking further down the sandwich board, you quickly search for other news, which orders itself as secondary to the initial headline. You soon find it......-

HEAT WAVE TO HIT BRITAIN THIS SPRING!

Was there indeed any degree of sense in casting these two pieces of news together in their intense diversity? Neither one cancelled out the other. They might as well have been headlines from two separate planets. Surely the journalist, who thought of the latter, deserved to be placed on a different planet. What right had they to align any similarity between England's temperatures and people's lives?

Joining the queue of those waiting to purchase their respective papers for further expansion of these headlines, you watch the curious and varied attire worn by the people in front of you. The changing weather has chanced a daring assumption that the actual air temperature has risen by some considerable number of degrees. You beg to differ as you once again, tuck your collar up around your neck. There is certainly an amazing and extensive variety of fashion displayed this afternoon on the street, which exerts a strong feeling for an urge to change from normal winter clothing to something which Yells …'Summer has arrived in Britain! Footwear and all kinds of clothing are experimented with on a day like this, mainly among the ladies. Some still wearing sweaters appear slightly over heated, but not enough to remove their offending layer. Oddly some have decided to attach sandals to their feet, maybe to offset the warmth of their sweaters; their un-stockinged feet, presumably less uncomfortable and perhaps slightly refreshed when they inadvertently step in the occasional puddle. Your eyes follow a lady conveniently dressed in a rather flimsy T-shirt, perhaps her favourite one, which until now she hasn't had the opportunity to wear since she bought it. Across her breast area the shirt reads - FCUK. The letters are each stretched in a vertical persuasion, by the wearer's curvaceous body. The slogan is one you remember seeing for the first time, not long back. You had read it on a billboard as you had been negotiating a tight bend, in your car. It had taken you completely by surprise and suffice to say, had immediately caught your eye and made you look twice, in between checking the road ahead of you and realigning your car against the curve of the kerb. How did they get away with that? But then you knew why - It was clever, and the psychology worked. It had worked for you and right at this moment, it was working well for the people passing you in the street, and those in the queue ahead of you, not to mention those behind. There is nonchalant nudging, inadvertent tripping, all taking place at speeds of half a mile an hour, as people's eyes meet with the advert. In your case a speed of thirty miles an hour, behind the wheel of a car, had been a little more hair-raising, not to mention slightly more dangerous. You would have liked to have raised the issue with the council at the time, but then you rather liked the advert too, so you had let the notion drop.

The queue begins to move forward; the vendor's calls becoming clearer and louder as you approach the head of the queue.

"Papers! Papers! Get your Evening Papers here!"

Your turn arrives. Almost deafened by the sound, you make your request.

"Yes! Can I help you? Yes! What was that?"

Trying to raise your voice above the din you repeat your request once again. This time your voice squeaks but you have obviously been heard.

"Thanks. There we are." Handing you a warm copy of the newspaper his other hand darting out in a pleading fashion, he waits for your change.

"There we are!"

"Not enough, sorry."

Hastily you search for further change, as you mentally note how inflation has hit the newspaper industry, whilst you have been away.

"There we are! … Thank you." You clutch the paper and step to one side, allowing the queue to move along.

"And many thanks to you! - Yes! Next please!"

Waiting for a moment to decide what your next move will be, you glance down at the paper in your hand and quickly flick the fold so that it drops open in front of you and the cover is revealed. Your eyes are beginning to widen, and you caution yourself not to read but although your mind does not want to, your human curiosity drives your keen eyes hurriedly across the page and then with equal keenness, your eyes follow down a thin column of words, to the right of an explicit picture. There is no colour required to decorate this image or dress it up. The stark black, white and grey ink speaks its own news in one forceful and unequivocal blow.

Within a bold printed line for a frame. A single large plane sitting on a curiously deserted runway. The airport lights and those from within the plane itself, outline the image, and create a further starkness to its forlorn and desolate appearance. Around the plane, a small distance apart, stand a circle of armed guards.

Your mind is registering the impact of this picture, and quickly piecing together its contents. You assume that the armed guards that you see, must be on the side of the Hi-Jackers',within the plane. Surely no one else would want to get that close to danger.

You are beginning to take in the words, which your eyes have just scanned. You must have scooped up the important facts and put the story together as a colourful mental picture, without actually realising. For the story in comparison to the picture that stares at you from this front-page holds an element of foreboding, which makes the two almost incomparable.

The Headline begins: -

NEGOTIATIONS REINSTATED AFTER FIRST
CONFIRMED EXECUTION.

Following the headline, the reporter's efforts had pulled
no punches in examining and detailing the News. -

Palestinian and Israeli diplomats
are still locked in talks tonight in
a bid to pursue an end to the hi-
jacking, which began on Saturday
evening.
All reports so far state that one
Israeli hostage has been killed,
And that at lunch time today his
body was thrown from the plane's.
emergency exit.
No further communications have
Been made with the hijackers since
this incident took place…...

The impact of this report stabs you unremittingly and you
feel weak, as you did earlier, when Ken had first shocked
you with the news.
Persuading yourself to try and block your mind to the
incident and concentrate on the 'now' is hard. Suddenly your
work with TOP has taken on a transparent worth against the
larger problems of the world, but nevertheless in their own
undistinguished   ways   -   Hi-jacking,   Obsessional
Compulsive Disorder and People's Phobias, all have their
respective importance to each individual, living and
working together, on this rapidly rotating planet.
As you refold the paper, the STOP PRESS column
catches your eye, and another headline strikes close to
home.
JOURNALIST AND INFANT DIE IN STREET
COLLISION…

Again, your heart sinks. And in the words of A.A. Milne, you sincerely believe that "You can run from bad luck - but you can't hide!"

Deciding to deliberate no further, you turn yourself around and head back up the street in the direction of the Marylebone Road. You will pick up the car and drive to Waitrose on your way home. You had made do for breakfast and yesterday's T.V. Dinner hadn't been bad, but your body is slowly leaning towards a desperate yearning for some descent fresh vegetables and fruit; not to mention a descent piece of lamb or perhaps beef. If it hasn't gone out of fashion since you've been away! Thoughts of food push your salivary glands into over-drive and realising that you cannot hold out much longer, you dive into a corner shop for a Mars bar. Somehow you feel it will have a more dramatic effect on your sugar levels, than the odd polo or two, which you have been trying to sustain yourself with, for the last half an hour or so.

"Will that be all?" The disappointed face of the saleswoman looks at you in such a way, that you feel you ought to commit a crime or two to make her melancholy mood worth her while, ……. then you think better of it! She stands almost motionless in her elaborate Sari. Her bindi stares at you from her forehead like an evil eye watching you, delivering telepathic spells. Her piercing brown eyes follow suit.

"Yes, thank you." Your affirmation causes her face to drop a further degree; though you were not sure this was humanly possible. Never mind perhaps tomorrow would be a better day for her! Maybe she wished she were nearer home, Bangladesh, Pakistan or wherever. Had she really had a say in being placed in such a culturally different world? Was she in fact better off standing in a cold, isolated sweet shop, or would she prefer working in the warmer environment of a paddy field some ten thousand miles away? - Who knows? -You wish her 'Good day'. If your thoughts are not too patronising, you feel sure that she will feel a little happier maybe, when this Heat Wave comes along. -You hope so! You do feel genuinely concerned for her, and you know that your slightly racist thoughts come not from you, but from a slow filtered deliverance over the years from your parents.

Nibbling the Mars bar, you make your way energetically back to the car, the pull of Waitrose helplessly evoking you to conjure up images of plates of delicious foods and tempting desserts. These images are almost enough to re-evoke the temptations of those smells from the East - and indeed you salivate, both mentally and physically.

Reaching the car park you search hastily for your ticket, without it you will be unable to exit, that is without a rigmarole, involving security and the Local Council. You have experienced the protocol already - only the day before your holiday. This evening you aren't as keen to repeat the pantomime, and feeling your keys deep within your pocket, alongside your ticket, a sudden relief draws the tension of concern from your brow.

CHAPTER SIXTEEN

Sitting in the driver's seat of your car, you lean across to the passenger side and fumble around inside a large briefcase, hoping to discover where you have placed your mobile phone. Countless pens, writing material, a thick Diary, all pass through the course of your searching hands. As your search becomes desperate and deeper, the odd remains of a polo packet or two become available.

to you, but you decline; their stickiness unappetising, after probably weeks of festering in the gloomy depths of your case along with……Oh what's this? A few old rubber -bands…. A number of tissues… A bottle lid! Wherever had that come from? - Best not ask! And oh lovely! ... Whatever is this? ... It feels like a sock. - No surely not, but it's definitely cotton. Freeing the article from beneath the other matter, you uncover an old sling! When was it that you'd injured your elbow playing tennis? - Must have been at least eight months ago! How on Earth had this article found its way in here? And had you really not had the opportunity to sort out your case in all that time. Oh no! One more thing! Surely not? This felt hard and unusual; you cannot make it out. … Of course! An old apple-core! … How lovely. …You were despicable! - There was no other word for you. - If this had been someone else's briefcase you would have been horrified. No wonder you couldn't find that retched phone.

"Bloody hell!" The sound of your own voice startles you a little, and you suddenly hope that no one else has heard. But how can they? -When you're sat inside this car with all the windows tightly closed. - Out bursts like this are out of character, and seldom happen. Besides you don't want anyone to witness your alto ego in full play -but of course it's safe. You can if you want to, curse and swear as much as you like for there are no bystanders. Probably no one in ear shot, no one within a hundred yards or more. Contented you chose no further expletive language for the moment, as you reach for the glove box, the flap collapses down and there happily sat between the box of kleenex tissues and the de-Icer is your mobile phone - Jesus Christ! Your prayer to Saint Anthony had been answered. But he could have been a bit quicker!

It has long been your argument that mobile phones are an unnecessary commodity. In your heart you firmly believe that this is true but having been encouraged to get one by countless friends, you have noticed that whenever you lose the thing, the situation becomes a matter of life and death. How easy it is to get hooked like the rest of the world, on these fragile articles? However, the offending article is now *back* in your safe hands!

It 'Peeps' at you as you try to register your personal identity code. The screen flashes alarmingly but does not react as fast as the 'peeps'. -Who says light travels faster than sound? - Not when it has to transverse the 'Orange phone' satellite, obviously.

'Low battery' The massage flashes itself across the screen relentlessly. "Blast!" - Did batteries just decide amongst themselves when they were going to run out or was it really down to physics?

Well, you had better plug it in to the cigarette lighter and give it a bit of a charge up. But you don't really want to sit here for too long. You decide to switch on for a moment, just to see if there are any messages held.

"Oh great!" Five all told. Now your curiosity is getting the better of you. You don't want to wait till you get home to listen to them. You want to listen to them 'Now!' - Perhaps you'll just listen to the first couple and save the others till later. Here goes!

You press the necessary buttons -

"The other caller has hung up……." Having pressed the switch, to hear the next message, there is a momentary pause. And then -

"Caller Number two. Please await message" You wait.

"Hello Didi. This is Wayne Burlington here. Hope you don't mind me tracking you down. Thought I'd try to ring you at the office; but it seems that I've just missed you. I caught Ken, and he didn't think you'd mind if he gave me your mobile number. Hope that's Okay?" …..

You inquisitively listen on.

"Thought it might be nice to have a get together now that we're back in England. What do you think? Collette seems keen to join us so it will probably mean that we'll end up talking shop. But I don't think you'll mind, will you?" His voice hesitates for a second. "There may be a couple of my colleagues from the department, coming along too. Perhaps you'll give me a ring and let me know if you can make it. Next Friday's looking good as a suggestion, rest of the week's a bit tied up with lectures and conferences. Do give me a call when you can. My mobile number's…." You listen and jot the figures down on an old envelope. "Thanks. Bye!" The message ends.

You press 'replay', just to check the number, and then pressing 'clear'. You turn the machine off.

Putting the car into drive you move round the maze of parked cars, until you are eventually approaching the exit. Your window wound down, you hold your ticket at the ready, waiting to place it into the mouth of the machine, when its visual display demands.

Exiting out of the car park, you turn out onto the main street and combine yourself with the rest of the prevailing traffic, slowly but steadily moving forwards towards the Marylebone Road. The fading daylight persuades you to put your sidelights on. You feel dazzled by the other drivers, but it is that time of year when this half-light seems to continue for a while before the real darkness eventually sets in.

Following the straight line of traffic, you move in stops and starts, as the rush hour allows, and you begin to assess the best root for your journey home. It is always a gamble, getting caught at a couple of sets of traffic lights can vary the travelling time by a number of minutes and accidents can sometimes lead to hours of delay. It would be easier, though maybe no quicker to use the bus or the tube, but you never know when you might need the car to visit another office or get to a meeting. So having reasoned with yourself here, you have to agree and accept that your own vehicle is really essential and that the daily journey through the traffic comes as part and parcel of this overall decision.

You turn on the local radio station to hear the latest news headlines being played out by some loud orchestration that signifies an annunciation has just been made. The chosen music is always cleverly composed. Enough to grab your attention before the news and punctuate it immediately after it has been delivered. In a way you are rather glad that you have missed it as you were hoping to mentally switch off a little and concentrate on your driving. You feel that you have already heard enough news to keep you going for the rest of the week. Though you're sure you'll hear plenty more before the weeks up! You wonder whether to pop on a music CD, when suddenly the introduction to another old seventies hit blasts out and immediately you choose to keep the radio on. How strange that you should have thought about Gerry Rafferty earlier. You listen and hum the tune. The words are there but you can't quite remember the title. Why are you always quizzing yourself with these things you wonder? This is what you were doing yesterday when you were sat in that pub, and you still can't think of the name of that Stevie Wonder hit! Oh well perhaps it's your short-term memory loss beginning to herald the start of many other afflictions which will no doubt encompass and bombard you now that middle age is upon you!

NO! Wait a minute! You feel suddenly, much better. Yes! You can remember this one after all. It's - 'I feel Love' - That old Thelma Houston single. The one that was exhausted at the time by every disco that you went to and you must have gone to an awful lot over the years! You turn the volume down, smiling to yourself. Twenty odd years ago it had been impossible to play it loud enough, and now here you are feeling the need to restrain the blast from your eardrums.

Whilst you hum quietly along to the radio, your mind relaxes ………

'TOOT, TOOT, T-O-O-T'!

Heavens, what was that? You sit upright, realising how relaxed you actually were. Checking all your mirrors, you can see nothing wrong, but a taxi has pulled up beside you and through the open passenger window, the driver is now challenging you verbally. His mime is not sufficient for you to make out what it is he's actually saying, so you politely wind down your window in order to listen.

It's not Bert but it could just as easily be. Oh, why is it that all Taxi drivers look so alike? Well maybe they don't, perhaps it's just that they all have a similar character and a cloth cap perched on their head that could convincingly fool a lot of people into thinking they were all related at least!

"Crikey Moses! Watch it – Yer nearly 'ad my wing off!"

"Sorry"

"Who taught you to drive - the bleedin' army?"

"Yes as a matter of fact they did!"

Feeling a little perturbed by this incident, for you are sure you were doing nothing wrong. Your mind flashes back to the days before you took your test, albeit some years ago, remembering that your driving teacher had indeed been an ex-Army Instructor.

"Think you're bleedin' funny, do yer? Drive-in's daft enough without clowns like you trying to be clever!"

You glance as the lights ahead change to amber. The taxi driver continues to shout some further obscenities in your direction, but they are drowned out by the impatient horns of other motorists, as they 'Honk' ferociously, urging the taxi to move on. Eventually he gives up on his sermon, but you know your ears will be burning later, when he retells this scenario, down at his local pub.

Passing through the lights you increase your speed a little. For some reason most of the traffic seems to have dispersed now, and the road ahead is almost completely clear. Turning left at the next set of lights you turn onto the Edgware Road. You notice a faint drizzle beginning to pattern itself on the windscreen in front of you, illuminated by the multicoloured signs radiating from the buildings on either side of you. Their effects are kaleidoscopic, and you feel yourself drawn into the centre of this picture. Wanting to take part in every movement and to hear every sound. Next to Paris this city is your favourite, the warmth and charisma that is generated by the spectacle around you is both enthralling and exciting.

As you approach Marble Arch, you brace yourself as the traffic increases around you. Looking up at the monument ahead, you marvel at its solidity against the weakness of the rain, and the dazzling lights, as its intensity blurs the edges of all its surroundings. Taking the park Lane exit you begin to feel on autopilot, as you saunter along with the steady flow of Jaguars, BMWs, Mercedes and the odd little Metro, which someone has bought with the simple purpose of parking on their mind rather than driving. Very wise! Its indefatigable means of weaving in and out between the majority of the traffic, gives it a head start over all its rivals. You watch it now as it disappears ahead of you, turning on Hyde Park Corner and disappearing through a mist of traffic.

As you approach the last 'bottle neck' of your journey you look over towards 'Speaker's corner'. The poor illumination and probably the rain as well seems to have finally dampened the enthusiasm of today's philosophers and philanthropists, and you watch as they begin to dismount from their soap boxes and pack up their troubles, their reasons and their answers for the day. Heading towards Knightsbridge now, you feel the call of home welcoming you. Just a short shopping spree then you would be able to kick off your shoes and relax for the rest of the evening. These thoughts begin to invigorate you, and feeling more comfortable you execute your plans.

CHAPTER SEVENTEEN

The path through your back garden leads down from the garage steps along to the kitchen door. You were lucky when you moved in. At the suggestion of the previous owners, you conveniently managed to secure the garage, a spare - belonging to the flats that back on to your property. The access gained through a small green wooden door, built into the wall. It remains almost hidden from view, camouflaged by the surrounding ivy. Xindi greets you as you step into the kitchen. You had asked your Spanish housekeeper to pick her up from the Cattery on her way in this morning. As usual Ella had carried out instructions without question. The only time she ever fails to carry out a task is generally due to a difficulty with the language rather than obstinacy. She greets you now and rushes to relieve you of your shopping bags, which hang off your arms in all directions.

"Hola Didi! Ow, are you?" She smiles and her grin displays her missing tooth (You wish she'd get it fixed) – "I av missed you and Xindi as missed you too! Aven't you? My little guapa?" She gently lifts the cat to her breast in a dramatic demonstration of affection and concern. Xindi, with her claws out attempts to retaliate but Ella pulling her closer, allows her no little movement; almost asphyxiating her with the amount of bosom that only an elderly Señora can display.

"Hello Ella. I'm fine. Everything all right here?"

"Si, Si, and Why should it no be? When Ella here, everyting is always right. No? - You grin. Sometimes you have no reply to Ella's conversation. She often gives you no means to dispute her. And why would you want to anyway? You are lucky to have her.

"You want to come inside?" Ella beckons, whilst taking your last bags of shopping from you and placing them on the kitchen table. "You ave bought somethin' good?"

"Yes Ella, something very good!" You often find when talking to Ella that you are affected by her accent and find yourself almost mimicking her speech in order to help her to understand you, although it is not your conscious intention.

"You wan me to peel potatoes before I go, yes?"

"No, no, Ella that won't be necessary, Thank you. I'm sure you've worked hard enough already. Please take yourself home!"

"This is good. I go home early, yes?"

"Yes Ella, it is a little early for you, but please do go."

Fetching her hat and coat from the hallway, she proceeds to put them on. Despite the milder weather Ella continues to wear her thick winter coat and a rather elaborate fur hat, which makes her look about to jump into action and perform a Mazurka on the spot. She obviously feels the cold despite having lived in England for some thirty years or so.

You know that she will not shed a clout until May at least, and then only if the temperatures reach into the seventies. Maybe these people are wiser than we are. They don't ever seem to catch as many colds.

What was the old saying? When in Rome do as .... But maybe the British didn't have that kind of cultural persuasion about them anymore. We always seem so undefined. Our fashions; our tastes; our politics; our attitudes; all are so unidentifiable. - How difficult it must be, for anyone coming from abroad, who is trying to find a means of copying or mirroring our ways, because seemingly, we have none! - Anything goes!

"I leave now Didi. Be Good and Be careful!"

"Yes Ella, I will!"

"Then I will see you tomorrow, No?"

"Indeed Ella."

Proceeding up the small stairs leading to the hall, Ella carries her buxom weight in an awkward fashion as she negotiates each stair. Every few steps she stops to exhale in an exasperated manner.Eventually she makes it to the top. You hear the clicking of the front door catch and a muffled squeak as the door opens; a small draught finding you as it marks its way along the hall, down the stairs and disperses itself around your shoulders as you stand rooted in the kitchen doorway.

It always feels very quiet and hollow in the house when Ella is not about. Just knowing that she is somewhere around; sweeping a carpet, or tidying a room, brings an element of warmth to the surrounding atmosphere. You often listen out for the occasional creak of a floorboard, which generally signals her presence as does the patter of her size four feet scurrying across the wooden floors above you; periodically muffled by her stepping on the occasional rug, here and there. Now at nearly six in the evening these sounds are absent, and no matter how hard you lean your ear to try and find them, there is nothing, no sound. You are alone.

Casting aside your briefcase, you fetch a bottle of white wine from the fridge and delicately poor a small glass as you play back the messages on your answering machine. Somehow their importance, has depleted, since you have arrived home, hunger at this instance, taking precedence. Removing a folded envelope from your coat pocket, you find a pencil and wait to jot down anything important. Switching on the tape you listen quietly……

'First message' The recording then goes on to state that this and the two other supposed messages are non-existent and confirms this accordingly each time - 'the other caller has hung up.'

You notice that none of the numbers of any of these incoming calls so far have been recognised, except for Professor Wayne's, which tallies with the number you already have in front of you, which you wrote down on the envelope earlier whilst in the car park.

Not overly disappointed and spoilt once more by the temptation of 'quick cook' food, you place your supper… another T.V. supper, in the microwave. Despite the shopping trip for fresher food… here you are yet again! Yesterday it was 'Spaghetti Bolognaise.' - a real treat and not as bland as it has sometimes tasted. For this evening, you have chosen 'Cannelloni'. Hopefully you will enjoy it with equal relish. Italian food always tastes good because of course it is good! What more can you say on the subject, except that when you haven't cooked it, it always tastes even better!

Pressing the correct setting on the microwave, you check the timing and switch on. Leaving your meal to be bombarded by infra-red particles for the next two minutes, you run upstairs to see if any further messages have been left on the answering machine connected to the hall phone, pausing for a moment to close the bathroom door on the half landing. No matter how many times you remind Ella, she always forgets; the same as when she misplaces things; often picking up your reading glasses, when she is dusting and putting them down in another room. You remember the time you had found the daily newspaper tucked between a pile of towels by which time the daily stories had become three-day-old news. Ella meant well, and that was that. Everything could be forgiven about her, because Ella was Ella. You question this forgiving statement as you approach the hallway, seeing that the Ella you have so understandably forgiven, has just happened to leave one of the downstairs windows slightly open. Your heart sinks in dismay. But Ella is Ella.

Continuing to listen to the message on the answering machine, you close the offending window tightly shut, trying to avoid catching the net curtains which are flapping with the persuasion of the gentle breeze that is seeping in.

'You have one more message' states the polite voice - Always so 'Very English'. You wonder if one day your ear will meet the voice of a Mancunian or perhaps a Glaswegian, maybe. But you know that the argument still holds at present, that this is the voice that can be most commonly understood by the majority of listeners.

A few clicking sounds and then you hear your message....

"Hi Didi! Didi are you there? It's me, Rachel. Perhaps I've missed you. It's possibly just after eight. I'm still here in Tel Aviv, but I'm hoping to return home sometime on Friday, probably Saturday morning. Hope all is well. There's been a lot of talk here about the conference since you and most of the others returned home. It seems to have got a lot of American publicity too. There were apparently a few top American psychologists at one of the talks, and they are really impressed with the way that these treatments are going. They seem to claim that the methods that you have talked about were their own discovery, but that's nothing new............Oh Didi, I think I'm talking too much, perhaps your tape is running out? But there is just one other thing I have read all about the incident at the airport after we said Goodbye. It must have been terribly frightening for you and now to think of all those poor people still on that plane. I expect you will have seen all the news your end. So, I do not need to go into any more detail. How unfortunate that you got caught up in all this. I am sure you would rather not be reminded. Didi, don't try to ring me, because I may be travelling around in the next few days. So I will contact you again when I return to England. Take Care won't................

The tape finally cuts out, not surprisingly. You are pleased to hear Rachel's voice. There is always an element of compassion and understanding about her, which seems evident in whatever subject she is discussing and whoever she is talking to. That personal touch! Which, you don't always get with too many people these days. She always delivers concern and reassurance in the same breath. And noticeably hits you with the good news first.

Lingering over the message, you capture the smell of your supper wafting its way up the stairwell beside you, and following the mental dinner gong that has been set off in your head, you hurry down to the kitchen with a relaxed air of urgency and relief.

Picking up your half empty wine glass, which you set down on the table a few moments ago, you take a further sip and prepare to exterminate your hunger.

CHAPTER EIGHTEEN

Having taken the Piccadilly line from Kensington High Street, you are now travelling north on the Northern line. You jolt about in a tightly packed carriage; Friday evening is never the best time to travel. It doesn't seem to matter whether you are coming away from the city or entering it, every conceivable means of transport is always heaving with passengers, tenfold to the normal number on Mondays to Thursdays. It appears as if the population of London doubles at this point every week, just for an hour, just for the convenience of making everybody's life a little more hectic and awkward.

Perhaps someone should devise a system of coloured tickets in order to stagger the flow. Blue tickets enter stations between five and six, green tickets between six and seven. Sounds absurd but then most new inventions are laughed at initially. The English aren't one's to acknowledge change with open arms, even if there is admissible strength in its suggestion. Oh well until that inventor comes along to pioneer your idea, you will have to settle down with the rest of London's passengers and enjoy the ride!

Mind the gap! Doors closing! Hampstead station. Mind the gap! Doors closing!

Abruptly you come to with a start, realising your whereabouts; daydreaming at a time like this is never wise. You jump up quickly and head for the doors of the carriage, stumbling over bags, umbrellas and the occasional pushchair, reaching the doorway just in time. Jumping onto the platform, you quickly get your bearings and drawn in with the swarm of people around you, you soon arrive at the archway marked 'Exit'.

Feeling in your pocket for your ticket, you begin to wonder if you really ought to have got a taxi instead. Bit late now though! You carry on forwards drawn by the wake created by the passengers in front of you, who are in a far greater hurry than you or so it seems. You wonder where they are all hurrying to. Momentarily you look forward to the evening ahead. You are glad that you have accepted Professor Wayne's invitation. His sister has apparently booked her favourite restaurant in Hampstead, 'Fagin's Kitchen' and you understand that they have each invited along one of their colleagues. It is going to be an interesting evening; you are sure of that.

Remembering the directions that you were given on the phone last evening you stand at the entrance to Hampstead Tube Station, and look around you, to get your bearings. Then turning right, you begin to make your way along the ascending road in front of you. As you travel along the light is beginning to fade, and at certain points along the street you witness the shop windows illuminating themselves; encouraging you to become more aware of their displayed contents. You notice a few specialist food and health shops and then a few glamorous fashion boutiques; one heralding a colourful mannequin dressed in the new spring collections fresh out of 'Vogue' and 'Harper's and Queen'. You know because the magazines have been used in the displays too. Dotted here and there in a creative, eye catching and subliminal way, allowing you to follow the order and connect with the ideas, a paradigm of cosmetic thought. Radiating from the array of garments and magazines, there is an obvious smell of wealth and splendour. Poverty is far from the image of this place and yet you know that in Kentish Town, not a stones-throw away from here, lies the shadows cast by people's desperate means to survive. It's dark under-world creeps beneath the surface of the streets, providing a weird illusionary foundation, with an under-current of drug deals and prostitution. These well sought after jobs being as popular as, banking and retail jobs, commonly fought for on the surface of society.

Yes indeed! Who needs wealth, surely having just what you need is a far more important goal, than trying to succeed and exceed. And how must those people in Kentish Town feel, when the Hampstead yardstick extends further than theirs does. Imagine feeling so deflated? so demoralised. You close your mind to your sudden socialistic attitudes and further scan the window display in front of you. It is appetising, tempting, all this richness beckons to you, and you can see immediately how the rest of society are so easily drawn in by the media and advertising. Everyone wants to be that someone that they weren't yesterday. Someone – 'SPECIAL'. Someone – 'DIFFERENT'. No one seems satisfied with the person that they are today. And yet no one can tell them that the person inside never truly changes. Does the man who wins a million, wear a smile on his face for the rest of his days? Does he keep smiling when the press, come snooping? When friends start begging? When the government says it wants more tax? Let's hope he does!

Further down the street you pass a charity shop. As you pass by you notice the sign above the door: -
'Care and Share.'
Does this prick the conscience of the shopper who has just spent his three-figure sum in the shop back down the road or does being rich buy you a clear conscience? Who Knows? You imagine yourself in an 'Yves Saint Laurent' suit, and saunter along as if you are someone different. Intermittent glances at your reflection in various shop windows assures you that you look good enough, dressed as you are. Feeling slightly smug you walk on.

Glancing at your watch you check the time –Seven-fifteen, you thought it might have been later, bearing in mind all the queues at the tube station. You had agreed a meeting time with the others, yesterday. Seven thirty in the restaurant bar. You know you haven't far to go, and as you continue to negotiate the irregular cobblestones which inter-lace themselves between the concrete pavements, you progress along the street.

Fagin's kitchen stands out on the other side of the road. A beautiful Tudor frontage enhanced by the theatre-like curtain of Ivy that adorns the length of the building and trails down like waterfalls at either end. You cross the road. There is a heavy oak door, which encourages an entrance from you and as you lift the latch carefully, the door slowly begins to open onto a room that seems slightly lower than the street level. You carefully avoid tripping on the pair of narrow steps, which lead down to the floor level. The wooden floorboards creak as you place your shoe softly upon them; trying to avoid the loud 'Clank' that such contact normally procures. Your footstep is silent, silent above the noise of the room. There is much jovial conversation and merriment and the whole place seems to shake with the internal sound that pushes against its walls. Above the din you think you here music, but you realise that the only music present is the echoing voices of the occupants. There are a few Irish voices among them, which you quickly pick out listening to their harmonious sweetness.

You look around for the familiar faces of your friends, and spot them, sat huddled together at a large table squeezed into an alcove. Moving over towards the group you appear engulfed in a mist of cigar and cigarette smoke, everywhere taking on a hazy appearance against the somehow, stern dark red walls which encompass the room.

Ghosts live here, this passing thought creeps through your mind. As only it does, when that kind of thought is inexcusably evoked. You imagine the history behind the building and all the Tudor drinkers who must have spent many hours looking at these very same walls, though of course none would have had the opportunity to appreciate, the William Morris style wallpaper, as you do, now. At last, you are approaching the table, and everyone is beginning to turn to look at you as you announce your presence."Good Evening, Everyone!"

Professor Wayne's outstretched hand greets you as he stands up to welcome you further and begins the ceremony of introducing you to those present at the table.

"Caroline, I'd like you to meet Didi,"

"Hello Didi. Pleased, to meet you." Caroline's voice has a slight Russian or Polish accent to it, and you are surprised at first, for no reason. It then occurs to you that some people just don't look as if they have an accent.

"Pleased to meet you too Caroline, I gather you work with the Burlington's? Is that right?"

Caroline clears her throat before she replies "Only sometimes. I'm a researcher and I spend a lot of my time in America. But I prefer to work here in London when I can."

You notice the Professor trying to regain your attention, and looking away from Caroline, you follow the direction of his hand as he introduces you now to the second friend.

"Didi, I would like you to meet a very old friend of mine Professor Sophie Ingram."

"Hello Didi, please just call me Sophie, I hate using titles with friends! Though incidentally, I love the way you address our friend as Professor Wayne! I think it really suits you, Wayne!" Turning towards him to share this statement she laughs in time with the professor. You hadn't really seen anything amusing about this nickname, but obviously it has struck a harmonious chord with these two.

"Now Didi!" Sophie turns to face you and a broad Cheshire cat grin reaches across her face, highlighted by a pale pink lipstick, heavily painted on, in a Barbara Cortland style. Behind the smile, a row of gleaming white teeth share a brief display with you. "I have heard so much about you from Wayne and Collette." Sophie goes on. "And I have been so looking forward to meeting you. No doubt we will learn a lot more this evening. It was so good of you to arrange to join us. We quite often come out like this for a little get together. Although we all have such similar jobs, our lines of work often keep us great distances apart. And so this is like a little homecoming - Isn't it everyone?" Another grin steals the moment as she amusingly turns her head to allow herself to engage with the rest of the party.

Everyone nods their agreement, and you can see by their enthusiasm that their infrequent get togethers' are important to each one of them. They are truly a close circle of friends.

Professor Wayne takes the initiative in this brief moment of silence to conveniently interrupt and ask.

"Anyone for drinks? Didi?"

"Please. A gin and tonic if that's Okay?!"

The others take the opportunity of sharing their individual choices, as Professor Wayne mentally takes down their requests.

The waitress is summoned to the table and the various beverages are ordered.

"Let's order a wine for the dinner, shall we?" Professor Wayne is obviously keen to make certain that the evening's drinks are well organised and in continuous flow.

"Yes Wayne. Good idea!" Colette is the first to agree, without hesitation. Obviously as enthusiastic as her brother at keeping everyone's thirst quenched. "What's it going to be then Wayne?" It seems to be taken for granted that Wayne will do the choosing; obviously the expert on the subject or at least he gives the impression, that he knows what he's about as he does with many things it would appear. An extraordinary level of confidence pleasantly free of arrogance. Perhaps he is a Gemini and has the ability to skim over the surfaces of a lot of subjects, appearing to know them very deeply by his manner. Perhaps you will question him later, if the conversation requires re-stoking.

"I volunteer that we try the Borolo!" No one attempts to make an alternative suggestion and with nods of heads all round, the wine is ordered. The waitress having taken an opportunity to pass round the dinner menus, now scribbles down the drinks order and wishes everyone a pleasant evening; telling you all to let her know if there is anything else you need. Keenly she informs you that her name is Della. From listening to her speak it is apparent that she must be from the local area. She has that Londoner's warmth and sensitivity about her which provides a charisma that you can't help feeling comfortable with.

Della returns to the bar, to sort out the required drinks. In the meantime, your little group hurriedly gets to work, exercising thoughts and exchanging knowledge and opinions. It is the kind of conversation that you enjoy. It is like a spilling over of the thoughts and ideas that often govern your own mind privately. You find it both stimulating and calming all at the same time, undoubtedly in a way, a rather strange phenomena which perhaps makes up for the inert and uninteresting conversation that sometimes takes place around you during your normal daily life.

As the evening sets in, you feel the slow emergence of your body from its quiet dignified composure, that business-like approach which you tend to adopt during the daylight hours. Now that the night is upon you, and the effects of the alcohol are starting to endorse themselves upon your tongue and your co-ordination; you are beginning to feel more at home with these new friends that you have found. At first you had felt that you were impinging on their intimacy, that perhaps they would feel unsure about saying certain things in your presence; they are obviously used to their own company in an informal setting, but they certainly aren't used to yours. Yet it doesn't seem to make any difference. You feel accepted. There seems to be a mutual understanding between these people that you are to be appreciated and respected. As it should be of course! But for so much of your life you had felt uneasy in the presence of educated people - those 'People' with knowledge - those 'People' with letters after their name -

those 'People' with experience. You had always imagined those people to be of a different sect, one that you were not worthy to be a part of, because you had such little knowledge in comparison to theirs. Of course, you have no letters after your name but indeed you know now that the way you used to feel was altogether wrong; your early beliefs and perceptions categorically untrue. Your own measurement of psychology holds equal ranking and understanding, to that placed upon these intellectuals, though not only your knowledge but of course your own first-hand experience. You know as much and perhaps more besides, though you haven't quite got used to admitting it yet.

Looking around as you do now, you notice that it doesn't matter how fantastically clever you are, the effect of alcohol eventually takes its toll on even the cleverest mind.

Noisiness erupts all around you, in the form of uninhibited speech, but also in the knocking of misplaced articles, as co-ordination and perception are slowly lost to the contents of various coloured bottles. You know that you are keeping a careful watch on your own intake; not yet enough to spoil the evening, but sufficient enough to make you feel aware of the effects. You know your tolerance level, and in the present company that you are in, you don't want to make a fool of yourself, although it seems that in the eyes of these people, you can effectively do no wrong.

"Didi!" Caroline carries a more serious and studious look than Sophie, her stern face has remained almost unaltered so far even though she appears to have consumed a vast amount of Brandy during the course of the evening. There is a radiant glow to her face, but no real hint of a smile. Somewhere deep in her eyes, there shines a sensitive intrigue, seeming to announce a genuine concern to discover more about you. Slowly she continues as she follows your changing expressions. You feel almost as if your mind is being read. "You have a very intriguing history. Having listened to your story earlier, it is quite amazing how you are able to detail so much of your past as if it were yesterday."

"I guess it comes from my love of storytelling. I certainly can't think of any other reason" Your answer is steered by the manner of Sophie's gaze, which continues to lie questioningly upon you. She remains silent as Caroline attempts to continue the conversation.

"Perhaps you're right. But one thing that intrigues me about you is that you never mention your family in any of your stories, Didi. I assume that you have a family?" Quietly and passionately, she asks. "What happened to them? Or would you rather I didn't ask?"

"No, I don't mind! You're quite right, though; I don't speak of my family much. Some things are often best left unmentioned, I feel it doesn't necessarily mean that any underlying problems will disappear or get better for I know that only too well. But it does strike me that if you have tried numerous ways to resolve or improve a situation and nothing is seen to be working, then it calls for a more radical approach. You may think I'm sounding rather subversive in what I am saying here. But I really think that after going through the complication of tearing myself away from other problems such as my illness, that I can't now afford to let my health suffer any further, trying to cope with putting up with things that I can't change." You stop at this point, realising that you are almost talking round in circles, in order, to expose what you are trying to say. The faces watching you, watch with intent interest, waiting for you to resume. You can see this, but do they really want to hear every single detail of your personal history? - The 'Ins and Outs' - The 'Whys and Wherefores'? You doubt it! So, you continue to pause, to regain your poise and dignity and to give yourself time to consider what to say next.

"Do go on Didi" Somehow, Caroline's obvious perplexity is providing you with a reason to continue. Yet it is mostly the soft pained understanding that emulates itself from Sophie's sweet smile, which is more persuading, making you feel that you want to go on, because you want to believe that these people really care. Sophie's smile tells you so, it is convincing, reassuring and most of all trusting. To have all these profound attributes all in play at once is a rare sight to behold. But feeling encouraged you try to pick up from where you left off, searching for the appropriate words, as best you can.

Before you can compose yourself any further, Caroline has stepped in. Obviously, she feels the need to reassure you. The rest of the group has become rather silent, and all attention seems to be on you.

"Didi, you have obviously separated or isolated yourself from the rest of your family? Am I right?"

"Yes, that is true." You feel relief that this confession has been acknowledged, and that these people are still on your side, but you feel an urgent need to back yourself up with a reason or two.

Caroline continues before you can reinstate your cause. It is almost as if she wants to tell the story herself because she knows it so well. Probably she does. Probably she has met many cases like yours before.

"Was it because of your illness?"

"Yes, that's right! They……."

"Didn't understand?"

"That's right." You feel yourself beginning to feel a touch of melancholy at these thoughts. This is a subject, which you try hard not to touch on too often. Even though you feel that you have addressed the problem, you haven't ultimately solved it, and nor do you think, you ever will.

"So, what happened?" Caroline presses you with her further questioning.

"After many years of counselling and being told that my mother appeared to have a personality disorder and was probably suffering from a chronic depression, I finally got to a point where I couldn't try any harder. What I mean *is*, that I gave up trying to make my mother pleased. I had spent all my life trying to please her. And I really had tried hard, really hard. If only she had known just how hard I had tried, but it was seemingly impossible." You hope that your emphasis here will allow your listeners to find the grace to understand and believe you. You don't want to sound like some martyr or a pathetic actor. Those years of struggling had brought great hardship on you. They had caused you to feel so desperate at one stage that you had even tried to take your own life. But although these thoughts trail around in your mind you do not share them with your listeners. Some things are best left to the imagination, and you are sure that these new friends will successfully use theirs in order to picture the scene; after all they are paid to understand, and for one or two of them, it is their life's work, to further their understanding. Not so that they can then go 'There! There!' but so that they can begin to see the wider picture, and so use their knowledge to then prescribe various methods and ways of coping and recovering...

You taught yourself those methods, and you knew how hard it was to put them into action, mentally and physically it was exhausting. There were some that didn't make it, you were very aware of that. Some just accepted and lived with their illness all their lives. Others gave up and made a better job of suicide than you had, but looking back now, you could safely say that you didn't envy them. You had so much to live for now, and you could see the waste. However, at the same time you could appreciate that feeling of absolute emptiness and desperation. Those feelings had been with you for many years and all those negative thoughts had bled your mind clean of any pure or rational thinking. When your mind is that weak, suicide takes nothing. And you have the ability to know that feeling as well as understand it. It makes you no simpler or cleverer. No more naïve or wiser. It makes you just another human being, in the human chain of history. But ultimately you feel that during your life, not only have you existed but most assuredly you have *lived*!

Caroline begins to home in on your thoughts, and although so many ideas and pictures have been whizzing their way through your mind, you are aware that less than a minute has lapsed since you stopped to take stock of this conversation.

"This is not new Didi." Caroline manages to confirm your own thoughts, by means of how her mind is thinking; you obviously have a reasonable telepathy passing here between you. She continues "But of course not everybody has your strength and ability to make such a profound recovery, as you have."

You quickly stop Caroline here. For you want her to be fully aware of your feelings on the subject of recovery. ...

"Caroline, I don't feel that I am fully recovered. I don't think that Obsessional Compulsive Behaviour is, as you might say 'curable'.There are always scars but what does happen is that each day becomes slightly easier…just a little more bearable, because with this illness there is just such a huge mountain of a problem to tackle.It is only as the mountain becomes smaller that it becomes easier to climb. I seriously think that the mountain is always there. Sometimes you can smell the alpine flowers feel the tender breeze through your hair and look up and admire the sky. Other days, the scent of the flowers is hidden, the breeze is like a gale, and you look up to the heavens and all that you feel is dizziness and an overwhelming loss of control."

Caroline looks at you now, in a somewhat bewildered fashion. You feel that you have taken her to that mountain which you have described and left her to the perils of the elements. In some knowing way she certainly seems to have connected with you. Looking as serious as ever; she prepares to fire another question to you.

"So why do you think that you have managed to survive this experience. What profoundly gives you that extra energy to fight, even when everything seems to be against you? What is it Didi? What is that secret?"

"I don't think there is one. I think it is just a primeval urge to survive that maybe kicks in. But that's only an assumption."

"Strange that one moment you feel suicidal and the next you have this amazing ability to survive at all costs?"

"Well, that's just it, probably. Because you have reached such a low ebb; you quite literally have nothing to lose and perhaps everything to gain. It depends how you visualise life itself. I have always felt that life is so precious and so special. I always wanted to live. The reason that I found life so frustrating and felt such desperation was because my illness was preventing me from living. So, in the end I just felt that I would live anyway and push my illness out of my mind. Amazingly my philosophy worked. Every day I wake up and get going. I fill my day with interesting things, I concentrate my mind on my work at the office and try to plan my next move each time, so that I don't allow myself too much time to sit down and wonder what to do next. I believe that these moments are the most dangerous for a mind that can wander, imagine and question. You have to rid the mind of the opportunity for it to dwell.

"And think 'Positively'!"

"Yes, in a word that's true. Yes…I'm sure you're right there. I do still get negative thoughts, but I manage to dismiss them. I don't put them to one side and come back to them later. I used to, but it doesn't always work. You just dwell on them at a later time in the day; possibly when you are a little more tired and less able to cope. Hard work is always best attended to straight after breakfast! Don't you think?"

"Possibly Didi, possibly?"

You pause once more, you really think that you have said enough, but this time Sophie, takes up the conversation.

"If you can put the past behind you, then you can move forwards. You have proved this without doubt. But it is extremely difficult for someone who is conscientious, to do this, as you must well know." She raises an eyebrow in your direction before continuing. "I think a lot of people could do what you have done, and move on, but their lives are probably still riddled with guilt, and this hinders their future, in quite a crippling way. What they don't always realise is that they can still remain caring and understanding. No one can take that away from them. They just have to learn that to be in control does not mean that you can please everyone. And sometimes for the sake of their health, it is important that they do take control." Sophie stops here, obviously believing that she has capped the evening's philosophy with her summary.

CHAPTER NINETEEN

It is eleven O'Clock. You are looking at your faceless watch, judging the time by the position of its hands. Over the years you have grown clever at doing this with a quick glance of the eye. You enjoy this instrument. Others you know would find it very frustrating -Those that dislike change, those who like to see things at face value with no hidden puzzlement to camouflage the meaning. Yes, those same people that you were reminded about only the other day. How tiresome they would find you. YOU, always prepared for the unexpected. YOU, always looking further than the picture, Searching for an in-depth meaning to everyone and everything in life. For you it was healthy, the only answer. Yet for some it would be far too extreme. Life was tough enough, in one piece, without dissecting it!

Sophie, Caroline and Colette have already left; their decision made by an agreement earlier that they were all feeling the effects of a busy day. You had already explained that you had organised a return taxi for half past eleven and were happy to stay on with Professor Wayne, who has decided to share the drive with you albeit for a few corner - turns to his home just a few streets away.

It had taken a while to say goodbye to the others; everyone wanting to exchange telephone numbers and addresses. There was a definite feeling that everybody was very keen to keep in touch and you were made to feel that your presence would be very welcome at any future get-together.

"Well, Didi - Just the 'hard drinkers' left!"

Sensing the stern amusement in Professor Wayne's voice you make sure to keep a straight face as you reply.

"Yes, certainly looks like it!"

"So Didi, what shall we discuss. Seems like we've covered everything this evening, doesn't it?"

"I'm sure we haven't put the world completely to rights, but we've certainly had a jolly good go!"

"So, back to you. Did Caroline hit on a really sore point when she mentioned your family earlier?"

"No, not really. I can bare it."

"Were they really that terrible?"

"Who...My parents? No not really. In fact, if you were ever to meet them you would think that they were the sweetest people. They would always show concern and try and give advice. Unfortunately, they couldn't accept failure very easily. If I didn't do the things, which they considered right then I was looked upon as disobedient and ungrateful. They couldn't seem to see life from my perspective at all. And when I used to try to explain the way I felt they just refused to listen. It was hard to separate myself from them both. My mother was the one that I just couldn't seem to get on with, but I never wanted to let my Father down. That was very hard. But they worked together, they were part of the same team, invariably they would finish each other's sentences. I had little hope of achieving a win against them."

"Exhausting work, Eh!?"

"You could say. Not just physically but mentally, it was absolute torture. You know that there are people out there putting up with far more than you, and you feel that you should be grateful and satisfied but somehow that attitude becomes so difficult to adopt. You can't always be charming and dignified just to impress everyone... Sometimes you just have to be extremely selfish and do what pleases you for you and you alone."

"You sound like a psychiatrist talking!"

"Do I? I'm not surprised, I've listened to them repeat these things to me over and over again, through the last decade or two. Strange, how you sometimes have to listen to something too many times before you actually believe it!"

"Oh, I think you believed it Didi, you just didn't have the built-in strength to accept it. Keeping the status quo was far more important."

"Yes, I guess you're right! How perceptive of you!"

"Families are never as important as your own survival. But that is always hard to believe in times of peace, and sometimes harder still to believe, when the family is in conflict."

"That's true! But I was made to feel that my family was more important than other families were, being......"

"But that is.something we are all led to believe. It comes from the primeval urge to survive, first as a species, then as a nation, and finally as a family. Look at the family in Lorna Doone. They were in constant conflict and yet they were never allowed to forget that they were all one family, seemingly blood is thicker than water. But when the blood becomes poisoned it can work through the system very quickly, creating irreparable damage. The sooner it is diluted before it reaches this stage, the better, for one and all. That is not a selfish thought, Didi, that kind of thinking lends itself to wisdom."

"Mmm …Maybe, but what I was about to say was, that my Mother always claimed that we were descended from Lady Fairfax."

"Marvellous! So Didi, what does that make you, some illegitimate member of royalty?"

You feel a tingling sensation in the depth of your spine a centre point reacting to your overwhelming embarrassment. Put, this coldly and cynically, you find yourself feeling almost nauseous at your own profound arrogance; the mere suggestion that you are something special, that you are placing yourself high up on some mental pedestal. Why for heaven's sake? Why was it so important to you? No one else cared, so why should you.

You mumble a few words in your defence, laughing at yourself as you do so.

"Yes, silly isn't it. Obviously, I'm lucky! For instance, say I was prince Charles going through this with 'her Majesty' then it would be almost impossible for me to walk away. I'm lucky, for when I walked out on my family, it didn't hit the headlines, because I am nobody special, and that's what I have to remember."

"Nothing's so hard, that it couldn't be harder!" He looks at you affirmatively.

"Yes, you're definitely right!"The evening has finally drawn to a close. That fresh air had hit you both as you had walked out onto the street. Neither of you had felt the drop in the temperature. Your bodies warmed by the refreshments of the recent supper. A mixture of choices had been on offer steaks, salmon, beautiful dishes of various cuts of lamb. The smells of the accompanying sauces had further whetted your appetites, the aromas of cranberries and brandy had sufficiently kept the taste buds screaming for more. Whilst you had felt so full at one point, your stomach had quickly kidded you into having a little more. No that wasn't correct - in fact, it had been a lot more. Those ice-creams and meringues had been far too good to choose from, so you had finally ended your meal with a plate of cheese and biscuits. Consequently, you are now feeling sufficiently assuaged of hunger that you feel you could happily retire from eating for a week.Placing your hands in your coat pocket, you look across to Professor Wayne. Whether through desire or complete exhaustion, he now seems completely devoid of further conversation, so out of courtesy you remain quiet as well. The obviousness of this silence seems determined to be broken, and sure enough the professor soon allows himself to speak.

"Must go and answer the call of nature! I'll just nip back into the restaurant a moment. Don't hold the taxi for me if it comes ... I'll walk!"

“Of course.”

You watch the professor negotiate the awkward set of steps leading through the entrance. It is always difficult for one drunken mind to assess the compass orientation of another, but you quickly note the ataxia to the professor's gait. His speech had become slurred a while ago. And at one or two moments in the evening you had felt somewhat embarrassed for him. Never mind come the morning, he would probably have forgotten all about it. Through either natural or convenient memory loss!

CHAPTER TWENTY

The cold air is beginning to reach you, especially your extremities You feel your fingers start to glow hot and cold, as if they are unsure how to respond physiologically to this temperature change, especially as the rest of your body is feeling so flushed and full of warmth. You feel like a patient with Raynaud's disease, as if your hands are struggling to cooperate with a bizarre Malaria-like fever. Slowly your toes begin to act in the same way. One moment feeling so painfully hot and the next so painfully cold; yet the pain becoming the same as if touching fire then ice.

Believing that you must address this problem, you decide to exercise yourself, hoping that by energising your body a little you will restore some warmth and life back into your limbs. You can't wander far, obviously, for fear of missing the taxi, but the road is straight, the only deviation being the rapid incline, either up or down, depending; and so providing you follow the pavement your figure will easily be seen by vehicles approaching from either end of the road. You stroll a little one way, and then the other, just a few yards at a time. There is no need to go far. Gradually you feel the blood starting to pump back into your extremities. Slowly at first creating a small tingling sensation, noticeably painful in itself, then slowly subsiding to bring about a more obvious sense of expected feeling. Yet as you place each foot down on the pavement, you can't help being aware of a stranger sensation, as though, the bones of your toes are touching the pavement as if there is no flesh or shoe, forming a separation between the two. You remember cycling to school as a child and experiencing a similar phenomenon, but as a child you had cried, tonight you do not cry!

As you continue to pace up and down, you are aware of the darkness that has spread itself around you. Some nearby windows have extinguished their lights, as the inhabitants behind them, creep slowly to their beds. As the odd light here and there goes out, you imagine yourself in a room full of candles, trying to move slowly and carefully so that your breath or your movement will not create enough displacement of air, to allow another candle to be blown out. Somehow the reduction of noticeable light seems to intensify your feelings of loneliness and detachment. You follow the line of street lighting, which runs the length of the road; Shielded here and there by the overhanging branches stretching from the avenue of trees aligning your view.

…The quiet noises of the night adjust themselves as if a bell has been rung to announce that all further sound must be submissive. Slowly the noises of the day give themselves up, surrendering without question, apart from the odd revving of a car engine in another street or an impatient youth or two, shouting to their mates. A strange squawk from a nearby tree grabs your attention for a moment. You try and recognise the call, a night inhabitant, perhaps an owl, although you can't begin to fully know, as these noises are not ones you have ever paid particular interest to before. It is not often that you find yourself alone amongst these noises. Somehow as you listen, you realise how intriguing the sounds have become and you realise that when you are preoccupied these sounds become unusually invisible and silent.

Still no sign of the taxi; you briefly look down at your watch, the hands now luminous against the surrounding blackness. You follow their position as usual and realise that it is half past eleven gone. You are now standing about fifty yards away from the entrance where you left the professor ten minutes ago, but strangely there is still no sign of him.

You feel a little mystified and your imagination starts to explore the possible whereabouts of the missing. Could you imagine yourself inside a story, where you were just about to be abducted by mysterious creatures from another world? Was it possible that you had reached a dream like state as Alice had done, and slipped off into Wonderland without even realising it?

Could this be the beginning of a story? So many people claimed not to have a story in them. Yet you couldn't imagine anyone standing here right now and being incapable of using their imagination and conjuring up some kind of weird and wonderful tale of mystery and suspense. You continue to ponder and air your imagination, though you are beginning to feel a little eerie, scared off by your own thoughts and the vividness of your own imaginings. Looking for further objects to focus on in order to while away the next few moments, you wonder if you ought to retrace your steps back into the restaurant and check on the professor, but some element within you, persuades you that all is well, and to stay put, outside. Suddenly a small rustling sound behind you makes you turn, and you find yourself glancing over your shoulder, at a small narrow ally way, almost hidden between the walls of two adjacent buildings. Perhaps, the noise had been made by a cat, siding past something. It is hard to make any objects out in the dimness, but you thought you noticed what appears to be some wide sheets of metal, or maybe they were wooden pallets, lent up against the wall at quite an acute angle. You felt that if something had brushed passed these panels, they could easily have been caused to wobble but on closer inspection it looks far more likely that they would fall. No other objects seem evident within your visual field, as you try to look further down the ally. Everything is cast in a deep black cloak of darkness that doesn't look ready to give up any further secrets for the benefit of your knowing. This death like shadow holds itself tightly in position, bonded in the same fashion as a shell to the creature within it; un-remitting to separation.

For a moment you are once again finding your thoughts intertwined with your imaginative realms of thinking. Suddenly the shadows are becoming figure like and appearing to move, sometimes in opposing directions, sometimes, inconveniently, towards you. You feel the nerves in your spine begin to twitch, and your position begins to feel uncomfortable, like the dream-state where you desperately want to run and find sanctuary. Instead, you stand statue like and feel as if all the forces within your body are remaining on hold. As if they are patiently waiting for that moment when the adrenaline reaches its climactic level, and your hypothalamus has to conveniently decide upon the options of fight or flight - neither is chosen, or so it seems. Your body appears to have remained locked, your feet firmly rooted to the ground and your mind wedged in a state of limbo, unsure what it is, that is really scaring it. You prefer to feel like this, it seems less scary. You feel totally out of control, but at least the numbness that you feel, is helping to cushion those real emotions that are reacting spontaneously to the stimuli set around you.

You remain rigid, and you are unaware of the minutes that pass. Perhaps they are only seconds. But like a prisoner held in a timeless cell, you feel unreal to time. Only the moment itself stands out and embraces you as if time itself has become conveniently immeasurable. If it had been possible to continue to imagine and imagine, you would by now have taken yourself hastily back to the entrance of Fagan's Kitchen, but for whatever reason your sense of imagination had been swallowed up completely. Remaining in a trance like state, you begin to hear a quiet voice calling you…'DiDi'...(silence) …'DiDi'.

Perhaps your imagination has returned after all. Maybe you are creating delusions out of the familiar sounds that pierce through the darkness all around you -The murmur of the breeze, tickling the leaves above you … Quite possibly, or the fluttering of torn newspapers lying on the pavement … Who Knows? Gradually the voice becomes less transparent, as if at the pivotal moment of a dream, when you pass from sleep to consciousness. When everything around suddenly becomes enhanced, and impressions make way for reality.

…Your senses become alert and the weight of the surrounding body of air which bears upon you lends its firm hand upon your shoulder as if becoming the touch of another human, making their presence known. It holds you and presses against you and in some discouraging way it forces you to remain rigid and in defence-mode.

But surely it is only the hand of a dream. The innocent hand of the energies around you, groping about harmlessly in the darkness???

I call to you now, as you stand sublimely innocent and mentally naked. Remember that you will never change the world, for you are no more than a small handful of dust, given to this moment of history. No more, no less. To another your dust is as worthless as all dust is. To another your dust is worth the dangling price tag which it confidently displays.

I want you now to rest; for your journey so far has given you a rapid momentum, one which it is important to recover from. Spend a while re-energising, and whilst you do, hold in your mind all the strength you can, whilst your body slowly ……..slowly becomes weaker……..weaker …………Feel yourself dropping and if you can let me catch you……… ….

PART TWO

OPENING CLOSETS

CHAPTER TWENTY-ONE

Over the East end of London, a heavy mist spreads itself like a tightly woven blanket, extending itself around every part of the neighbourhood, and further stretching itself outwards in order to touch the next town and then the next. There seems no reprieve from this claustrophobic form. It represses and depresses those in its path and leaves behind it a wake of cold, miserable, unimpressed characters that slowly go about their business; anxiously waiting for this weather to abate.

Tiny coughs echo around the narrow alley ways, leading to nowhere and coming from nowhere; a mysterious connection of tiny thin routes linking one street to the next and then the next. The passages smell of yesterday. Yesterdays' leftovers, yesterday's perfumes, yesterday's tobacco smoke, yesterday's urine and faeces, yesterday's living, if that's what living is. Often these ally ways smell more of death and finality. Their material left unmoving, unbreathing, and cold; waiting to be discarded. Sometimes that's how its people felt too; like they were just smells and odours; just existing, not really living. Waiting to win the lottery and take themselves' off to some remote desert island, where they could then recline in splendour and watch the rest of the world continue to struggle and continue – 'not really living.'

It was hard to picture anyone wanting to dance at the prospect of being brought up in such squalor and dirt. But for some this was all they knew, and for many all they would ever know. The low hanging washing strung along makeshift lines dividing the narrow yard ways between the rows of terraced houses, their chimney's smoking. The people that survived here hadn't quite given up yet. It was only Tuesday after all!

Colin Brown was one of the survivors he hadn't given up yet either. With his large hands thrust in his trouser pockets he walked the alley ways and streets, making his way to work. It was the second week of April, and this was his first day in employment. He had tried hard to get a job, harder than most. He needed the money, or rather his family did. It was already assumed that some of his wages would be given to help top up the weekly budget, a recognised and accepted Jewish custom.

The Brown's were not a typical Jewish family, far from it. Colin's mother had been born Tanya Guilfoyle, and her parents had brought their young family up in the heart of Palestine amid all the trouble and unrest of the sixties. She had seen her fair share of despair and anguish until her family had finally been driven out, pushed back across Europe, to settle in this poorer part of London's city. It was here at the age of twenty-six that Tanya had met Kenneth Brown an atheist electrician from the East End. Within the year they had married and were looking forward to the prospect of raising a young family and continuing the family line, as everyone does. Bar Mitzvahs and Bat Mitzvahs marking the passage of time and progress. They were typical of everyone else in their neighbourhood, apart from the fact that Tanya had become a lapsed Jew. She had been shunned by her parents and the rest of her family and although she felt strong and will-full about her decision, the underlying guilt remained a source of provocation to her, and she had, as the Torah had told her she would, fallen on rugged ground.

For Colin his whole history seemed to provide him with a feeling of non-belonging and an overwhelming desire to feel demoralised. He felt neither respect nor understanding for either of his parents. And any feelings of justification in anything that he ever did for himself were quickly washed away by his parents' indifference. To think that any hard work that he performed would undoubtedly be carried out, not for his benefit, but to help keep his mother in cigarettes and the occasional sherry, and his father from being kicked by the money lenders on a Friday night, was not encouraging. Such a strange cycle of events but nevertheless it continued to rotate that way, year in year out. Not only for the Browns', but also for the Millar's, the Courtney's and the rest of the families up and down the street. They weren't all as lucky though, they didn't all have a Colin to send out to work.

Stacking supermarket shelves - Well it was a job after all. Colin began to feel his confidence rise as he shook hands with his new manager. It had been less than three weeks ago, that he had said a final farewell to his old Headmaster. The handshake that day had not been quite as courteous.

Mr Williams had been the Headmaster of Colin's old school for at least twenty years, but boys like Colin always made his life difficult as it did for many of the other teachers; who's thankless task it was, to create some sort of socially acceptable product. Mr Williams had never been certain, which way was the best. No matter how hard working you made boys like that, in school, you knew that they were just going to go straight home, put their 'bother-boots' on, grease their hair, smoke a few dubious roll ups, and go and scare someone no-where near their own size; in between collecting a few ounces of verbal abuse from their mother's and a good half-pound thump from their father's What a rewarding existence! Mr Williams hated the parents, not the children; the children were innocent. The monsters they became were not.

Maturity in Mr William's eyes should provide a social justification for the way people behaved. But society had turned this around. Mrs Thatcher had described Britain as 'no longer having a society.' Mr Williams felt that this was pure denial. No one liked what society had become. Society today defined itself in other ways and maturity was not one of them. The youth today wanted attitude and identity, in either order. As a Headmaster, his job was one of the hardest; trying to proclaim to those growing youngsters that these two factors were secondary to being Human.

Colin felt mature. When he looked in the mirror every morning, he saw what to his peers was conventionally acceptable. He wore trendy jeans, casual trainers, and a T-shirt top, never a shirt. His favourite brown bomber jacket went everywhere with him, when he once thought that he had mislaid it, his heart had sunk so fast and to such a depth, he had thought that he had a terminal illness. His clothes were, to Colin, a lifeline; a constrained link to others of his age, who sighted the same philosophy, to live young and to live cool. It was not quantity but quality that really mattered after all. Colin had only a collectively small wardrobe and yet, because he had these clothes, he felt he had all the worldly goods he required for true survival. What appeared on his dinner plate was secondary and yesterday evening when Colin had sat down for a brief while and had done his sums, he had begun to realise very quickly (in fact extremely quickly), for someone who had had to be coaxed for the last two years on the art of performing math, that with his weekly wage from the supermarket, he would be a lot better off. He had miserably deducted a fair percentage for his parents share, but this made him feel slightly annoyed and bitter, and so once he had completed the sum and written it down, he tore up the piece of paper, so that he would not be reminded. Despite making allowances for this deduction however, he would still have a comfortable sum left in his pocket. An amount left to him to do as he pleased. Perhaps he would build up his wardrobe. He could hit the nightclubs now, perhaps once or twice a week? Suddenly a whole New World seemed to be opening up in front of him; a world that had always been there but had never been tangible. It made Colin feel powerful. He would no longer have to beg money from elsewhere, it was a comfortable feeling. He felt encouraged and almost lightheaded, with the thoughts and ideas that were spiralling around inside his mind.

During his day at work, Colin became mindfully resentful of factors that were influencing his performance. Although he had estimated his deductions, if he had done his sums more effectively, he would have realised that for every pound he was earning, thirty pence were being robbed from him by his parents not to mention the taxman's cut. Effectively he was working ten hours for free. Colin just wasn't that kind of person. Charity was not up his street. Poverty was close to home, but charity was just a running man. Had Colin become the mathematician that his school had so desperately tried to make him, he would have been easily unimpressed. These feelings were the sort that would encourage Colin to go out and kick a few dustbins in those discrete alleyways. This was usually his vent, when he had had a fiery row with his father, or like the time he had put his mother to bed because she had disgraced herself in front of the neighbours. Having drunk herself silly; for an encore, she had passed out in the back yard, landing in a suitably indignant heap so as to display the absence of her underwear.

Each customer to Colin could easily have been misplaced as one of those jeering neighbours who had happened to be around to witness this 'Piece de resistance'.

"Poor love - Ever hopeful aye?"

"What's der matter Colin – Yer family too poor to afford knickers?"

The taunts had been heightened, by their meaning and emphasis. Vengeful thoughts towards the culprits, who had placed them, were secondary. The memory of those taunts remained. Colin tried to forgive but he knew he could never forget.

That scene in his backyard a few months ago had highlighted to Colin that his life was a fixture. It lay bare, ineffectual and without substance. And those cutting remarks had hurt far beyond the pain of poverty itself.

Little did Colin know just how difficult that first week would be; the fantasia of feelings, emotions and desires. Mentally he had already spent his wages and yet here it was, only Monday and there would be no pay cheque until Friday afternoon. This could have represented the day in Colin's life, when his mind suddenly become aware of the benefits of personal wealth but there was an un-naturalness in his almost immediate desire to make more. His 'two-penny-half-penny' wage from Sainsbury's seemed marginally inadequate against the enormous mental shopping list which Colin managed to produce during the course of the next few days. When his wage was finally placed in his hand at five-thirty on that Friday evening, the notes looked transparent and weightless against the bill of assorted items which he desperately wanted to go out and purchase.

Thanking the wages clerk, he backed away from the finance office, almost afraid to turn around and disclose his disappointment to the employee standing directly behind him in the queue.

"See you Monday Colin unless you want to join me for a drink?" A cheerful voice from further down the line seemed determined to catch his attention.

"Right, yeah, see you Monday!" Colin smiled at his new acquaintance, Geoff, whilst disregarding his invitation. Unlike himself, Geoff was one of the hundred or so quietly contented employees in the establishment, who had worked and survived for nearly a decade on his small wage, a wage that probably kept his head barely above water. Geoff's smile edged itself around a feeling of gratitude and contentment, for Geoff obviously perceived himself as a lot better off than some, and he was most probably right.

People like Geoff left Colin bewildered. They were suitably happy with their lot. They didn't require any clandestine rules or materials to make their world any different. In fact, if their world had suddenly been transformed, they would have probably been frightened of falling off! If not true, that was certainly the impression that these characters gave. Geoff stood for the likes of those around the world who remain satisfied with their lot, because that was the way they were. Probably due to the way in which they had been brought up. Who knew? It was just that to the likes of Colin these people were just not in his class. They floated in the vacant air beyond the existence of his shape and all he stood for. He wanted more; they didn't. That in itself made them Poles apart - Worlds apart. At times in the past, he had been led to believe that whatever he wanted would always be just out of reach. But right now, all that had suddenly changed; he felt that he was almost touching that space, that it was just a few small centimetres from his fingertips.

Today for one reason or another, a big difference was being made to Colin's life. Since the touch of those few ten-pound notes had met the palm of his left-hand Colin had felt some kind of revolutionary epiphany begin to uncover itself in front of him. Somewhere between the apparent impressions of fatigue within his eyes, (brought on by the past weeks' hard work, no doubt!) the impressions of dollar signs were beginning to manifest themselves.

Colin had known poverty through the last seventeen years of his life. It had not been fun; in fact, it had been hard; harder than most people could imagine. He could relate easier than most to the Oxfam posters that graphically enlightened those of us in the modern western world, to the starving who currently existed in the third. Colin's world now, was luxury in comparison, but only just!

A small band of contempt often links us to what we have and what we want. Today Colin's band was being stretched from a point to which it was unlikely to return.

CHAPTER TWENTY-TWO

Retracing his steps from earlier that morning, Colin followed his shadow through the streets. The day had continued to remain pleasant, despite a few small showers, the darkened clouds had passed as quickly as they had come. And for the likes of Colin who had been effectively tucked away inside an artificially lit building, and busy working, the inclement weather had gone by more or less unnoticed. Apart from seeing a few customers coming through the store with specks of drizzle patterned on their coats and noticing a few dripping umbrellas tucked into shopping baskets, Colin had had his mind on his job. Well - almost!

Now as he ambled along, he toyed with the idea of meeting up with a few of his old school mates. He knew instinctively where he would find them, propping up the bar, no doubt, at the pub on the corner by the post office. His legs twitched indecisively at first, not knowing whether he ought perhaps to be going straight home, in order to share the account of his day's work with his family. But when he began to think about it he didn't think anyone other than his older brother George, would be in the least bit interested and George would probably have already finished his supper, and be en route to the night clubs and bars, for his frequent Friday night pursuits of drinking, betting and chatting up the girls. He was never short of finding fulfilment in all these requirements. He made life good for himself, because that was specifically all he wanted. He was much like a Geoff as he was a George, though unlike Geoff he didn't give the appearance that he went to church every Sunday and changed his underclothes every day. Because George had never sought employment and happily collected his dole each week, without remorse, his payment towards his keep was overlooked. George was seen, by both their parents, as someone who should be pitied, and therefor despite his ability to blow fifty pounds quite easily in a few hours, a blind eye was turned towards his ways.

Colin's other two elder brothers were not part of the family portrait anymore; both had moved away nearly five years ago now. Both were comfortably married with young families of their own, surprisingly they had managed to break away from the East End life. One brother had a job in the city, 'Shifting other people's money about' as Colin's father liked to describe it, the other brother dealt in the property market. To say that neither had done well at school, they had both proved themselves through their own determination. Hard work and effort were all it had taken. There was also the fact that both their lives had substantially improved, once they had detached themselves from the family home. They had both met 'fine' girls as Colin's Aunt Annette always told him and furthermore reminding him that - 'It's the woman you marry that makes or breaks you!' Colin always cringed when older generations would come out with these little anecdotal phrases. To him it just wasn't fashionable to be that philosophical, but somehow, he always had a slight soft spot for Aunt Annette, and he had to give her, her dues, for what she said was often very true, and couldn't easily be disputed.

Colin's feet shifted again and then led him off in the direction of the pub. He knew that for a lot of reasons this was not where he should be going. Most of his friends were like his brother George, having no real enthusiasm or intention to do a day's work any sooner than they were forced to. Colin didn't quite know why he was different to them. In some ways he felt that he had an inborn grudge against himself, and forcing himself to take employment was in a way some sort of a self-punishment, but he didn't

really know what for and thus it remained for him another-
one of life's mysteries.

He knew that his presence would cause ill ease amongst
his peers. And that he would probably be assigned to buy
the next few rounds now that he had the available cash.
Colin was begrudging of this idea, for his money was
already accounted for. Yet his legs were carrying him
nearer and nearer to the pub and no matter what he said to
himself he just couldn't seem to turn himself around. Well
of course he wanted to be there, he wanted to be with his
friends, why should he have to isolate himself, just because
he now had a few pounds in his pocket. Why should money
change him? Why should money change anyone?

The group at the bar eyed Colin as he walked through
the doors. At first, he couldn't seem to recognise anyone,
and then he realised that it was their expressions that he
didn't recognise; the sheer amazement that his presence
seemed to have evoked made Colin feel very uncomfortable
and wary. Gradually the ice began to break, and Colin
noticed a few familiar smiles begin to warm the faces of his
old friends. It was hard for him to forgive them for their
cold reception, when they had probably spent the day
loitering around street corners. Smoking anything that they
could get their hands on and being generally menacing to
the rest of society; whilst he, 'the fool' had been working his
backside off, loading shelves and heaving heavy boxes
around, for the best part of eight hours. He felt anything but
pleased about his status, in fact right at this moment, there
was an uncomfortable feeling at the back of his throat, and
he felt able to vomit had he wished to do so. His audience
prevented him and instead he maintained his dignity and
quietly joined the rest of the gathering huddled around the
bar.

"How's life then?" came the first break in the silence.

Colin hesitated for a second, realising that any slip here would make or break his future position in the eyes of his so-called friends. He answered hesitantly, hoping that his voice would stay level and he wouldn't show his fear.

"Life's fine thanks. How's it with you?"

"Oh - So-So! Done a bit of 'bird pulling' ... lots of beauties about today, they've all broken up from school early ... Studying for their exams - so they say." The speaker's face holds a broad grin, and his eyes begin to twinkle as he continues. "I found me-self a nice blond at lunchtime. Really chatty she was. Course I didn't get to find out whether she's a true blond, but there's always tomorrow, ain't there?"

Colin never liked answering rhetorical questions, he never felt that he could do anything more than answer them with a yes, even if he wanted to say more. Today however he tried.

"That depends, Rob."

"Wow, what words Colin. You learnt lots of big words today – ave you? Now you've got yer job an all that. ... Well Colin, what does it depend on then, if you know all the answers? You an expert now on deflowering the ladies, or are yer just try-in to sound clever?" Colin felt himself starting to tighten inside, from his groin right up to that big lump which had started to reawaken itself at the back of his throat. He knew that he would have to reply cautiously.

"No. I don't know all the answers. As a matter of fact, I would have said exactly the same last week and I hadn't started work then, had I?" Colin was beginning to feel a little braver inside, but he still knew that he had to play very defensively. He didn't want to try scoring too quickly in case he suddenly found himself offside. He wanted to try and remain smart but dignified. He knew it wasn't easy given the impatience and mentality of his audience.

"How did the day go then Colin?"

"Not too bad thanks, bit of a shock, the hard work and the long hours, but I guess I'll get used to it."

"Cor! You're a real martyr ain't ya Colin?"

By now Colin was beginning to feel a little ruffled under the collar. He sensed the resentment among his so-called friends. Perhaps he would have been better off taking Geoff up on his earlier offer, at least the conversation would have been a little easier going, and he wouldn't have had to watch what he was saying or wonder what everyone was thinking. Although he didn't have to be a mind reader here; the room stunk of bitterness and hatred. He was still standing there after five minutes and no one had made any attempt to offer him a drink, despite their full glasses standing lined up on the bar. Everyone else was smoking; their cigarettes all at varied lengths, hung from the corners of their mouths, or were being waved around by gesticulating hands as they spoke. Again, not one person had taken the opportunity to hand his opened packet in Colin's direction. The atmosphere and suggestiveness of the scene spoke volumes to Colin. He was not in with the gang tonight. Whether it had been a point of discussion amongst the other members was not an issue. The obtuse manner in which these feelings were being displayed was enough to make its mark clearly on the recipient of these powerful vibes. Despite feeling parched and hungry for a smoke, Colin began to retreat, making excuses which he knew were poor, by the deliberate and detached manner in which he delivered, them.

Slowly edging himself towards the door he continued to prepare his departure from the scene using all sorts of reasons, - He had remembered a phone call he was expecting. (No one ever phoned. They had given up - the phone was so often cut off because of the unsettled bills.) - His mother had promised him his supper at a certain time. (Nice thought but almost impossible to perceive.)

Colin lived in a world of dreams. Dreams of hope and ideals, which were always lodged far in the future. As unreachable in a lifetime as the farthest star, but at times they held themselves up like a masterpiece in front of him until they were almost tangible and believable. So convincing to him were these visualisations that Colin could talk about them as if they were absolutely solid.

…Finally reaching the doors of the pub, Colin breathed a sigh of relief as he entered into the fresh air. The damp air of the evening made the smell of the street unusual. Whilst it smelt stagnant it also seemed to have the pleasant lure of a natural essence, which Colin couldn't immediately place. He followed the scent along the road outside the pub, until he came to a nearby lamppost. There he stood for a few minutes fumbling in his pocket for his roll-ups and his matches. Leaning against the post, with one leg crossed against the other, he carefully fashioned his cigarette and lit it first try. The odour from its ignition soon cancelled out the smells that he had noticed earlier. It even helped to extinguish the smells of the alley as Colin turned between the next two buildings and followed the dark separation that lay between them, giving up his shadow to the dark abyss ahead of him.

Because only imagination can transcend the images of the mind and displace them so erratically that they become distorted and unrecognisable; then what happened next could only be described as Colin's imagination hard at work. A curtain seemed to move ahead of him, but it could have been a sheet hung out on one of those familiar washing lines strung out between the buildings on either side, further up the alley.

As he widened his eyes to see more clearly, he thought he noticed the shape of a person slowly moving towards him, but all features and limbs were hidden and contorted by the presence of the sheet or curtain that had fallen over them in their advance. This was like some strange trip, though Colin seldom used, he was one of the lucky ones that had tried a dose once or twice and had not been hooked. He still of course had the memories of those strange apparitions that he had experienced at the time. An experience in itself, Colin prided himself on. The knowledge that he had been somewhere that not every human being had had the opportunity to visit, and having had that opportunity, he had then had the good fortune to return back to reality knowing what was on the other side of the fence, so to speak.

But right at this moment reality and rationality were telling him that this experience was both real and unreal. It was like the moment when he had made his first parachute Jump - A charitable event which Aunt Annette had got him involved in. He remembered that moment when he had had to finally let go - he had shut down all his thoughts of fear, and just stepped out of the plane as if he were someone else not himself. He remembered that experience now very clearly. He also remembered that first 'trip' when he had felt himself flying. He had held his arms stretched out on either side of his body and not recalling how his feet and legs had responded to this artificial position, he had felt his body being lifted into the air, as if by some stranger force, rather than the air around him. And then he had been carried up, up way above the gardens in his mind, to some high position, somewhere beneath the clouds. He recalled dodging the birds and flying across gardens noticing the fences between them, but never landing, though he recalled that he had had an urge to do so at the time. But of course, he had had no power over this urge, he had been, to all, intense and purposes in the hands of his dream. Memories of the past were not helping to serve Colin well, in trying to make any sense of what he now saw in front of him. It was unreal and irrational.

Perhaps he was having some kind of flash back from his days of abuse or maybe this was some sort of anxiety attack brought on by too much hard work, lack of sleep and his body's desperate need of a decent meal! Whatever it was, something made Colin proceed along the alley, all-be-it into the jaws of whatever loomed ahead. He felt an impulse to close his eyes and feel his way along the side of the wall to his left. Making his way cautiously he moved forward in this fashion for a few hundred yards or so it seemed, until cautioned by a strange sound he came to an abrupt halt.

CHAPTER TWENTY-THREE

His hand had been feeling its way over her body, for the past few minutes. In its initial position his hand had rested on her left breast, whilst his fingers had circulated around her excited nipple, before it had moved itself steadily downwards. Sliding its way along the side of her slender body tracing the outline of her hipbone, where the flesh stretched away from her sleek waist. Feeling her buttock, which he swallowed into the palm of his hand, he began to grapple with the material of her skirt, scrunching it into his fingers until he eventually drew up the edge. She never wore her skirts very long; he'd noticed that when he had watched her during the last few weeks. Soon his hand was feeling its way beyond the warmth of her thighs to a position where warmth and moisture intermingled, making his fingers eager to explore more. He felt his own desire enhanced by the feel of her keen response, and he knew that she wanted him. Slowly he made his advances until the nakedness of their bodies were touching; their sexual display, discretely hidden by the fall of her skirt folds.

He kissed her repeatedly, his tongue searching for a rewarding solace each time, as he thrust deeper and deeper... The rhythm of his tongue jerked with his body. Amongst the dark shadows, only her gentle moans signified to the onlooker that she was being entered.

"Stewart there's somebody there." The girl quickly placed one hand on her ruffled skirt as she turned her head in the direction of the sound, she had just heard. It was not that dark, and she could easily make out the figure further down the alley, which seemed to have stilled itself at the very moment that she had called out. Not, however, before she had noticed, that it was feeling its way along the wall, guided by its left hand.

"I don't think they can have seen us, Stewart." The girl's whispers were hardly audible to her listener. "The person seems to be blind."

"You what?"

"Well, they're feeling their way along the wall as if they can't see."

"Well! What yer worried about?"

"Stewart! It doesn't mean to say they can't hear us."

"Look Darlin', Just moan quietly, ay."

She could feel his swelling touching her thighs, drawn out of her by her sudden reaction to the noise earlier. This touch seemed to suddenly cancel out all her awareness of what was going on around her, and once again she felt her body responding.

She felt her eagerness awaiting the touch of his excited body, once again, but she couldn't seem to help turning her eyes towards the stranger standing in the shadows. In some way she felt excited at the prospect of being watched from afar. Perhaps it was everybody's hidden desire to be turned on in this way: how was she to know. It certainly didn't seem to be putting Stewart off, but then he was a 'man'. Surely, she shouldn't be experiencing these kinds of thoughts herself and yet strangely they seemed to be with her, in a surprising fantasia of eroticism.

As she felt her body being pushed heavily against the wall, her mind became aware of a soreness at the base of her spine, yet the pain was bearable, for the pleasure within her far outweighed it. And she felt Stewart continue to swell inside her.

"Don't stop, don't stop!"

As Colin watched and listened, he felt himself becoming excited too. The feeling of arousal within his loins becoming increasingly more uncomfortable, and although he remained silent, it was difficult for him to remain still. He tried to adjust the position of his feet, but it was awkward, and his shoe made a scuffing sound against the paving stone. He wondered if he had been noticed, but still felt sure that he hadn't. To move away now would make his position too obvious, using this as a positive excuse he decided to remain still. It was a poor excuse for after all, he was enjoying the display.

At the far end of the alley the two dark shadows cling together as if they are one.

"Yes, yes!"

He could feel his excitement increasing, and leaning against the wall, he found himself cupping the bulge of his erection with his left hand. The whole experience made furthermore uncomfortable by his circumcision. (The only Jewish blessing bestowed upon him by his mother, before her segregation from her faith. He had thus been spared the humiliation of his Bar-Mitzvah.)

The entwined shadows continued to pulsate.

Moving faster and faster against one another the two bodies continued to impact until passionate sounds combined in an explosion of ecstasy.

Colin could feel his own moistness through the material of his trousers, warm against his hand. He didn't feel that he had committed any sin, in placing himself in this position as voyeur, but somehow, he felt an unnatural resentment, realising that it had been a long time since he had been allowed the feel of a woman. Feeling her mentally was not the same as a physical encounter. He was aware of the amount of gratification he had felt by his observation, yet strangely perhaps he was also aware that he would rather have shared the pleasure with another human being. A human instinct, no doubt. The primitive brain kicking in; awakening inborn urges, that render you useless and thus are unable to explain.

Further up the lane the shadows begin to move on. Quiet voices exchange clichéd conversation-as only post-coitus language can. The illumination of two cigarettes, guided by the hands that hold them, discreetly advance into the future blackness of the alley, until finally their light is swallowed by distance.

Moving from his cramped position, Colin steadies himself momentarily, whilst his legs come back to life. Deciding to light up a cigarette, he waits for the sound of the footsteps ahead to abate, then slowly and cautiously he begins to move forward, passing through the light cast by a nearby window which had acted as a spotlight earlier, over the uniting lovers.

For the first time in a while, he was becoming aware that the strange cloud of terror, which had pinned itself over him whilst walking into the alleyway, had now vanished. Colin was forced to remember once again how strange and uncomfortable he had felt for a while, but he can't seem to regain that feeling of tension. At this current moment he felt more relaxed than he had done in a long time. He felt confident and sure of himself, almost in a way that he had never done before. Gripped by this positive persuasion, he felt ready to take on the world. The only thing concerning him was whether the two lovers would ever recognise him again. This made him feel embarrassed and guilty, but it was a Jewish thing, he felt sure of that, and he felt certain that his mind would get over it.

CHAPTER TWENTY-FOUR

The next few minutes held a strange momentum of emotional thoughts and physical persuasion for Colin. He would never be able to explain exactly what had happened to him at that precise moment. Though he did try years later, having been asked to detail the events to an interested party, he was heard to describe how he had undergone some psychological change, which he had seemed to have no power over.

Standing in the alley, he watched the two figures ahead of him slowly moving into the final point of his visual range, growing smaller and smaller until their defined images were eliminated by the surrounding blackness. And as he watched he once again began to feel the strange eerie feeling of unease and anxiety which had first pierced the boundaries of his attention, some while previously. A sudden impulsive urge grew inside him like the brewing of a volcanic eruption and slowly he began to feel the wretched force against his head and limbs as his flesh pulsated with the increasing rise of his blood pressure. As the intensity of this feeling worsened, he began to feel the necessity to run, but he did not know where or why. He was only aware of the energy which was being used to hasten his legs from a steady slow trot into a raging canter, his body carried, as if spiritually through the passage steered by the decisiveness of his eager legs.

Through the alleys …..along streets …..across roads …..hitching bus rides …..knocking passers-by without the means of an apology. Driven only by the force of the night, a hidden force, which would be unlikely to rear itself in the presence of daylight.

He moved as if possessed, fearing his own demise. Yet his fear was thrown aside by the rapidity of his journey, inertia splaying all his thoughts to the wind. Caution was not on the agenda, a mere hypothetical equation, set to the tempo of this physical assault, there was no conclusion evident. Feeling defeated by his body, Colin tried hard to hold on tight to his mind, it was not easy. Whilst aware of his surroundings he felt that he still had a grip on his sanity, but as to his inappropriate physical behaviour, he had to let go, and allow this detached disembodiment to do its worse. Despite the energy that was escaping from him, there was no evidence of a reprieve. It was if his body was regenerating fuel from this exhaustive journey. Feeling confident that his body would eventually find its point of rest, he continued to allow himself to be projected about like a piece of iron filing attracted by a distant but powerful magnet.

Patiently he continued to passively occupy his mind with the passing treats of civilisation that he was witnessing on his course, hoping that whatever was persuading his body in such a forceful manner would unveil itself soon and disclose its form and reason.

He struggled hard to memorise his journey. Unlike Hansel and Gretel, he had no clues to place, in order to retrace his steps at a later interlude. Everything was now in the present. No obvious threads tracing back to where he had come from and no signs of any lifelines, to give an indication of where he was being offensively lured to.

Mysteries are fascinating when they are presented on the screen or between the leaves of a book, but somehow this was different. Colin would follow such events avidly when they were being portrayed to him in the fictitious world, often able to foresee the predictable conclusion. But the situation he was in now was different. It was unpredictable to the point of being totally inconclusive. And in a split second of digressional thought, he decided that if he were not playing the starring role in this spine chiller, it would most definitely be a great story.

No convenient means of help seemed to be available to him and realising that if this momentum were to keep up it would probably lead to some sort of mindful or bodily overload, he decided to brace himself for all possible consequences. Though, he truthfully didn't have an idea what any of these consequences might be.

Trying to hold on to the edge of sanity, Colin momentarily found himself in a position of brief reprieve. He was aware that he was sitting on a hard backed though fairly comfortable seat. Opening his eyes cautiously he found himself on the London tube line. Training his eyes above the heads of the people sat opposite, he followed a diagram of the train's route, mapped out across the wall of the carriage.

Tottenham Court Road - Goodge Street
- Warren Street - Euston.

Looking closely at the map, Colin knew that he was heading along the Northern line, though he had no idea, which station he had come from nor indeed which station he was heading to. Trying to disguise his feelings of worry and confusion, he cast his eyes over the other passengers, but no one seemed to be looking his way. He did meet with a quick non-communicative glance from a young girl further up the carriage, but he guessed that like himself, she was only scanning faces inquisitively and had not selected him out for any particular reason. He half smiled in an involuntary way, but her eyes had already turned from his direction and were beginning to read an advertisement held in a frame at one end of the carriage. Colin followed her gaze.

'Let the train take the strain'!

185

Colin read it with amusement. Seemingly he was supposed to sit back now and relax and let all his worries and troubles be absorbed into this train journey, how wonderful! Well, here he was waiting for it to happen. But not surprisingly there didn't seem to be any obvious transference of his present feeling of stress, as was being suggested, by the persuasive image on the advert - A young couple spread out semi-naked on a tropical beach, with a warm sun blazing down upon them. Well as far as Colin was concerned this journey was providing no conduit, in evoking for him the feeling of warmth and satisfaction that was eking out from the image. He felt as if he had been totally abandoned in this carriage, like a piece of lost luggage; and if anything, this poster was making him feel more ill at ease, in its mere affirmation that he was indeed not feeling or believing, anything of the tonic that was being prescribed.

…Noticeable physical needs were beginning to make themselves apparent to Colin, as he slowly became aware just how hungry and indeed how tired he was starting to feel. His stomach had been rumbling for the last few minutes in a vain attempt to capture his attention. Of course, it had, but he had been consciously trying not to connect with the thought, in the hope that the feeling might abate. Indeed, it had not, and now his imagination was slowly taking a hold and encouraging oasis-like pictures of food which might have tempted even the fussiest, connoisseur.

He felt into his left-hand trouser pocket to see whether there might be an odd sweet or piece of chewing gum, waiting to be discovered. But unsurprisingly, there was nothing, except an old crumpled up bus ticket and the inevitable piece of fluff that somehow collects in all pockets over a lost period of time. Feeling the fluff more inquisitively for a moment he rolled it around between his thumb and forefinger in the reassuring way that a child feels the edge of its comfort blanket or favourite toy. It is said that the dying or delirious patient's hand searches for the same comfort in the act of carphologia. Colin was not sure which of these interpretations were nearest to his own purposeful need at present. He sighed. What more could he do than sigh? Somehow, he felt that there was little likely hood, of this journey taking him to some restaurant or even small hamburger bar in an effort to create a mistakingly pleasant conclusion.

No! He definitely felt that he had had his chips for today. Yet the pains of his hunger were mounting. Moving his other hand into the pocket of his jacket he felt somewhat relieved to feel the presence of a few coins. He twisted them around in his fingers for a few seconds trying to exact the amount. It seemed possible that he had a few pound coins, at least, although he didn't really want to present them for inspection in front of everyone else around him. He began to add the possible amount together, and the total, he reckoned, allowed him a hamburger and chips, and perhaps a can of coke. -Some places charged considerably more than others did, and he knew that he would have to choose his watering hole wisely. But at this moment in his present state, he felt like a beggar and indeed he knew that in falling into this category, the possibility of choosing might well be off the menu for this evening.

CHAPTER TWENTY-FIVE

As the train pulled into the next station, people quickly began to jostle about, rising from their seats and moving towards the doors in anticipation. The passengers standing by the exits were already at an advantage except that they were now starting to get a little squashed. No one seemed particularly annoyed with the next person for being elbowed or having their toes trodden on. With an accepting politeness everyone in turn seemed to forgive the next person, in what appeared to be a school dinner-queue mentality; pushing and shoving in the ever-hopeful attempt, of being the first person to escape through the train doors at the very moment it stopped. Eventually the exodus began and in contradiction to the gospel teachings - the first were the first and the last were the last.

Colin watched unmoving, something within himself told him this was not his stop, and so he watched the disembarking passengers with little if no interest. Perhaps only enough to notice the cosmopolitan assembly of culture, wealth and humanity, which had for the last few minutes been congregated together in this narrow metal tube, whizzing through the under-paths of London. The exodus complete, the mass of new travellers began to embark, in a similar assembly to those who had just escaped through the doors.

'Mind the gap. Doors closing.'

As the announcement came, Colin glanced up, just as a young fair-haired girl was manoeuvring her body through the closing automatic doors. She was quick. -She was lucky, -she just made it! Colin admired her nimbleness. As she regained her breath and stability, she looked along the carriage dreamily until her eyes came to rest on Colin, who's eyes had remained focused on her. Recognition lit up her face.

"Hello Colin. How are you?"

Feeling a little taken aback, Colin readjusted his gaze from his earlier lecherous look, and studied the face ahead of him in a manner that required him to search his memory bank for help in recognising this person. She had a heavily made-up face, patterned with numerous patches of colour. Bright pink cheeks offset with a bluish grey eye shadow. The detail around her eyes was pencilled in like the outline in a child's colouring book. Everything about her façade was severe. But the voice that spoke through the face was tender and quiet. Colin began to show his quizzical apprehension, and the girl seemed to immediately gain pleasure from her masquerade.

"You don't recognise me Colin, do you?"

Colin didn't think he really needed to answer, but nevertheless he did. "I'm not sure. Your voice sounds familiar." Somehow, he didn't want to appear too slow, and he certainly didn't want to give the girl too many points for being impressiveness. He hated giving people what they wanted too quickly, he liked to see them sit up and beg. He couldn't do it with his own family, but whenever possible it was fun to do it with other unsuspecting characters, -and this girl was sitting bait. He sensed an ensuing bat and ball game commencing.

"Oh, come on Colin, you must remember me?"

His immediate thought was 'why'? But he didn't say it. Something in him made him aware of her possible sensitivity to such a remark, and so he trod warily. "Help me out, I've got a terrible memory!"

This made her smile. Colin noticed how pleasant and warming this smile was despite the overall negative appearance of her face. And he found himself warmed by this reaction and his face for the first time that evening began to smile too.

"Oh Colin, for goodness' sake, I'm Frances, we sat next to each other last term in geography." Again, she smiled, or rather her smile just grew larger, a bit like Lewis Carroll's cat, it didn't seem to begin or end it just seemed to be there. Colin felt comforted slightly by its warmth and slowly he began to feel a little more relaxed. He settled back into his seat and laid his hand across the back of the head rest, in a pose that prompted Frances to immediately sit down and settle back and adopt a relaxing pose herself. Something, she seemed able to do, without any degree of difficulty.

Colin meanwhile was a little unsure how to continue the conversation. His memory was just starting to serve him with a little recognition of this enigmatic character who was now perched beside him. How quickly he had forgotten her. Yet she was hardly recognisable. Transformations like that must require a change of passport. He must look to her like somebody very ordinary and mundane, in the fact that he had chosen to remain so static in his appearance. He reckoned that he would probably be one of those faces that changed very little with the passage of time. Well! ….He half-hoped anyway!

Although preferring the silence, he knew that it couldn't last, and trying quickly to take charge of the conversation ahead of Frances, he began to search for anecdotal things to say, to pass the time. After all he didn't know how long Frances would be sharing the ride with him. Maybe she only had one or two stops to go or maybe she was with him for the duration. He was sure that she would certainly have a better idea than he did, in regard to where she was heading. He didn't however feel that he wanted to ask, because obviously it would draw attention to the subject, which was just what he didn't want to do.

"Have you left school now as well?"

"You could say." Frances interjected with yet another smile. Surely someone who smiled this often, had to have had lessons, it just wasn't normal. "I'm working in a bar as a waitress at lunchtimes but I'm starting a computer course at night school, soon."

"That's good" Colin shuffled more comfortably into his seat, somehow the direction of the conversation was going in his favour, no less than he hoped. All he needed to do now was keep it there.

"What do you hope to do eventually then?"

"Oh, you know, be rich and famous perhaps and not have to work at all. That would be nice, but I don't suppose it will ever happen!"

"Well, it'll be a bonus if it does!"

"Yeah, I suppose you're right."

"I'm always right." Not quite feeling himself again, he feared what his reaction would be to any further conversation. It felt as if his alto ego was beginning to nose in on the act and whilst normally, he would think perhaps a little curtly at times, he could normally find the dignity to curb these thoughts before they were carried on a sound wave. He didn't like this new freedom that his body was beginning to exhibit, and he felt a little out of his depth.

Frances having more dignity than him, at this present moment in time, quelled the situation a little with her next remark.

"So, what makes you think you're so clever then Mr No-It-All?"

"Just a notion; nothing else really."

"Pardon me. I seem to have lost you!"

Colin had to be careful not to allow himself, to say 'feelings mutual' but he kept going as best he could. "Suppose it's what some people might call their sixth sense. It's that feeling that you feel when you are certain about something. In my case, it's proverbs and little sayings. I grew up with them you see. My aunt was always using them, and they always seemed to be true, so I began to believe in them. Funnily enough I used to cringe when my aunt used to use them, but now I find myself repeating them, just like earlier, when I said about things being a bonus for you if things come up trumps. I believe in the saying. I really believe those bonuses happen for people if they try hard enough and I'm sure it will happen for you."

"Well thanks for being so sure about my future." Her smile dims for the first time. "I just wish I could believe in myself as much as you seem to Colin."

"It's all down to confidence!"

"I'm sure you're right."

Colin quickly found himself covering his mouth and grinning. "I nearly said 'I know I am', but I better not upset you!"

"Thanks Colin."

"Think nothing of it."

"Oh Colin. This is beginning to sound like some script from a movie. You seem full of those little 'one liners'."

"I think you mean clichés, Francis."

"Probably, if I understood what they were. How is it you know all these things Colin, I don't recall you ever being this bright at school?"

"Don't you?"

"I didn't mean to insult you. On the contrary, I was trying to pay you a compliment, actually."

"Compliment taken."

"Good, so are you going to answer my question or not?

"I'm afraid I've forgotten what it was."

"You're just so much more talkative than I remember you, Colin. I feel like I'm talking to a different person."

"Really!? So what was that question again?"

"How come, you seem so clever all of sudden?"

"Cleverness is not necessarily a thing that can be taught, Frances, which is where school let me down. Cleverness comes from one's own personal experiences, and observations. Observation is the key method and it's probably the simplest, because after all animals use it. Think of the 'simple' duck, and the imprinting process!”

“I suppose you're right, well of course you know you're right! So, I guess I should be, believing you without question. After all you really do sound convincing!”

“Why Thank you.” For the first time since the conversation had begun Colin felt that he was safe. He was no longer looking for escape routes to keep the conversation on track. Its mundanity seemed to be keeping it effectively buoyant without the need for Colin's brain to interject. For this he was thankful. If he could just keep things running smoothly for another few minutes more. He felt that there was a possibility that the train would have by then reached the buffers. The ensuing conversation had caused him to lose all perception of where the train might possibly be at this precise moment, but from the map which he was now studying again, he reckoned that they must be somewhere well up the northern line.

“Well, here we are!” Frances leapt up and Colin's eyes followed her rapid action. “Nearly missed my stop chatting away with you. Thanks for all the tips you've given me!”

“You're welcome.”

“Just one thing.”

“Yes, what is it?”

“Well, I hope you won't be offended.”

“Depends?”

“Well, it's just that…it's eight o'clock and…”

Colin was startled, he had lost the last few hours of his life, but he tried not to let it show.

…Well, you look as if you've just come out of work…and…Oh I'm sorry it's none of my business…..”

Colin watched as Frances disappeared from view amongst a stream of passengers; once again he watched as the disembarkation process played out.

CHAPTER TWENTY-SIX

Colin's mind was wondering. He wasn't sure whether this was similar to some imminent death experience. For his life seemed to be paying him a quick visit in instantaneous pictures, which were flashing past his mind; although imaginary he was aware of their potential realness, and whilst the experience was eerie it was also fascinating.

There was no apparent order to the images, he was aware of this more or less straight away, by the fact that Aunt Annette's wedding was the first picture that he met with. Of course, this was her third wedding, he recognised her new husband straight away; Uncle John had only come on to the family scene in the last ten years, and Colin knew immediately that there was far more pre-existing history to his life before this comparably unimportant event. He watched the scene with avid interest, but it did not appear to move. In his imagination he could move the characters easily, but the true picture remained static. It was as if his mind had taken a photograph at that precise moment in time and filed it for future reference safely within his memory album. As he continued to watch, the present picture began to fade, and a new image began to emerge, as the outlines and the colours became clearer, he soon identified the scene before him. It was the birthday party of one of his elder brothers - probably Christopher. He could see himself in the background of the picture sat in a highchair holding up a large wooden spoon. His face wore a wide grin as did the faces of all the other participants within the frame. He had been told many times during his short life about this particular party. This quiet picture had apparently been the scene, before the event - That being Colin's unfortunate head dive out of his highchair due to an unfastened catch on his reign. He could not remember the incident at all, but the rest of the family had put this down to a severe concussion, brought on by the fall, just to make the story a little more sensational and of course more plausible.

As this picture began to take on a more transparent feel, yet another picture appeared to take its place. Colin began to feel a little curious as to what was coming next, he felt that he was being taken on a journey through time; it was as he had always imagined a journey in the Tardis would be like. Though of course he didn't want to get too excited, for he wouldn't be arriving in the future, or at least he didn't think that would be the intended agenda. Colin had once again lost all concept of time, whilst still managing to remain in touch with his present surroundings; these being the repetitive furnishings of the rail service's uninteresting seating arrangements and the awareness of a few other human beings who were still sharing these travelling facilities with him.

Colin wondered if the train had already hit the buffers and began its last fatal journey beyond its rails, careering into some solid and un-penetrable object. Perhaps he was part of this conclusion already. Perhaps back in the real world, people were already mourning his loss. Well he could always hope!

The images kept coming and he could do nothing other than gain further intrigue and pleasure from them. They remained haphazard in their order, this he found enlightening. Whenever he had heard the expression 'Their life flashed passed them' he had always imagined the flashback starting from the moment that person's life had begun, flashing through in some kind of daily, monthly or yearly sequence. With the current evidence he was beginning to question the credibility of his previous judgement and beliefs.

Within a tiny corner of his mind, he was beginning to give himself up to his fate as further images began to sequence themselves around him in a comforting way, making it possible for him to witness several scenes at a time from various eras. Everything seemed disjointed yet at the same time everything seemed to pull the four corners of his life together in a tight and neat way like sweets tied into a handkerchief. He tried to hang on to this secure feeling. In doing so he found himself clenching his fingers into fists, whilst at the same time he could feel the muscles of his face tensing into the formation of a heavy frown borne low on his forehead.

Anxiously awaiting the next move in this psychological quandary, he began to recognise voices that were trailing into his mind. Feeling un-threatened, he listened tentatively, becoming aware that this mental soundtrack was actually playing itself in time to the accompanying images. It made it more interesting, but unfortunately it didn't begin to explain any clearer the weirdness of this whole scenario. Colin, however, tried to sit back and enjoy the picture show. Listening to the conversations that were centred around him in the scenes where he was only a young child made him feel quite devilish. It was like being a fly on the wall, but not only being able to watch others but quite excitingly being able to watch yourself. It was, Colin thought amazingly absurd.

"Excuse me sir."
Colin looked ahead in the direction of the voice.
"Sir, I'm afraid I'm going to have to ask you to disembark." The policeman, stood before Colin, was trying to perfect a firm but un-alarming tone to his voice. He did well. Colin did not move immediately but stared into the policeman's face, searchingly.
"There's been an incident further up the line, no trains can continue further than this station."
"Thank you. I'll wait!"

"No sir, I'm afraid you can't do that. There'll be no more trains along this line before the morning at the earliest."

Colin felt anxious. The sanctity of the train seemed to be his one last hope of exempting himself from anything, which was about to happen. The thought of leaving this haven made him nervous. Feeling that it was important to know his current whereabouts he asked the first obvious question, which sprung into his mind.

"Which station is this?"

"Hampstead, Sir. Now come along we better get you off now in case they have to close the station."

Not feeling in the mood for any further retaliation, to this request. Colin nonchalantly picked himself up and then having made his way through the open train doors, he walked towards the archway marked by the exit sign, closely followed by the policeman. He could hear the mumbling of the disgruntled passengers further ahead of him, who were obviously annoyed by this unforeseen disruption to their journeys. He however remained calm and quiet in contrast to the behaviour of the other travellers. Somehow, he felt that this would validate his appearance of being in control.

Moving forward he felt the firm hand of the policeman upon his left shoulder.

"Well done! I thought I was never going to get your attention back there on the train. You must have been far away with the fairies, there. People were falling over your feet and still you weren't moving! Wish I could sleep like that on a train."

"I wasn't asleep!" Colin heard a curtness in his voice.

"Oh, weren't you? Well, you could have had me fooled!"

"I wasn't setting out to fool anyone, but I really wasn't asleep."

"Oh well. Fair-enough!"

Colin felt in a strange position here. It was almost as if he were in dispute with his own mind. It was as if he were trying to make an escape. He desperately wanted to explain and share his weird experiences, feeling that if he were to do this, maybe it would milk away the thoughts that he was experiencing. But somewhere else in his head this thought was becoming paralysed, preventing him from sharing anything with anyone. Quite clearly, Colin was on this ride alone.

Right now, he welcomed the feel of the hand upon his shoulder. It felt like he had imagined his father's hand would have felt if his father had ever performed this gesture, which of course he hadn't. There was an energy that seemed to transfer into Colin through the warmth of this contact; presenting him with the feeling that he was being supported in some way. The touch seemed to impose a feeling of acceptance in whatever Colin was about to set out to do. It was like the hand of the father upon the prodigal son, which said 'Go forth and do what it is you have to do.' There seemed to be no conditions set by this selfless touch. The gesture was free. Colin continued to believe that the hand was beseeching him to go. But he did not know which part of his mind was accepting and believing this message; the perceptive and lucid area which interprets the present or the more austere and frightening area that transcends the Corpus Callosum and reaches out for something that lies far beyond the infinity? He had no answers. He only knew that the vibes were strong and urgent!

CHAPTER TWENTY-SEVEN

Leaving the entrance to the tube station, the sudden daylight hit the lenses of his eyes with dramatic impact. Stopping immediately in his tracks, he reached his right hand into his jacket pocket to find a handkerchief to wipe away the resulting tears from his face. He re-adjusted his vision, and searched around him, though he wasn't quite sure, what he was looking for.

The street was busy with people bustling to and fro, all preoccupied, or so it seemed, with their own desires and interests. No one seemed to notice him stood there, waiting for the next moment to happen. He didn't feel conspicuous, but he felt noticeably different, like a piece of cardboard pasted onto the current picture of events, a figure in time, but not in the present. He wasn't sure whether he was transparent or invisible, or indeed whether there was any precise difference between the two concepts.

Patiently he waited. After a while a few people did exact a glance towards him and although he didn't want to be stared at, it was comforting to experience the acknowledgement.

And so with gratitude he smiled.

And in response the other humans smiled back politely.

As the darkness began to cover over the last remaining shadows, the streetlights illuminated themselves in response whilst further, more mysterious shadows began to present themselves around the street. From where Colin was standing immediately beneath one of these lamps, his shadow was completely obliterated. And the feeling of his incompleteness returned.

He watched as people continued to pass by and in his attempt to while away the time, he began to view these people more closely. He wondered about them; some were more interesting than others. He found that he was drawn in particular to the more attractive face, whether male or female. These faces seemed to contain more of a story held by their image - tanned faces, people who had recently been abroad, perhaps, was it business or pleasure? – vibrant faces, perhaps, describing a richness, not financial so much as cultural. Casting his vision over the hearts and souls of these characters, he began to paint mental images of their persona. And he did it with interest and with intrigue. Each individual held so much hidden material within their appearance that he felt like a scientist unravelling a genetic chain.

He liked watching. He felt he was beginning to know these people in a strange way it made him feel that he held some sort of a key for unlocking these people's being.They didn't know, they were unaware, but he knew.

It was easy for him he had given himself plenty of practice, just lately. He liked amusing himself with his imagination; though sometimes he really did believe in his thoughts - they were simply too real for him to hide away from. Trying to understand people from the inside - that was what he liked doing most of all, and he felt that he was good at it. He was brought back to the present by a sultry voice, which started to awaken the hearing in his left ear.

"Do you know the way to white stone pond?"

A thin, slightly built youth hung over him, like the arbour of a tree. A few inches taller than himself, Colin became aware of the dishevelled appearance of the man, before noticing the stranger's face. He reacted to the voice of the youth, which seemed worried and agitated; quickly giving the directions, he thought to be correct. He was ultimately pleased that the strange behaviour evident in this other individual might in some way be helpful in masking his own peculiarities.

But no one on the street was really paying much attention, anyway.

PART THREE

OPENING MINDS

CHAPTER TWENTY-EIGHT

You're feeling as if you're floating. Go with the feeling and don't let go. The feeling is a cushion around your soul, protecting you and comforting you. Lie back and release the thoughts that lie deep within your mind. Let your mind become transparent, as if in death. But remember consciousness becomes the body, and if your body is taken from you, your consciousness will remain. Allow your mind to transcend to that tempting Arabian evening, albeit a memory. Hold on to that which is solid, for no one can take this picture away from you now. And whilst you hold on, you cannot fall. Smell the charm of the night and engulf yourself in the essence of what appears to be real. Your mind is strong; stronger than you think. The solid objects of this Earth, which can disable your body, can never touch your mind.

Remain akin to this strength and force yourself to believe that from wherever your body is imprisoned, your mind can escape. Release the chains that imprison you and throw your arms high in a gesture of freedom. Let the evil minds that await you, cry remorselessly for their penance.

As the still of the night engulfs you from all sides, you engage your hearing to the noises around you. Far away the distant call from a fox catches itself on the wind creating a Doppler affect, which leaps over you. Reaching its peak at some high apex directly above your present position, it then slowly peters out, in an arc that is lost to some unknown point on the horizon.

As you listen you are beginning to feel an uneasy calm about you. The presence of some kind of bodily energy, and you are not really sure if you have ever felt this way before. You can feel the adrenaline beginning to rise in your system unsure whether it is going to trigger excitement or anxiety. You wait to see ... And you wait……

Words cannot exact the first feelings of realisation, as you slowly find yourself falling to the ground. You feel a throbbing on the left-hand side of your face, and slowly as your awareness intensifies, you notice a warm sensation touching your skin beside your left eye. Slowly this warmth begins to wind a pathway down the lines of your face, and you feel it tracing its way over your jaw and down the side of your neck. You have read this description in many books, and you know immediately that the heat that you feel is the warmth of your blood channelling its way out of your body. The feeling makes you feel physically sick, but you do not have the strength to turn your head on one side to vomit. Your head and body seem to be fixed rigid in a state of un-measurable shock. Yet somewhere in your consciousness you realise that if you vomit now you will probably asphyxiate. Your mind calmly reassures your body, and the nausea begins to subside. Long may mind over matter, preside.

You recognise these feelings as similar to the descriptions you have read in so many stories; however, realism is not set apart from visualisation.

- The fatally wounded hero, collapses on the floor, slowly slipping into oblivion, as his life's energy seeps through an open wound, in his side.

You can affiliate to the part of the character, and yet you can feel no pain. There seems to be a kind of numbness; an unreceptive area which has disconnected your brain from the pain on the outside. Your body appears to have shut down from the touch of the surrounding world, and you lie as if levitating on the air around you.

You feel no ground beneath you, as if you have been swallowed into some kind of weightlessness, and there seems to be no stimulation from any other object around you. Inside you feel both hot and cold, at the same time, and there is a constant throbbing, which although it seems to be projecting from your big toes, appears also to be situated within your skull. The beating of this pulse is like a noisy drum, which is at the same time, both stimulating and harrowing to listen to. You listen, without avoidance, and the sound begins to get louder. In your body you desperately want to run, but in your mind, you feel as if you have reached a state of peace.

Feeling that there is still a little bit of wilfulness about you, you remain motionless, believing that you must be supine, but you know that you have lost your sense of orientation and for all you know you could just as easily be upside down. The sound of the beating drum persists, and its artificial rhythm feels uncomfortably out of tempo with the pulse of your own body. Yet the harshness of its threat holds you to its regularity and you begin to feel hypnotised and unable to escape from its noisiness and confusion. Like the ticking of the clock the sound is injected through your system as it continuously connects you to the essential passing of time. Each second commanded to attention by the persistent thud.

Your ability to perceive time has been milked away in the same way as your perception to interpret space, and you act as if you have been transported to another dimension, where time itself seems to have been stolen from you, as indeed has space. A 'time warp' victim with no ability to enjoy the experience; that's what you would write, if you ever lived to see the end of this tale.

Unable to move, you use your only remaining sense to connect with the moment, your hearing has in fact become acutely sensitive - you suspect this is in compensation for your other sensory losses. You think you hear voices, but when your vision has been stolen from you, as it has, it is easy to distort what you are hearing or indeed, turn the words around in order that you can only hear what you wish to hear. You tune your attention to any minute detail which might enable you to interpret or understand a little more fully, exactly what is happening to you; trying at the same time to re-establish your whereabouts.

The sound of a human voice rests upon your ear and places you immediately back in the present. Planet Earth, *Friday 14th April 2001.* Why indeed has that date stuck in your memory? How did you manage to recall it so quickly despite having lost all perception of time? Was there any significance to this date above any other, which you might be able to recall to memory in the same rapid fashion? You doubt it. This date, you feel sure, is the present date. Although as you begin to contemplate events, you realise that considerable time may have passed and it may even by now, be tomorrow.

Your eyes are unable to distinguish light from dark. And you are aware that you are in a position shielded away from the knowledge of whether it is day or night; hidden away with no body clock to determine an estimation of the Earth's current position within the solar system.

Beginning to lock into this newly discovered voice, you hasten to listen attentively, like the submarine homing in on its radar. The voice is at first faint and so vague that it is impossible to distinguish between it being that of a male or female voice. The tone is level and without any visual help it is impossible to determine the temperament of the communicating creature. Your only feelings are that the character behind this voice is behaving cautiously impatient. The pitch of the sounds, remain unaltered and inexpressive, and just then you thought you heard the mention of the word - excellent! "Excellent!"

The word continues to echo around your head, seemingly unaffected by any other thoughts that may be issuing around. Floating, as if a butterfly, the beating of its wings, echoing the word in each stroke.

'Excellent'

'Ex-cellent'

'Ex-cell-ent'...

Your mind once again conjoins to the pulse of the word. Following each syllable in a raging rhythm, that is compulsively disturbing. The word is now dominating your thoughts and your awareness of the thudding pulse between your ears, has seemingly vanished. One intrinsic sound outweighed by another.

Slowly the word begins to fade into oblivion. The word itself becoming meaningless and then fading into an unnecessary sound, which fails to resound any further as an intelligible word. Quickly you remember games as a child where along similar lines you would repeat your own name until it too began to sound meaningless, and you too became non-existent. These had been the first experiences you had ever had of unrealism, but in the game, you had control, whereas in real life these experiences had tormented your body on a daily basis, and for many years. Despite the repetition of the word, you have been listening to, you knew that at this precise moment you haven't lost your sense of realness. Despite feeling deprived of your self-control, you still feel mindfully intact. You try to make yourself think that you are going mad, but nothing happens.

As ignorance is bliss, so acute awareness is trauma, and right now you feel as if someone is contorting the embodiment of your mind, into all sorts of weird and peculiar positions. Extending the ligaments and twisting the tendons until the element of pain suggested is beyond physical acceptance. Agonisingly you begin to cry out silently, awaiting the outcome of this torturous limbo. All earlier calmness within your mind has evaporated and now as the pain extends its way through to every crevice of your skull there is an awareness too of an agonising soreness on the side of your face.

You become more orientated, without doubt, as the pains in your limbs seem to be acting as if they are some kind of cerebral smelling salts, bringing you back to earth with an alarming jolt, reawakening you to the alarming present that you appear to be locked into.

You feel yourself being lifted up, and the voice you hear around you rises and falls, like the waves of the ocean. It is as if you are laid out on a lilo, embellishing the natural movement of the waters, but you remain un-calmed, despite the tantalising comfort, that is being induced around you. 'If only you could open your eyes' The desperate feeling of having lost control becomes paramount in your thoughts and you anxiously search for coping techniques to equip you in your quest to survive ... If survival is what you are fighting for? A sixth sense has already placed you in a position of extreme danger, for how else were you to interpret this 'happening'. You certainly do not feel that you are on some kind of extra sensory ride - If this is journeying into other time slots or experiencing outer cosmic sensations, then you really don't want to buy a ticket. This experience will be enough to last you a lifetime.

A sudden sensation of coldness travels across your body, followed by an increasingly warm sensation that remains with you. Only your suspicion tells you that you have been brought in from the cold and have now been placed in a position of shelter if not sanctuary.

The voice, which your mind has tried to track, now seems to be positioned above you, and the tone, although that of the same voice has begun to soften. Still, you painfully struggle to recognise the words, searching for clues and meaning, to help you interpret and understand the strange existence that has befallen you.

As a means of reassurance, your mind seems to have developed small images, those which, may help to explain your circumstances.

-Perhaps you have met with an accident, and having been placed in an ambulance you are now comfortably en route to hospital. -Maybe you fainted, and your mind is quietly re-processing thoughts, which are causing you to imagine all this pain which is circulating through your body. In a few moments you'll probably come to, feel a bit dazed, and then everything will be back to normal! - Perhaps you have been thrown into some kind of epileptic seizure, or you are suffering from a rare medical condition, which up to now you had no knowledge of. Again, maybe someone has come to your rescue and in a short while all will be well again pending a check-up at the local clinic!

Whilst you are linking with these thoughts, you notice that the pain has subsided a little and so you try desperately to keep your mind wandering along these positive pathways, connecting with material that seems to be cushioning your fall. - These are no woolly thoughts these are survival tactics substantiated by desperate and determined means.

The voice has silenced for a moment.

Your awareness breaks off from any other immediate thought, as you tentatively listen for the encouraging sound of another human's presence.

Eventually it comes! "Excellent!"

The word with no meaning! A statement; an expression; a jubilance; a word which when repeated has no existence within your lexicon and no semantic energy.It is of no help and yet it is all you have left to go on. Perhaps there is a cryptic clue? You fail to connect. The word continues to cry in your head, until the word is yours, and no one else's.

CHAPTER TWENTY-NINE

If today is April, then this is the coldest April day that you can ever remember. You feel your limbs shivering against a pressurising source, as if a lightweight material has been wrapped around you in an extremely tight fashion. It presses against your body in a way that causes a throb like the sensation of 'pins and needles' - A confused sensation which makes you want to escape it immediately, but of course you can't. You are trapped. Bound and unable to freely move your limbs. Held as a prisoner, but by whom and for what reason? You tense yourself against the restraints around you and try to use the moment to expel that tension as a force to tear you out of your restricted enclosure. But your tactics fail, and you remain bound and helpless.

Far away you begin to hear a faint whimpering, then matching up your own cries of desperation, you realise that it is your own sounds that you hear, echoing back to you from the walls of the cocoon that encompasses you. Your fingers are numb from the coldness and although you can visualise their movement it is impossible for you to feel the nature of the material that engulfs you. Your hands feel restricted, and a painful throbbing draws your attention to your wrists. The lack of feeling makes it difficult for you to determine exactly what is happening, but there is a suggestion that maybe your wrists have been bound together. There is a pressure at the base of your palms. Maybe the hands are actually pressing on one another, though it is still very difficult to tell. Your whole body feels in a confused contortion as if you can imagine where your limbs are and yet without seeing them you cannot be accurately sure that your predictions are correct.

As far as you are aware your legs seem to be curled up in some kind of foetal position and your arms are crossed over in front of your knees. Something like the position you used to adopt sitting on the floor in school assembly, all those years ago. Only this time you are laid horizontal instead of sat upright.

You begin to feel the throbbing on the side of your face and what you can only describe as the eruption of a swelling in the traumatised area. Your head and your face are the only parts of you that feel real. The rest of your body seems to have disengaged itself from your voluntary persuasion. Turning your head slowly you confirm your right to move this upper part of your anatomy, albeit in a restricted fashion.

The sound of a car engine, and the smell of diesel fumes awakens you to a new realisation, -the fact that you have obviously been placed inside a vehicle. Your thoughts turn to all those chilling thrillers that you have watched on countless occasions, where the kidnapped victim is hurtled into the boot of the get-away-car and transported away to meet their fate. Your further imagination sends shivers of terror up your spine and you are drawn to the firm belief that in the not-too-distant future you are going to meet a foul and gruesome end. Just like all the countless victims in those movies, except that the majority of their stories bore on fiction, whereas yours bears on simple naked truth.

The nature of these thrillers has always been borne out of bloody violence, and your thoughts link with the gruesome scenes imprinted in your memory. You always linked the minds of the villains as being those of fiction, never of truth. Yet they were indeed transposed through the mind of their author in each case, and so indeed the author was perhaps quite capable of committing their villain's crime, theoretically, but in Practice? -Who knows?

Maybe the writing of such scripts encouraged the demons to be removed from the author's mind and therefore become transferred into the mind of the perpetrator; invented for the purpose of committing the author's crime. Is the author therefore guilty of the crime they invent?

Sometimes without these stories, would-be criminals would be without a template, to work from. Or worse still is the author himself set with the potential of carrying out the crime which they report; constantly battling against an alto ego, to suppress their urge to run out and create havoc and mayhem.

For some reason you feel compelled to remain friends with your captor, and you comfort yourself by blaming the author, who placed the idea in your assailant's mind in the first place.

Lying still, you continue to inhale the diesel fumes. Something tells you that you are close to the vehicles exhaust. Could you possibly be in the boot? Quite possibly you suppose! You are beginning to feel a warmer air around you and a few small beads of warm liquid begin to run down the outer aspects of your face, and you feel them too on the upper aspect of your lips. Placing your tongue outside your mouth, you guide its movement across the area of moisture that you feel. Your tongue responding to the salty sweetness, confirms to your mind that this is sweat not blood and with some relief your tongue re-engages with the area, to try and assuage your apparent thirst. The evening's wine has reached its maximum dehydration level, and your body lends itself to sympathise with the lost soul in the desert, searching for the whereabouts of the next hidden oasis.

A sudden pain is gripping you, just behind your right knee, and you desperately try to extend your leg against the pull of the cramp, which has attached itself to your contorted muscles. Slowly the pain releases, although your movement is heavily restricted, by the tightness of the material that swathes you. Like a baby in the arms of a dying mother, you lie in a peaceful repose, whilst your life energy silently and surreptitiously vanishes, unknown, unheard, un-prevented.

You feel the pressure on your lungs as you carefully try to breathe, slowly and deeply - you don't want to pass out again. No matter how much it hurts you want to hang around to see the end of the show. Is this prudent or just human curiosity, taken to the extreme? More likely the latter! Wouldn't it be better to hide your eyes and cover your ears form the torment that engulfs you and wake up when all is over? Or never wake up at all?

Hear me now Didi and remember what has been said. Hold on to what is real, don't let go from your thoughts. Remember that consciousness provides the body, and whilst you are with these thoughts, your body cannot be harmed. Your mind is strong, though many arrows have impacted on its fortress, but you have been strengthened, not weakened by their blows!

Allow yourself the courage to place yourself into this situation wholly and be masterful of your own judgements and considerations.

No fool can conjure up the wisdom of a wise man. But no wise man can easily lend himself to the foolishness of a clever fool.

Mindful understanding is by far the most precious gift.

It is wise to admit to what you do not know. But perhaps wiser still to deny that which you do, for the sake of survival.

Survive, at your will,
Survive at your leisure.
Time can be held on your side, and the games and rules can be yours to declare.

I pass you now to the helm and through the guidance of your experiences, I leave you to steer yourself through this unexpected storm.
Take heed of my words and take courage.
Good luck Didi, you are on your own!

Almost at once you feel a sudden sense of relief though nothing physically has changed. The contorted positioning of your body remains held inside a dark encompassing space that has no beginning and no end. The weird smell of a manly scent entwined with the potent aroma of fuel, leaves your nose puzzled and drawn, although you would rather not be sharing the embrace of either of these smells. Overpowering and un-welcoming they do little to influence you in a medicinal way, as the aroma of myrrh and those other eastern smells that you are beginning to recall.

Those eastern nights seem so far away now, as if a dream, as if in another lifetime, a separate existence, looking through the open door within your memory, that night in Tel Aviv seems so far away. - So distant from present reality yet so clear in your mind's eye. You hold on to the picture as it skilfully places itself in the gallery of your thoughts, and as your eyes quickly scan the scene, you feel tears welling in their corners, as the memories linger in front of you. Albeit still yet moving in the presence of time. Slowly the reality of what you are regarding stares back at you like the sudden understanding of a language which is foreign to your tongue.

This masterful picture is the statement of your sanity built on the solid ground of your own past. This was once you as you were, not as you are now entombed, but as you were free and without restraint. Only held in the moment by the encapsulation of time; otherwise, free to do exactly as you pleased. How insane are your current thoughts for realising the existence of this freedom only when it is so obviously too late and seemingly lost for good.

Sparing yourself from further thoughts, you close your eyes to these memories, and adjust your focus to the present and the means of survival, which you must now seek to operate in order to preserve your justification for existing upon this Earth.

You hear the distant purr of an engine, and occasionally you feel the surge of your body as the vehicle you are contained in shifts gear. But as an object in a hidden space, you really cannot tell if the force of your weight is being shifted forwards or backwards. All you have is the sense of an orbital movement within the space you have been allocated.

Your linen clothing provides no warmth around you and yet you continue to sweat handfuls of a cool, almost refreshing liquid, which expels itself through every identifiable pore in your entire body. You imagine yourself appearing like a human watering can, with spurts of your sweat leaping up in parabolic patterns all around you. The picture is cartoon like and amusing and in your mind, you begin to smile but your face refuses to excite this gesture - Your lips are dry, and the pain on the side of your face, is worsened considerably by any movement of your intricate facial muscles. You continue to lie expressionless, whilst awaiting the moment of truth.

You note the passage of time, though you have no idea, what time has passed, and how fast present time is moving. Mystery stares at you from all sides, and yet you seem to be the prize of the mystery itself. With no perceivable head for answers, no mind to search for truth, and nobody physically able to transport you away from your fate. You lie here in the bosom of helplessness, held by your temperate mind in the conclusion that all is a dream and that if you can survive this dream than you can ultimately survive reality.

The vehicle stops with a jolt.

You hear the screech of brakes and parts of your body knock against hard objects all around you, as if you are being whirled about in some giant toy box full of angry metal toys. Eventually, inertia is interrupted, and your body stills once more. A car door slams and the echoes rumble around you. Footsteps as if on gravel, move towards you in a shuffling motion, restricted perhaps by the awkwardness of walking over tiny stones. Eventually they stop. A clicking sound from above; and the sudden awareness that the deathly black case that has been surrounding you for what has seemed an overlong period has finally been lifted. A brighter awareness of your surroundings occurs; probably made possible by a nearby streetlight or searchlight of some kind. You are still surrounded by what appears to be a thin plastic sheet. You hear the ripples of its movement against a faint breath of air that passes around your space. Everything else is still. No Earthly sound. No Human sound. No sound of life, only the unfamiliar feel of un-realism and disbelief. You remain still and silent. You play possum, and yet you know whoever it is knows you're there. There is no playful hide and seek to this adventure. Games have become gambles. And you are now the ace.

You follow the shadow as it moves closer to you. It crosses over the folds made in the plastic that lies across your face. Not a recognisable face, but the distorted contortion of another human being. Its head and neck appearing to lean unnervingly forward, hung like a willow tree, in a stooping-like fashion, as if the strength has been sapped from its trunk.You fear this façade as you acknowledge that any misperceptions you might deem to be reasonable are just a means of borrowing time. This figure must have power and strength, somewhere within the depths of its mind there is probably a hidden strength that has the power to create and destroy at random, and you are within its grasp. Your mind screams for revelation so that redemption can begin. Your body remains still but you can feel a small twitching above your right eye which you have no means of controlling. You try to ignore it.

Feeling yourself inhaling deep lungfuls of air, you slow your breathing down, wondering where your fresh supply of oxygen is coming from. Obviously, a small hole somewhere, for you can feel the plastic now settling itself across your face. Are you supposed to be gaining this fresh supply of air? Or is it already assumed that you are no longer a surviving member of the human race?

From beyond your cover, it must be easy for an individual to make out your features, through your plastic mask. -Your face appearing like a still Michel Angelo cast in pewter but with lips appearing to twitch, on each intake and out-take of air.

The shadow above you swarms around you, and you feel yourself jerked into a painful and uncomfortable position. You can only imagine your ensuing plight, thrown over the shoulders of your captor you are now being whisked off to the dark dungeons of despair, from which you will never return. You feel your body jerking with every uneven footstep. Your momentum slows even further when your carrier appears to negotiate a set of steps. There is a sound of a door opening and the footsteps now take on a different tone; that of clicking heels rebounding on a flagstone floor.

A few changes of direction as you assume you are being taken through a series of rooms. Then at last you feel yourself placed down in a sitting position, which is only just possible in your present contorted state. Feeling unable to move in order to gain more comfort you remain positioned thus and await your fate, as your captor exposes you.

CHAPTER THIRTY

You stare at the face ahead of you and the face of your onlooker stares back with a look of intelligence, profound malice and a firm contempt. You meanwhile bounce against this look with one of disagreement, fortitude and a questioning brow. (Indeed, this is how you hope you appear, realising the restricting presence of your facial injuries).

"Excellent!" You find the meaning of the word returns as you hear it once more. Then it is repeated again this time with reference to a subject or at least an object,

"Excellent article."

As you listen, you remember hearing these words before in a slightly different context, but at the moment your memory does not help you in recognising precisely where or indeed when. The voice too seems strangely familiar, but not a voice that you think you ought to know. Just one you have heard in passing perhaps. You home in on the face of your interloper as he carefully clears his throat. He then begins to manipulate the previously dormant muscles, enveloping his straight -lined mouth, almost as though, performing a theatrical exercise of the face, which only RADA might possibly explain. If he is about to make a speech, you feel it will not be long, in coming. Searchingly his eyes move in the orbital movement of the owl's eye, seeming to look at you from above, behind and below all at the same time, tracing the visual field around the vicinity of the space in which you are sat; yet they do not seem to focus upon you immediately or at all. It is as if you are not there in body but only in spirit. He seems to be experiencing your presence in a different form as if his mind has transcended to another plain. The coldness of his stare continues to pass around you and although he makes no eye contact with you, you can still feel the penetrating pressure of those eyes and the ring of cool abnormal temperature that encompasses you right now.

You remember reading Lewis Carroll as a child. The familiar pictures illustrated in your version of the story begin to appear life-like in front of you. You recall particularly the part where Alice is inside the house and begins to grow, until her limbs are contorted and begin to pop out of all different orifices within the house. The doors, the windows…The pressure must have been awesome. Right now, you relate to that feeling, as you slowly feel the room in which you are enclosed beginning to move in on you. Unlike Alice you have not drunk or eaten anything to make you shrink or grow more quickly than you can control. But rather you are experiencing some similar feeling in reverse, whereby the walls that stand around you, seem by some delusional coincidence to be moving slowly towards you in military timed slowness that makes you feel that it is possible that it isn't really happening. But nevertheless, there is still that element of doubt, which will not go away. And as you connect with the delusion you actually do begin to feel yourself becoming larger and larger, in relation to your surroundings, the pressure and tension around you begins to increase too, until you feel almost breathless and uncomfortably faint.

"Don't pass out on me now, for God's sake. After all this, let's at least see it through. Shall we?"

Coming quickly to your senses, you hesitate to make connection with the question then decide against doing so. After all it wasn't really delivered in the fashion of a question but more along the lines of a command, which in any case or circumstance is always best obeyed. Homing back to the statement, you try to understand what it is that you have been through, and what indeed there is left to go through. You hope that it will be less uncomfortable and over sooner than the opening of the drama which you have experienced so far. You realise that you have lost your weird sensation of feeling enclosed and threatened by the room. It seems that the voice of your captor has acted like a verbal slap on the face, ordering you to your senses. Though you are sure that the initial blow you received earlier was far more than imaginary. Although he is thin and scrawny you feel certain that both slaps were inflicted by the same individual, who's authority now engulfs you.

If a smile can warm the emotions, then the icy blueness of this man's stare could turn you instantly to stone. You read in his face the message of supreme hatred. It is as if he hates you right down to the core, every little sinew of muscle that stretches across you and holds you together, begins to feel the effect of this paralysis; you feel the first domino wobble, signalling a catastrophic collapse. As mindfully, you fall into a heap on the floor, the figure begins to move towards you, and placing his palm beneath your chin, as if in a gesture of support, he carefully locks his gaze against yours.

You feel an impact, as if you have been hit by an invisible bullet. Struck in the solar plexus unable to move or regain your composure. Your mind coughs and splutters as it tries to regain a degree of control. Somehow your thoughts begin to order themselves back into line, but you feel incredibly weakened. The eyes that stare towards you speak to you in a strange and foreign tongue. They do not appear as human eyes but as those that hide the complexity of hidden thoughts and aggression, which no other human being can tap into or release. This stare is more forceful than any chains or bars, which could imprison you, and it engulfs you in a wrestling hold, more forcible with each blink of the eye.

The look that bears upon you seems to beckon you to scream but you resist, with apparent ease. You try hard to hold on to some control in this situation, though you know not how. You feel no warmth of tears around your eyes nor are you aware of a furrowing of your brow. You try to imagine how your face must appear to your onlooker, but it is hard to transfer your thoughts away from your body and look back, as it were, over your shoulder. The trepidation of your ego is such that you feel it is better to know little, in order that your heart will not bleed so badly, but nevertheless you feel a further gush with every murmur of your pulse.

"Did you think you'd get away with it then?"

This questionable, remark, fashioned in such an ardent manner causes you to retract from providing an answer. For without knowing what it is you are supposed to have got away with, there is no foreseeable means by which you can defend yourself. Immediately you think that your captor has mistaken you for somebody else, and you feel sick from the fear and knowledge, that maybe someone, somewhere, is actually getting away with whatever it is you are being accused.

"Well, ... Didi!"

Your mind is alerted to the use of your name. And you feel violated already by this person and their unique informality.

"You didn't fool me! -There's always one person out there willing to stick their neck out to get the prize. Never forget that Didi. ...Never forget that."

The emphasis placed upon these last words rings solemnly upon your ears, and you know that no matter how hard you ever try it will be impossible to forget these foreboding lines. Everything, the numbness, the torturing words, the suppressive atmosphere within the room, bind together for a moment and you wonder where your sense of fear has actually run to. Your mind begins to transcend back to those days in your past when you were engulfed with those feelings of anxiety. You remembered how your heart used to race and your head used to throb, and your legs would turn to jelly even though you urgently wanted to run. No longer are these physiological signs respondent to your present feelings. They have been washed up in a tide of despair and somehow there does not seem to be anything to truly fear any more. The fear of the fear too has subsequently vanished. Perhaps because your body believes it can no longer be shocked or scared by anything, anymore.

You remember the story your mother used to tell of your grandmother, who had lost two brothers in the First World War. After her loss, she had become oblivious to the hardships and evils that the world surrounded her with. She firmly believed in her heart that she had already endured the harshest of pains and agonies in having to face up to the deaths of those brothers, whom she had loved so dearly, and she had been so close to. Her philosophy had not been cold and hard, but real, just like your present state, and you try now to filter some of that strength from the generations that have gone before. It warms your thoughts, and you continue to acknowledge the present in the most challengeable way possible.

"Did you speak Didi?"

Again, the forcefulness of the voice and its tone makes you careful to avoid answering in the wrong manner.

"No, I didn't."

"Speak up Didi, I can't hear you!"

"I said, No."

"Good, we wouldn't want you saying something that might upset me, would we? Very wise not to say anything if you're unsure. Sensible tactics, I expect you're good when it comes to being careful aren't you Didi…. Mmmm?"

The voice vibrates within your head and the feeling of nausea returns. The sardonic tones and patronising element attached to these words makes you feel physically repulsed, and you desperately want to retaliate in some way, but you know that you can't. Your hands remain tied both physically and metaphorically. And the measure of your tongue is equal to only a small syllable of any word, which would not make sense whether pronounced abruptly or phonetically.The moment remains silent. Whilst the words that you wish to shout out remain trapped within your mind, searching for small outlets to seep through and allow their presence to be known if not heard. Silence is golden, but not in this instance.

You wish your pursuer would ask those questions, which will allow you the opportunity to provide some answers and ask for clues as to the reason for this intrusion on your life. After all you feel that it is not a lot to ask. For the next few minutes, you wait. And you wait.

The silence holds an element of foreboding and discomfort, and you desperately wish to hear anything, even words of abuse, demand or accusation. Just to give yourself a clue. You hear your mind begging for something, anything, just to lessen the silence. Then the silence breaks.

"How much are you worth, Didi?"

"I don't know." You answer in the way that a person does when they believe that there is no answer, or indeed that if there is one then their questioner already, secretly knows it anyway.

"No answer, Didi? …But you are so clever, I thought you knew all the answers?"

You feel a whisper ebbing in your throat. "If only!"

"What was that Didi? Did you say something? Come on share it with me and be polite!"

"I said I have no answer."

"I see…We're going to play difficult, are we? Well, you better think again. There must be people out there who could put a price on you. Wouldn't you think?"

"I don't understand."

"You're losing that clever way you have about you. Usually you have all the answers, and you're cunning with it. Are you losing it Didi? Have I scared you into some kind of amnesia some psychological trance? Where's the one that knows all? Did they run and hide? Did they get scared Didi? Is the game too hot for you now? Are you in too far - that you forgot when to jump off the roundabout? Shame! Shame on you! You've let the side down and now you must pay the price. Unless of course someone is going to pay the price you're worth!"

You feel a need to know and understand more about what is being said. So much is confusing, and you feel totally in the dark. Feeling a sudden surge of confidence, you urge yourself to ask one question, at least, that may help you to understand.

"Why are you putting a price on me?"

"Because you're worth it! Ha Ha……!"

The agitated laughter ripples round you and once again you feel your confidence removed from you, as the force of these ripples draws everything backwards in a centre-petal force, everything drawn away from you. You begin to feel dizzy but quickly regain your composure, hoping that the expression on your face has not altered in a way that is likely to have shown your momentary loss of control. Your face still hurts, and you are sure you would not have moved it voluntarily. You struggle to adjust your position on the hard wooden chair on which you are sat. Wriggling yourself slowly from left to right; you find it impossible to make your movements discreet.

His hand grabs your right arm, and his thumb presses hard on the area where the biceps muscle crosses over and stretches itself into its insertion with the bones of the forearm. The pressure is painful, and you grimace, your pride prevents you from screaming out, and inwardly you digest the pain of the experience silently and without consideration. The moment passes and you feel the relief extend itself in the form of a pleasant tingling throughout your system, but you are aware of a tension inside which cautions you and prepares you for a repeat of the agony. You wait. The agony does not come.

Glancing down at your hands which rest forlorn and pathetic upon your lap, you scan the rope that binds them together and notice the reddened soreness that has appeared, there is a persistent itchiness too which won't abate, and you feel progressively more aware of the restriction procured by the rope. The areas above your wrist are scratched and bruised and a small laceration on your right hand is weeping. You try to exercise your fingers, perhaps to assist the restless feeling within your hands. Moving each finger in turn first and then altogether, the latter being a little easier, but your movements are affected by the swelling of your hands, and the pain of this operation makes you ease your exercising, and you lay your fingers gently still again. Trying hard to believe that this discomfort will soon be at an end, you nevertheless feel your equanimity begin to fade.

Your arm is grasped again. Tightly - In a hold which does not weaken. Tighter and tighter. The feeling burns. The pain surges and you feel your fingernails biting into the palms of your hands in a desperate ploy to refer the pain to a torture that somehow you yourself can take control of.

"Now that I have your attention, let us just discuss a few details together shall we, Didi?"

In the best gesture you can manage, you begin to nod. The continuing pressure on your arm makes you aware of your pulsating limb; it feels detached and heavy. You sink your nails further down into the flesh of your palms, and somehow the foreboding pain is slightly relieved. Then the anger of the voice you hear smashes into your eardrums with unprecedented velocity.

"Didi! I have to ask you – Why!?"

"Why?" You hear your own voice repeating the word as if it answers the question, but you do not mean to be sardonic. You wonder who is going to answer the burning question first. You or him? In the ensuing moment you wait to anticipate the reaction that your response may have instigated.

"Hell Didi! I thought you were the one with all the answers?"

"You did?" You answer quietly and his face does not acknowledge or show any interest in your reply.

"So look Didi let's cut out asking the questions, shall we?"

"If you say so!"

"Good, now you really are beginning to listen."

Obviously, the sarcasm evident in your voice during this last reply has gone un-noticed. His eyes begin to blaze once more, igniting a sense of alarm that burns with every glance that he directs towards you.

"What I want to know is, exactly what is it you want to achieve by your interests and your actions."

Pausing before you try to reply your mind wanders back over the question. What effectively is the answer that this man is looking for? Your immediate reaction is to connect this question with you work with TOP. but why on earth would these lines of questioning be focussed towards your involvement with the charity? It just doesn't make any kind of sense. Could this be a revengeful kidnap in response to someone you had helped previously, perhaps? It appeared to be the most obvious answer but it just seemed so totally bizarre and unthinkable. And why were you the chosen one? Why couldn't he have picked on Ken or Michelle? Or maybe even someone his own size, perhaps. You wonder this as your eyes quickly scan the height of the man in front of you, thinking hard you realise that in fact his stature would probably be hard to emulate.

Appreciating that you have not yet answered the latest question, you quickly switch your mind from wondering and try hard to connect with some kind of answer, which will show that you have been concentrating. You don't want to be accused of making light heart of this situation, and not taking things seriously enough. You have, however, noticed that you are losing your initial sense of fear and that the terror and uncertainty that was with you earlier has begun to dissipate. You think a little harder; then reply.

"I think you must find my work very interesting to want to know so much about me, and what I do."

"No Didi! I do not find your work interesting, in fact I find it callus and inhumane."

Your face changes expression even though it hurts. You realise that you have obviously touched a nerve in your inquisitor.

He continues."This is why you deserve this, because people like you take their work so complacently. You offend and direct your curses on other human beings, and yet you remain so unaffected by what you do."

These words would perhaps deserve a lighthearted reasoning in any other context, but in this present situation, you can see that this man is incensed in his beliefs and is powerfully opposed to what you do. You search deep in your memory to try and link this person to someone whom you may have encountered recently at one of your meetings - Someone with a grudge, perhaps, who found the methods and teachings of the group too hard to follow? Or maybe and you thought this was probably your best guess, that you were witnessing your first psychotic episode. Neurosis, being your field, you suddenly feel tremendously out of synch with this character.

He seems so detached from and yet so fixated with his cause, so unrealistic in his outlook and yet seemingly confident in presenting evidence in light of his reason. Through his eyes, it was you who stood in the dock at this moment not him. Your unjustified crime seemingly, far, outweighing, his own. Yet you had been kidnapped, beaten, presumably to an unconscious state. Tied up and hurtled about for many miles in the confined boot of a car. And here you were now, having to answer in your defence, without a witness or a lawyer to help you justify your purpose.

What sort of civil liberty does this grant you? The civility of this creature before you is of a kind fitting to the barbaric times set in the reign of King John. 'Execute first and ask questions after!'It is obvious to you that your liberty was stolen in the moment, some hours earlier when your body received that first retaliating blow. Freedom now is a faint speck on a dark horizon; that no longer beckons but only stares.

"Well let's see now Didi, if you're not going to respond sensibly to my questioning, I'm going to have to find out the answers to my own questions, aren't I?"

You remain silent; it seems by far the most sensible decision.

"Firstly! Let us see. Ah yes! That burning question, just how much are you worth? Well quite frankly to me you're worth sod all, cause the likes of you don't have a worth. You"re scum! Absolute bloody scum! You have no remorse or conscience in you. You're just boiled up from the stew of human leftovers. That's what you are. I wouldn't put you in my mouth to spit you out you're so bitter and tasteless."

These words ring stern against your ears, and echoes of 'feelings mutual' would have escaped from your lips, if you'd been in the mood for stark replies.

"The heap of human remains that you leave by the wayside in your feeble attempts to prove your cause lie putrid in the arms of those left to pick up the pieces. In fact, Didi the Earth is filled with the stench that people like you leave behind."

You listen unimpressed.

"Now regarding this issue of your worth!"

You're thinking 'Cut to the chase' For God's sake get down to the bottom of this issue and let's sort this out once and for all. But of course, you know that this is not going to be possible now. Already any simplicity involved in this matter has been washed away by the tidal wave of emotions that have already been expressed. Any triviality has already been saturated; any compromise waterlogged; any mutual understanding drowned in a sea of despair. You are washed up in a world that has no fruits or shelter to sustain life. You have no ready means of survival; this is a dead end that ends in a vicious circle, drawn by the waters which define your seclusion.

The voice continues and you return your thoughts to the room where you sit.

"The only way to find out who loves you, who cares about you, who wants you, is to ask. Isn't it? Who shall we ask first Didi? ... Your Mother? ... Your Father? ... The Almighty? What justification would any of them bring to your present case? Do you think they'd miss you if you weren't here, or in their eyes are you a worthless piece of flesh?"

Realising the manipulation that is at play here, you are reminded of your childhood and the guilt and rebuff you listened to and endured for so many years. For so long you worked with these thoughts and after many years you had managed to break from the conditional love that was your torment during your childhood and early teenage years. How had you broken from that process then? You had been forced to believe so readily that you were without a price; you were never quite good enough, never quite in the queue when the praise was dished out. But how had you ridden yourself of this torment? Years of hard struggle and determination, of course, but you hadn't years to play with now in order to straighten your mind and prevent your sanity from exiting on the next bend. Somehow you had to reach out quickly for that cord in your mind, and with it, pull your thoughts into some kind of order.

How had you managed?

Then you remember - All those rituals that you had felt so compelled to carry out; the ones that would seemingly make everything all right and to some extent they had. You had ordered a control over your world, which made you feel omnipotent, you thought you had it in your grasp, these rituals of checking, repeating, and washing, they made you feel in charge of life and the world around you, yet the monster had swallowed you up. Why? Because you had let it! But did that make you weak? No, you didn't think so, you just had had no means of knowing at the time, how to control the beast. But now you did! Now this beast was no more than a tiny shadow that stood on the horizon and beckoned to you occasionally. It had no power over you, other than making its presence known. You were the one in control because - You were special, if only because you had life. You were equal to the next man because you were body and soul. You were worthy because you had the ability to earn credibility. You were justifiable by your own justification. And above all you were a human being who could see hear taste touch and smell the belief in this person; the person that was you. Right now, you believe this more than ever before. If this man can break you, then he has the power that breaks belief, and you are certain that that is a talent which this human does not have the means to personify.

CHAPTER THIRTY-ONE

"Dear, Dear Didi! What have you done?"

As he speaks you feel the fingers of your right-hand straining against the grip of the rope. They move and you follow their movement in a not too detached way; your index finger tapping out its message on your lap. First one tap followed by two more …. Wasn't it 'Three for good luck' and then, oh yes - not forgetting 'One, for good measure'!

How familiar that little ritual feels right now; how comforting and seemingly controlled.

You sit fascinated by the easiness with which it has returned after so long a wait; almost relieved for after all it had been a familiar imp to you for so many years and now here it was once again holding out its hand and waiting for you to come out to play.

There was no degree of uncertainty within you that this felt incredibly safe and real, and that you were handling it in the most mature and sensible way. What if this were superstition gone too far, an extension of a childish whim. What you needed right now was some means of furthering your own reassurance and a way of finding something which you could attach to and be comforted by. Suddenly you feel as if you have found that object not in a lucky charm, or a philosophical saying, but in the re-annunciation of a ploy that has helped so readily in the past. Your mind begins to deploy a multitude of connected scenarios, where you have used this method to your advantage, albeit so long ago.

It had started relatively simply, just checking. Checking whether doors were locked; Checking whether forms had been properly filled in; Checking your clothes for pieces of fluff. Why? Because it had made you feel comfortable, until of course the next compulsive urge had taken charge. A synaptic roundabout, you were always dizzy, and you could never quite manage to jump off.

Gradually however those compelling urges had increased, until you had distanced yourself from the safe number 'four'. That was far behind you and in a short space of time; you had begun to check hundreds of things every second of the day. Re-checking, double-checking until your mind had checked so many things that it felt numb and blind yet at the same time it was hurting and the pictures it was seeing were real, and far beyond negating persuasion. They were tangible delusions and they preyed on your mind constantly every single day for many, many years. You had washed so many objects in some strange desperate measure of wiping the thoughts clear from your mind. But instead of diluting the feelings, they had been churned about as if they had been placed inside some enormous washer and were being thrashed against the inside of your scull. They had desperately wanted to be released. But whilst spinning around so fast and so randomly it was impossible for them to find a means of escape. It was like each thought was searching for one tiny wormhole in the midst of a football pitch, the only means by which it might find an exit.

So you had washed your thoughts and tried airing them to the psychiatrist, but all he had been interested in was yesterday's dirty washing. It had been no help at all. And all the while you had felt yourself getting worse, because you were quite obviously not getting better. You had never got to the ironing stage until some years later. It had not been as if a single day had been set aside as 'washing' day, as in Grandma's time, but rather that the day had lasted years, and even then, some of the stains had never truly been eradicated.

For the last few years, you had lived in a world where nothing was pristine or perfect. You had already realised that this was very much a false illusion, which could never quite be met. On the other hand, you had provided yourself with a world where you felt aesthetically comfortable and so far, that had been good enough for you. Objects around you were now seen to be as clean as they were in the next persons mind; there did not have to be a sanitary cleanliness as much as an organised and acceptable cleanliness which you and the majority of the world, you hoped, could accept and enjoy. No more false delusions or scary realities. Everything had happily reached a status quo. The unfortunate fact that you had left your parents unsuitably by the wayside whilst having travelled along this route was by far the saddest part of the process. Though an experience, no doubt, which many a fellow traveller might experience too. In becoming more grounded in reality, of being yourself and experiencing a oneness with the Earth, you had become alive. You had indeed 'Found yourself'! Friendships though important were now secondary. No one can invent friends any more than they can pretend to lose them. But new, somewhat, stronger relationships can often manifest themselves after a time of revelation. For all your losses and gains you had come to analyse and contemplate less. The ambiguity of right and wrong which had haunted you all your life; now gone, allowing you to feel locked inside a sense of freedom that no one can snatch away. You are free. Except right now you are a physical captive, within a world which up to now, you had so carefully mastered mindfully.

CHAPTER THIRTY-TWO

He studies you. You feel the intensity of his contempt around you, and you wonder what it is That this mystic gaze has been allowed to witness. Has he seen your hands and fingers twitching? Did he notice the strange blinks of your eye? -First the right, then the left. Or was it the other way round? The order of the ritual mattered not. Like the symbolic acts which certain sports stars had recently disclosed to the media, you wondered whether the slightest interest or notice would be taken of your mindful props, if you weren't to verbally draw attention to what it was you were doing. Indeed, was there any need to explain in the first place? -Seemingly not!What else were you doing to evoke this feeling of control and concentration? There were hundreds of little ideas buzzing through your head right now. Amazing how quickly they returned to you after such a long absence. Neglected and hidden away though obviously held in reserve, as was being demonstrated right now. If your observer were to notice these things, would he see them as an inadequacy on your part? Would he conveniently see your mind buckling, your knees weakening, or would he just as easily be totally unaware? It was hard to know; impossible to perceive and just as difficult to guess. You couldn't begin to conclude an answer and yet you believe in your heart that you are indeed as powerful as this person who stands before you.

How can you make this person submit to you? How can you turn this seat, which you are inconveniently tied to, into a throne as opposed to a stake? You watch his eye, just the right eye. Searching for the truth of an identity, that sits there beaming at you. Who is he that holds you like a snared animal, and refuses to release you or put you out of your misery? What inhumane act does this person intend to carry out in favour of possessing you and ultimately bringing you to your downfall? Does he already know that hidden answer to the burning question…Why? Or is he calling your bluff and waiting impatiently for you to finally surrender and submit all that you know? You hope not, for you have no ace card to play. Your poker face is evidently no asset to you here; well clearly not as helpful as it has sometimes been in the past. The game that is being played here, is by far more serious, and all eventualities at present lie firmly in the hands of the dealer. It would be as hard to turn the other cheek as it would be to turn the tables. You could try! But physically you know it would be impossible. The structure of this man far out-weighs your own complex building blocks of evolution. But mentally you wonder if perhaps the barriers that he has surrounded himself with are as structurally sound as the ammunition which you can bombard upon his mind? You know that you are clutching at straws.

Power is power at the end of the day and the power is his till dusk at least on this occasion.If pride comes before a fall, then submission only lessens the bump on the knees when the final defeat is witnessed. What have you to lose? But there again what have you to gain? If you step into the tiger's cage, will he necessarily roar because he wants to eat you? Or might he just be resentful of you disturbing his peace and quite obviously invading his space, when after all he is perhaps just trying to rest and quietly digest a meal which he has already eaten. If you were to show submission would your captor, not be easily persuaded that you were of no threat? Might he not see you not as an equal or a threat but as some trivial being? And treat you in a manner of sublime indifference? 'You had nothing to lose'. These are the only words of reassurance which you can find to write on your mental coping card. But it will do for now…You hope. Besides you are already in that tigers' cage so to speak, any further dangers have only to be decided for you by a third party. You had no choice whether you went into that cage or not. You have been placed there and so now you must apply your tactics for what they are worth, in order to move forwards with any hope of success. Somewhere in your mind there is a little area of uncertainty, questioning the apparent suitability of your reasoning at this level. It is obvious from past experience that you are not the inherent gambler by any means. But you were once taught never to make yourself a fool to others and somehow that advice has stuck. If you don't stick your neck out now you never will, and in the light of the present situation you might never get the opportunity again. So here you go, elbowing your way through the garden of uncertainty, trailing yourself along the path of realism and rationality, if ever you could meet on an even keel again with either of these two assertive assets.

Mindlessly stubborn and determined on the one hand yet feeling consciously feeble on the other, you stride forward holding with your thoughts trying to make real your plans though at the moment they seem intangible and reflective of your current state of weariness and fatigue. If all else fails, they will not be able to say you hadn't tried! But who were the 'They's? Who cared? Who really worried whether your plight was successful or not? What was it to them? You had lost so many family ties over the last few years, which made you feel rather omnipotent. Despite seeming very selfish, it was quite obvious that the only person that was ever going to benefit from your actions was you. Did this make it right? Did this condone your feelings of revenge and complacency?Were you really in the right frame of mind to make these decisions - to award yourself the permission to take the situation into your own hands? Well, there was nobody here who was going to provide you with an answer to these rather thin questions, right now. You could only work with intuition. Follow your senses.

Move with what feels right. No one was going to tell you, help you, or advise you. The world was tough like that, and right now you were in the toughest place on the planet. There was no room here for compromise. No far-reaching offer of understanding. You were at the raw edge of existence, and no one was paving you a smoother road, or providing you with a sign post of clear directions in order to make your decision more comfortable or obvious. You are alone and it is as if you are in a garden, surrounded by brambles, yet still able to smell the perfumes of flowers hidden from view, representing the freedom that lies out there waiting for you. Right now that garden feels dry and humid, uncomfortable and unimpressionable by its lack of substance. If there were only a gate somewhere, a significant opening that could justify your escape and could lure you in the right direction. You stretch your mind out like the hands of a blind man trying to feel the night. The gesture is weak. The symbolism of your thoughts is far-fetched and holds no further answers. The world as well as the room is seemingly closing in on you now and your time feels short against the invisible clock which has accompanied you on this experience so far; seemingly there are no bones to time. You have no idea of your position at this moment. No accounting for your present whereabouts, apart from knowing that you are far from your original setting last evening; the bright lights of Hampstead seeming far away. The warm embracing atmosphere of 'Fagin's kitchen', has at this moment vanished completely. It is as if you have been transported not only from you original physical setting but also from your mental one. No longer does the calmness that has surrounded you for many years lay with you like a blanket. For in an instant, it has been whipped unceremoniously from you. You are naked in a dismantling way that makes you feel both vulnerable and sordid at the same time.

CHAPTER THIRTY-THREE

Amid the years of countless longing to escape and be free spirited, the gauge of embracing a mental freedom seemed an entirely impossible conclusion. It's possible failure seemed to far outweigh even the slightest hope of any eventual success. Set against the possibility of a physical freedom it had seemed absolutely impossible to the point where any kind of physical entrapment seemed easy to escape from. Visualisation concerning these matters always consisted of Houdini type logistics, which funnily enough, always worked. Where the physical aspect of movement was concerned it was always so much easier to perceive one's limitations and indeed one's capabilities, whereas of course with the mind it was always so much harder to calculate and know what to expect. The mind always seemed such a frightening force to deal with; its abject failure a much more daunting and frightening conclusion to live with. In the physical sense if you fell you knew to some degree the possible nature or extent of the injuries, which you might incur, pain could be endured more easily because it could be perceived. You knew this was true it had indeed been shown in research carried out by some of the top psychologists. If a number of phobics were placed in their phobic situation i.e. a dental surgery or a surgical ward in a hospital, it had been noted that those who had been accurately told about the procedure, which they were to undergo, or indeed had had their treatment explained as it was taking place, then that individual would show a very obvious decrease in their anxiety levels, if not during the procedure then evidently their anxiety would fall much faster afterwards, thus accelerating their overall recovery in most cases. The evidence of this knowledge was easy to believe, but performing the same sort of mental preparation was far harder. It was easy to think about physical changes and procedures, but certainly very difficult to allow yourself to actually think about changing thoughts and beliefs within your head. Your past experience had taught you to analyse these changes in thinking very carefully before carrying out tasks.; the minutest inaccuracy causing devastating and long-lasting effects upon your ability to cope, and indeed, accept the overlying affects. Could you accept this responsibility? Could you be strong enough in yourself to work with the inevitable changes, which in most cases might request you to work with an element of guilt, laid neatly without reprieve upon your doorstep? The matter to some degree was in your own capable hands. You had the present advantage of being placed in the approved position of being allowed to pull the hidden strings of the mind. There was a manipulative element to this line of thought. One which you certainly were not used to, yet you felt quite in touch with all the same. If you pulled those strings with the right force and with a degree of furtive restraint, then there was a good possibility that you could work this process fairly accurately and with a good chance of getting things right first time; well, you had to to give it a go. There was definitely no turning back now. This was to some extent the point of no return, and yet you were holding on to that last thin line of hope…… Or was it thin? Perhaps it was only as thin as the comparative strength of the mind that was pulling it. It certainly was not a frail piece of string. More like a fine line of steel wire. Incredibly tough compared to its small diameter. The discouraging lines of pain strike deep into your woven brow and you feel the discomfort of each tiny particle within you. They question and concern themselves with your welfare and ultimately your survival. The heavy weight of these thoughts causes the furrows across your brow to deepen but on the inside, you remain unchanged and reconciled. It is only the surface which is changing in its appearance. Inside your mind the structure of your thoughts is exhibiting an increased welling of confidence. Although mindfully aware of this situation you can do nothing to change your existence on the surface and you know that you are giving out certain obvious signs of distress. Perhaps this is not a bad thing - to fool your captor into thinking that you are fearful and scared. That's quite obviously what he wants and here you are performing beautifully for his benefit and spontaneously at that. You feel proud. Your body language is helping you out quite agreeably. You couldn't have done this better if you had tried. Nothing could have prepared you for this and yet it feels so natural, accepting these feelings that you seemingly have absolutely no control over. Or so it had seemed!

At last, you feel that you have given in, and a general calm acceptance of your present mood allows you to accept the tears and frowns that are happening involuntarily with an almost amusing indifference. You smile inwardly and hope that this gesture has not transferred outwardly. There is no mirror to confirm or deny your hope, but you know that you have become a pretty good judge, and your judgement reassures you effectively. Remembering back to the writing of D.H. Lawrence you remember a passage which you once read, which highlighted Lawrence's understanding that certain aspects of the body and mind often as not were working in opposition to one another. It was his belief that these two fundamental and principal components of the body should be taught to harmonise more keenly with one other, in order that each could then function more wholly and successfully. That had seemed so obvious and sensible when you had first read this suggestion, but right now you felt that you were witnessing first-hand the heart if not the very core of this initiative in practice. Mr Lawrence had seen his hypothesis as a keen influence and healthy conjunction with normal living, but right now you seem to be placing these profound rudiments onto a higher pedestal. They were for you a necessity for anchoring yourself to the planet. Without working on these principles, both your mind and your body would be smashed to smithereens. Thinking on you remember the quote more clearly. 'The two conditions of thought and action are mutually exclusive. Yet they should be related in harmony.' What else had Lawrence pointed out? Something to the effect that 'We should act according to our thoughts and think according to our acts. But while we are in thought we cannot really act and while we are in action we cannot really think.' Well, if that was true you had better get practising. Right now, you wanted all your thoughts to be portrayed through your actions. And you wanted all your actions to be seen as harmonising with your thoughts. It was imperative! And despite what Mr Lawrence said in regard to the difficulty and general absence of combining these phenomena, a 'Way' had to be found, before it was too late.

The recurrent trailing thoughts within your head have prevented you from judging the passage of time and it is with little doubt that you realise that the time for sleep is slowly nearing. Your judgements and interpretations of all that is happening, will, you know, be impaired if you do not acquire some rest soon. You feel your eyelids closing heavy against one another, and the intimidating sounds caused by your inhibited hearing, echo in intermittent blasts. Your head is feeling weary, and you are sure that the outward signs of your body must be exhibiting the tell-tale signs which silently announce the arrival of imminent sleep. Sleep the final frontier! The most acceptable place for the non-committal mind;.the place for assured respite - providing nightmares take no precedence. They would not do so tonight! The ambience of tranquillity is a welcoming arm after the exhaustions of the day and by its restful

qualities its most profound comforts will hopefully suck
you into its warmest dreams, where all the pleasures of
illusion will transmit themselves upon the inner lids of your
tired eyes and once more the penetration of the moment will
allow you the presence of mind to believe your thoughts and
nestle relieved in an enlightening embrace.

CHAPTER THIRTY-FOUR

It is a revived fresh youthful figure that crosses the room and walks towards you now. The small glimpse of rays from a hidden sun, streaks its way across the wooden floor and in an accurate straight line it bends and rises up the green painted wall to your left. It stops somewhere but it is hard to say exactly where, and it doesn't seem to matter much. It is merely comforting to witness the presence of an outside force, which this cheerful youth has no immediate control over, although he could of course choose to close the large wooden shutters through which this challenging force has found a means of entry. You hope he doesn't! This single element of the sun's existence within the room somehow makes everything more natural, calm and bound together. A feeling of the tonic, which only the sun can procure, splashes onto your mind like the sprinkling of the morning dew upon the virgin grass and mosses; the beginnings of a new colonisation of positivity. You do not feel invigorated by your half sleepless night, sat precariously in the chair where you began your unceremonious conversation with your new friend, the previous evening. Although un-refreshed, you feel somewhat encouraged by the touch of the sun.

When did you last relieve yourself? Must have been last evening, shock must still be preventing you from feeling an urge to void the contents of your bladder or perhaps you had disgraced yourself? There is no smell, and your rear is so numb that you can't tell if your underclothes are damp.

The youth looks at you with the same piercing eyes as before, but they hold freshness in their stare, which only sleep could have placed there. Somewhere in that faraway look is the lingering essence of detached dreams and the infancy of twisted thoughts metastasising themselves before you. The world is a strange place when reflected in these eyes. Reality is lost in the haziness and confusion of the lurid blue lenses which stare at you, languid as in the absence of a human breath. They mock without movement. They question without sound. They tear across your body, ripping at you with the power and the destruction of a lion's energy. And hungry like the lion they rest on you and laze.

You search around your mutual point of contact and close in on the pointed features of your onlookers' face. A mane of hair sits dark in contrast to the paleness of his face. Small wisps of fringe half covering his right eye. A pale line of freckles trace themselves across the bridge of his nose; gradually tailing off as they rise up upon his cheekbones, like wandering insects, un-camouflaged against their surroundings. Their trail leads around his face introducing other features and pulling them all conveniently into one. - A thin pointed nose heralds itself somewhat off-centre, and a small thin mouth lies in a complimentary position just beneath. The lips occasionally twitch just enough to show a small line of yellowy teeth, which lie at ridiculous angles to one another, but as you often find with peculiarities in features, they have a striking effect, paradoxically drawing your attention towards them, even though you would rather look away. Ears usually do this, but this character's ears are conveniently hidden by his hair, which trails itself like a frame down each side of his face, resting itself in a thick band of heavy curls just at the shoulders, leaving no contrast against his black sweatshirt …. A Marc Bolan, or Noddy Holder, look alike; you can't decide which. But definitely 1970's, he certainly doesn't do much justice to the present decade. He was very much a fashion unto himself. Someone who cares about his appearance but obviously doesn't care what others think. He looks shy, even though he is being scaffolded by his aggression. A 'loner' perhaps. The only thing that seems to typify him as a current day teenager are his jeans; hung splendidly around his waist defining his body's shape and curves in the way that a well-cut dress defines a woman. He was proud. His body knew it and he wanted the world to know it. In his mind he might be shy, but his body had the confidence of a legion.

His mind and body looking equally hardened he begins his dialogue. Possibly trying to pick up the threads of yesterday's conversation, he begins by wishing you....

"Good morning Didi!" A grimacing grin appears across his thin mouth; thick lips never make this gesture; they are genetically inhibited. This mouth does it with ease and determination. - What an early morning welcome.

"How did you sleep?" Not waiting for a reply, he continues. "I trust you have had time to think about your present predicament...? Well, I'm sure you have! .... Is there anything that you would like to share with me now my friend?"

"I have nothing to share. There is nothing *to* share!"

"Oh! Playing it cool are we, well that's fun! You can have as much fun as you like Didi. The both of us, we have all the time in the world to have fun. I ain't going anywhere, and of course neither are you, so we could have fun here for days and days! Couldn't we?"

Slowly his voice begins to alter in its tone, the recent frivolity and coolness is dissipated by a harsher tone which seems to extract itself from another part of this man. A more critical voice; a more manipulative voice; a voice which hungers for the sound of victory and is ready to flatten defeat with one foul swipe of its viper-like tongue. He spits words to you now, as if they were extracted teeth emitting themselves from a cannon-like faucet in the depth of his face. Each word hits upon the target and you jerk backward defensively, but only in reflex.

"So, you want to play hard to get do you...? You want to make life difficult for me......? I have brought you to this water hole but I cannot make you drink! Is that what you're thinking?......Oh come on Didi what do you take me for?.....Some kind of a fool?...I've got you this far, do you really think I'm gonna give up now?.... GET REAL!"

Silence falls for a moment.

"Didi answer my questions won't you...... Can't you see it's the wisest thing to do?"

Through your mind wander the words of the philosopher 'Wisest is he – (or was it she), who knows what they do not know. It may pay you in the light of wiseness, to remain silent after all, but you don't feel too reassured.

"There is no other alternative. You're at the end of the road here. There's only forwards now. Repent and maybe I'll show you some mercy!"

This is so difficult you really do not know what it is that his man wants. Apart from your head on a platter so it would seem. You have done him some injustice, you must have done, maybe last week, maybe many years ago, but your memory cannot stretch to any time or occasion when this man was previously a part of your life. You cannot find any common connection between you both and yet somehow, he has over-ridden your failing memory and successfully caught up with you. What is it that is making him want to get even with you, so badly? Why won't he tell you? And how are you going to gain his confidence and forgiveness if he won't give any clues as to why he thinks you should confess? As you sit allowing yourself to wonder, you experiment a little further with your little coping tactics of the past. Moving your body, albeit restrictedly, in small ritualistic ways. 'FOUR' Your magic number - Three for good measure and one for good luck! You carry on the process with your feet your toes, your hands, fingers even the blinking of your eyes. It is strangely mysterious - you have not done it for so long and now here you are doing it so well as if you have never stopped. You continue to experiment. Has he noticed? Doubtful! - Your movements are too discreet, but if you were to exaggerate them just slightly, would he notice? What would he think? -That you were cracking - maybe. Ha, Ha! – Let him think what he liked!

"I think we'd better visit the little room."

This sudden change of dialogue takes you off guard. Somehow there is a little too much humanity shown in this suggestion. Quite obviously your needy plight is being questioned and examined. And before you have enough time to organise yourself with a reply you feel yourself being hoisted from your seat in an ungainly fashion, and your body wrenched forwards without dignity. You can hardly move your legs; they feel so restless and tired. Your feet awkwardly drag themselves across the uneven wooden floor, once or twice you feel yourself going over onto the side of your foot, and the skin grazes against the tiny splinters woven into the wooden floor. Finally, you reach a small green door, through which you are pushed. Your helping hand accompanies you and assists in manoeuvring your clothing in order that you can accomplish the task of sitting on the lavatory seat. Bliss!

"Now wash your hands!" He gestures towards the sink. "Quickly we must get on with some more talking!"

Not wishing to forestall him in his urgency, you wash your hands; but something is wrong. You glance towards your hands still bound together; they do not feel clean! They look clean, they must be clean and yet they do not FEEL clean.

"Come along! Hurry up now!"

"I am!"

"Quickly!"

"Alright!"

"That will do!" He looks inpatient. "Just stop washing your bloody hands will you!"

"I can't!"

"What do you mean? They're clean for God's sake. - Now come on!"

Tearfully, you feel yourself pulled away and you can feel the drips of water from your hands stinging the grazes on your feet, intermingled with these are the drops from your tears, their saltiness, stinging further.

CHAPTER THIRTY-FIVE

A glass of water is thrust to your lips. You assuage your thirst with its gentle trickle. The coldness and wetness bring an erotic pleasure to your mouth enhanced more so by this feeling's long absence; some twelve hours or more, maybe. The feeling is quenching and refreshing, in a strange way, equal somewhat to the relief which the voiding of urine had achieved some minutes previously. Replenished, you sit back in your familiar chair! Focusing you begin to notice small specks on your clothing, the kind that used to evoke the most uncomfortable and irritating persuasive urges to blow or wipe them away. But your hands are unable to reach these places now. They are physically and unkindly hindered from carrying out their compulsive task. The obsessive thought is there, but physically you have hit a buffer. The desperation in the forcefulness of this urge creates a massive panic within your system. Physiologically you are trapped You can feel your heart rate increasing and your palms begin to sweat, it is hard to tell whether your legs have turned to jelly yet because they have already detached themselves from any previous neurological connection with your mind. These motor and sensory losses depicted a deep melancholic ill harmony between body and mind. Who should we call upon to explain this D.H. Laurence or Drs' Guillain and Barré the pioneering neurologists?

Your eyes begin to blur slightly and slowly the room takes on a new appearance. You feel as if you are floating; not in a pleasant, relaxed way but in the fashion of a wild dream. Suddenly all the distant hidden horrors of the past begin to loom and rear their ugly heads, rushing towards you, they hold you in their stare. Their ugly faces made more intense by your distorted vision. Looking for a means of escape from these images, your eyes look towards the walls beyond. More images of dirt and grime, smudges, smears, the whole room seems alive with the enigma of foul and unpleasant smells; repugnant and putrid, as is the smell of rotting flesh. Everywhere there is a covering of an obscure and unusual emotion which exemplifies an extreme unpleasantness that you cannot see. But in your mind the ultimate question arises as it has done many times in the past. The ultimate question in fact, the one you cannot ignore. Stands erect beside the biggest scenario that any question can impose.....

What If...? What if, everywhere around you have been covered in contaminates? Touched by the dirty hand of some disgusting though possibly innocent passer-by. The 'What if' scenario might seem poorly justified by the rational thinking individual who is able to judge these cases by logical explanation, but for you it is beyond contempt.

There is no deep rooted or flippant remark, which can dissuade you from believing in the intensity of this thought. You are omnipotent without you the whole world must disintegrate into a foul pit, allowing itself to emit its stench across the planet from dawn to dusk; without you to check and clean and rid the world of all its foulness who else will do it? Who else will notice that this contamination exists in the first place? If not, you then surely no one; you had to work hard and fast. As your eyes pace themselves over the increasing number of blemishes and questionable marks, that appear everywhere around you; your eyes cast themselves downwards to a small puddle of water lying in the corner of the room. There were days in the past when puddles of water signified urine, and you would panic. Small damp patches in your handbag where your perfume had spilled, even the smell had not been enough to steer you away from that burning question...

'What If? It was always so intense, always so real and always so unkind yet you had kept on believing it, never, questioning it. Its power was like a tentacle that wrapped itself around you and held you tightly in its grip, whispering edifying words to enhance your beliefs. And so the blind relay race continues with the invisible baton.

Shoes! They were the worst. Always! They had to be. They touched the dirt. They carried the dirt, transporting it from one clean place to another. No wonder they were taboo. They were best not touched; they were best avoided at all costs. Your ploy was the most suitable that you could think of at the time, and it had worked successfully for a number of years. To be on the safe side you had volunteered yourself never to touch the ground. It had seemed like a safe bet, and you believed that it had been your safest guard. No touch - No contamination! - If only it was so. For right now those misplaced germs jumped at you from all sides and angles and somehow your delusions were so huge and vivid you believed them. Despite leaving in your wake hundreds if not thousands of fallen items, that had touched the ground and never been retrieved, you still felt defeated by your principle means of gaining control by avoidance. It was not the answer, but all those years ago you had struggled on, firmly wanting to believe it was. Because at the time it had to be - Yet you were no fool and every day you were reminded that it was failing.

Monsters are not nice and those that scare you most are the ones that touch you. Your fears not only reached out and stroked you, but they also bore down deep into your very soul, and the only way for them to escape seemed to be for them to bore their way suitably back out again.

Painful was their penetration and painful would be their exit.

CHAPTER THIRTY-SIX

As he walks towards you his left hand holds out a small piece of what looks like cake. His palm outstretched he encourages you to take the small morsel that lies within it. Kindly he moves closer to your restricted hands and allows you to remove the delicate crummy wedge from his. Appetising it is not, but you accept it graciously.

You had not thought of hunger but now food is being offered to you, you feel the overwhelming sensation of its presence. Like the first encounter with chocolate where you are presented with the passion and the taste, so that having been shown the open box your whole body just yearns immediately for more and more; until somehow when the box is visibly empty the body is psychologically full. However, you knew that would not be the case here. Your body was now so hungry that it could possibly and urgently fill itself with palmfuls of cake without any consideration for another person equally as famished.

Why so hungry? Your body has quite obviously been drained of its energy by the sheer terror of these last few hours. Your body's sugars have been burnt up like the fuel tanks of a rocket waiting to eject into space; emitting their energy with such a fiery exertion in order to obtain their full momentum. Similar to this you had quite burnt yourself out in the heat of the moment, and now you felt a strong and justified desire to refill those fuel tanks.

The cake tastes rancid and as you masticate it around the inside of your mouth, you notice that it doesn't really have a taste at all. You search the reaction of your taste buds, but they are not helpful. And you conclude that you must justify the eating by the filling of your stomach, no more, no less.

You wonder if there is anything to follow or whether this delicately prepared course is the beginning and the end of your meal. You wait with trepidation. But your wait is long. Just as he pulls his hand out of your reach, a final crumb deposits itself upon the wooden floorboards at your feet. You look longingly at the crumb and the crumb looks back. You can feel that urge to bend down and pick it up. His eyes follow you and you wonder if he can read your mind.

Does he think that you are too fussy to pick this crumb from its resting place? Probably! How can he know any different? Impossible! How can he know that you can no longer touch the ground? - The crumb signifies contamination, dirt, and repulsion. It rallies up all those other unpleasant feelings within you and becomes a trigger to a succession of uncomfortable reactions issuing on the surface with an explosion of panic, stewed together with an urgent wish that you could override this uncomfortable delusion and successfully eat the crumb. But alas the delusion wins, and the situation remains.

He's thinking. You can see his eye movements showing rapid activity as some deep thought process swirls around inside his head. Let him think on! You use the moment as a reprieve; knowing that it is unlikely to last.

Brushing his fringe away from his eyes he clears his throat. "Ah, Hmm …Is there something wrong, Didi?"

"No!"

"Are you sure?"

"Yes!"

"You look afraid. Scared perhaps?"

"Should I be?"

"That depends!" He grins. "If you feel in control of the situation, then I imagine you must feel quite smug by now. But really Didi I don't think you are!" He pauses. "In fact I think you're really quite scared of me."

"What makes you think that?"

"You just look scared, that's all!"

"Well maybe I am quite scared but not of you."

"What then?"

"Life in general I suppose!"

He looks at you in a curious way; pleased that you are showing a degree of trepidation and unease but obviously disappointed that his forcefulness and unpleasantness are not having the desired effect, that he was hoping they would. He stands with his head hung like a child who has just found his best toy broken .... angry, bewildered and frustrated.

"What about that crumb, Didi?" His head gestures towards the loan item on the floor.Maybe he knows. Maybe he understands and just wants to taunt you.

"What about it?"

"Are you going to pick it up Didi? Aren't you hungry anymore?"

"Not really!"

"Oh, go on Didi pick it up, after all you don't know when you might be getting your next meal, do you?"

This is not enough to persuade you, and you know full well it never will be. So convincing is the delusion that your mind is by now firmly convinced that the crumb is contaminated!

"Come on Didi! Beggars can't be choosers and all that."

"I can't!"

"WHY NOT?"

"I just can't!"

"I said, why not!?"

"I can't, I just can't!"

"Oh come on pick the bloody thing up will you, for Christ's sake. Don't try getting clever with me."

"I-I can-t." You feel a murmured hesitation to your voice; - its naturalness suggests that it is not put on.

"Go on - Be a devil!"

"I can't, honestly! I really want to, but I just can't, you wouldn't understand ….. I…."

"You're dead right I don't understand. Christ, what are you some kind of nutcase or something? All I wanted to do was just corner you, sort you out, make you pay for what you'd done, - so to speak. Make you pay and have done with it! That was all, really. I mean bleedin' hell, I didn't need all this. This is doing my head in, I'll tell you. What you tryin' to do, drive me round the bend *with* you? Christ I can't handle this. I don't deserve this."

You watch the beads of sweat building up on the furrows of his brow. The incomprehensible smile has been washed from his face now as the pangs of his inconceivable frustration write themselves in huge unmistaken lettering across the impregnable mask, which has served as his façade.

Where on earth have you found the power and means to break this barrier down?

Had it been as simple as just saying Boo!? Obviously, you had reacted in a way that was foreign to his expectations. He had wanted to 'Break' you with his determined skills of persuasion, manipulation and terrorisation, but where had he failed. His principles to some degree had worked in practice. You had indeed been terrified, washed up in his persuasiveness and had you known the answers to his questions you would have answered straight away. Coward or not you were certainly no fool either, that was a certainty. But somehow it seemed that because you had had no answers that you had laid yourself more vulnerably at the feet of this man, and this it seemed was what he found so difficult to respond to.

You had somehow given him a taste of his own medicine. You had provided some sort of armour for yourself by merely allowing your mind and body to become an easy sacrifice. Surely if this man had had to tear away at you both physically and mentally, he would have found his tactics easier to employ. But somehow you had diffused all the various implementations, which he had planned to use for the occasion. You had not done it meaningfully; it had just happened so naturally. You had endured physical pain, using some kind of mind over matter, and whilst doing so you had in some way successfully outwitted this monster, by using to all intent and purposes a weaker, submissive approach, once again in an un-calculated way.

As your mind continues to ponder, you watch the half-witted physical display of not the man, but the youth who stands gesticulating before you. Yes, he is definitely younger than you had first imagined. Now that you can look at him more closely it is easier to follow his body language. He is not a murderer or a criminal of any kind, but a simple human being, enduring simple human frustrations, whatever they might be. All he wanted was his money. His 'Price' as a compensation for whatever wrongs you had, in his eyes, been seen to perform. - A simple revenge, - that was all he had planned. 'An eye for an eye….A tooth for a tooth!' You wonder how many times he must have heard those words said to him on a Sabbath, as indeed they had been said to you. A biblical healing of hurt put to rights by the testimony of the scriptures. How easy it was to put the world to rights. Who needed political persuasion and internal morals, when we all had the freedom to go to our temples, on our Sabbaths, to justify our evils and our mistakes? - The excuse to wear our best clothes and to trundle in one direction for one day in each week for our entire lives. Sadly, this appears, not to be so.

Not one of us has in common the same attributes or the same detriments as the next person. To no avail can we justify the dissimilarities which exist between us. We recognise the differences as being diverse, and no similarities are seen as exact. We are by our human nature so different, how then, can we ever afford to think in the least like the next man if we have to defend our own ethereal territory; our own mind, our own being, 'Because'.

Like the word 'Excellent', the word 'Because' now takes on an intense meaning, which once again becomes milked down with its own predictable meaninglessness.

'Because', 'Because', Because what?

No man is an Island and so likewise no man can be a confederation. We are alone with our bodies and especially with our minds, whether we are physically alone, or within a crowd.

This prophet, who stands before you, and is so keen to remonstrate, has obviously failed to carry out his Lords' wishes, this day. Somewhere in some heaven, some God has placed justice or at least reprieve, in your court.

You must act wisely.

CHAPTER THIRTY-SEVEN

"Did you hear me Didi?"

Quite obviously you haven't. But the forcefulness of these last few words has returned you to the present with a jolt, and a sudden feeling of discomfort presents itself to you. Your physical position has not evidently changed, but you feel that you have made some ground in these negotiations in a different way. -A stronger way, perhaps, but not the most dignified way. Nevertheless, there has been some form of advancement in the proceedings, if only that there is now a contusion of disagreement and frustration, acknowledged by this present discontent. You feel a need to answer the previously presented question quickly, before tension again increases.

"No!"

"You're impossible Didi. This gives me no other option than to make the call."

You remain none the wiser. What is so important about this call? ... Why is such a fuss being made about phoning someone?... Is he going to shop you? ... turn you in or whatever it is that a 'grass' does when he can yield his power no further.

An urgent curiosity is to some extent aroused in you, and while with some caution you exercise your intrigue, it is nevertheless very evidently there. For a few split seconds, you side with your curiosity to such an extent, that momentarily, you almost forget that you are actually a part of this muddle and mystery. It is as if you are sat within the pages of a book, yearning to pace across the thin white sheets of paper in order to take a glimpse of what is written or drawn on the forthcoming pages. If only it were that simple! But you have no clues; nothing of any suggestion is being offered to you. You feel naked and vulnerable and tragically alone. Has anyone out there, beyond these walls, noticed your absence yet?

Perhaps Ella has arrived to the house early, and has already discovered that your bed has not been slept in. Then you grin mischievously to yourself. Ella would make her own interpretation of this discovery for sure! With her Latin blood she would have deduced her own mental picture of some Don Giovanni type escapade.

No! You could rest assured that Ella would be one of the least likely people to acknowledge your disappearance. To her it would be naturally accepted. And for that reason, Ella would not disclose anything she thought she knew to a soul. Her confidentiality could always be relied upon; though of course you had nothing to hide. No lovers hidden in closets or jealous entrails of some past affair stretched across time or the oceans like some threatening mantle. That was the trouble with your life to some extent, up until now; it held no drama, no shock, no untoward moments. In fact, you had created for yourself a life which conformed to particular patterns and routines, a comfortable existence until conversely, you had been caught, trapped, then questioned and challenged in this foreboding room upon this wretchedly uncomfortable chair!

Well, you had ruled out Ella as a possible hero, in coming to your aide. Perhaps Ken might be a possibility, but of course you wouldn't be expected at the office until Monday morning, that might be another forty-eight hours away. Suddenly the chances of being noticed, or not noticed in this case, prove a little frightening to you. You have no weekend arrangements planned. You had guessed Friday night would be a late one and so you had decided to have a quiet weekend. Well, you had been wrong in that prediction.

You amuse yourself in thinking that the first possible person to notice your absence may well be your nosy neighbour from around the corner. Perhaps these observant people did have a purpose in life after all!

There is a slight air of despondency matched with these thoughts as slowly you begin to realise that there are very few people close to you in your life. You had made it that way. You wanted it that way, but sometimes when the mirror is placed in front of you, you don't always like what you see. It is easier to imagine an image than to accept it at face value. Right now, you feel like that monkey again, who looks behind the mirror, wishing that the person you were staring at were someone else. But you know that that is not really true. You have what you have because you strived for it, and indeed that was the way you had wanted it - and the way you wanted it to continue. Freedom of the heart, the spirit and the soul is more important than any relationship with another human being. As you look purposefully at the man sharing this room with you right now, you realise how much better off you are in limiting your close human contact with others, if only for the sake of these strained and indelible reasons.

"Well, that's it!" With slow and heavily defined footsteps, your captor walks into the next room. A double set of painted wooden doors open enough to allow his exit, and then open a little further forced by the surge of his passage. Through the gap you can just make out the lay-out of the adjacent room. With dark green walls the room seems to be set out in the style of an office, a large oak desk taking centre stage at the far end of the room; piled high with books and papers. It seems unlikely that it is the personal desk of the young person whose 'jean clad' legs now perch themselves across its corner, a thin telephone wire coiling and extending itself across his knees, a receiver held firmly against his left ear.

You hear the dial buttons being pressed, a lengthy number, either a mobile or long distance? - But you might be wrong. A few muffled words exult themselves into the mouthpiece. It is difficult to catch their meaning. It is only when the voice becomes agitated that the words become a little more clearly articulated and intensified.

"Bloody hell! Where is he? … I can't wait that long. Is there another number that I can reach him on?"

Silence for a moment.

"Christ! Look! Perhaps I'm not making myself clear enough here. I'm not a patient person, so don't ask me to exercise my patience here, OK! I need to speak to him - Now! - Not tomorrow or Monday - I want him Yesterday. Am I making myself clear? Great! So, I'll repeat my question. Where can I reach him?"

You realise the change in the voices' tone. The East End drawl that was noticeable on and off earlier has suddenly vanished completely. This man can change his vernacular to suit his mood - and can seemingly sound very convincing by doing so. The voice you hear now could easily pass as that of a city gent, though not an impressive or dignified one in light of his recent strained and abhorrent attitude.

You listen in, as best you can, continually searching for clues, mesmerised still further by the obvious lack of them. The situation just seems to be more bizarre and confusing as time presses on. Evidently no one is going to hold up a card with the right answer on for you to read; providing you with some formula, which you will be able to jot down and retain forever. Something which you may well rely on for future use or indeed as a worthwhile piece of knowledge…No! That really isn't going to happen. This is all down to you to fathom out. There are no guidelines here or helpful hints. Everything is meaningless and hidden; opaque to the point of being non-existent.

However not to be seen to give up too easily, you continue the slow process of gaining more evidence about your case, you have no further clues than the ensuing telephone conversation which is now being conducted in the next room.

"So, what is it you're saying? - That I must join a queue like the other callers? - Blimey! - What do you take me for? ... I've already told you, I'm not a patient man."

For a moment his composure has been dropped. You wonder whether the person on the other end of the line, has paid attention to this. People don't. Everyone gets basic when they are annoyed and agitated. It could well be that you are the only one registering this swing in his mood and what good will it ever do you anyway. The man is losing his patience, what more is there to note? He is an angry man with an axe to grind and right now he is wielding it, in the face of some unknown human being, courtesy of British telecom. You feel a little unsafe and nervous and you hope that you don't appear to be listening in on the conversation for fear of enraging him further. After all, no one likes to be watched when they feel humiliated; you certainly aren't taunting him over what you are seeing and hearing, but you know that you have already set yourself apart from being one of his closest allies. Whilst furthermore, the recent advances in this present situation; have currently made you even more unpopular. You know that you must watch your back; though you are in no position to defend yourself further.

Meanwhile the dislocated telephone conversation continues. It is now becoming evidently a one-sided conversation.

"Fine - So you want me to hold!" A pause "No! That's not a problem. Is it a problem with you?" You note, an increasing defensiveness about your captor. "Yes, I'm holding! What's that?" There is another cautious pause. "No, I don't wish to phone back, I'd much rather hold the line thank you. I can wait, believe me I can wait. Wait! I can wait all day if it takes that long! I want to speak to him. And as far as I can see, unless he's left the bloody planet, there must be some way of getting hold of him."

Because no name has yet been mentioned it is difficult if not impossible to ascertain to whom the pronoun of this conversation is referring.This would be such a vital clue, but alas you are by no means any the wiser. Could this mystery person in some way be connected to stipulating the price that you are worth? Or is this person the one who is in fact expected to pay that price.

This should be interesting. At this moment in time, you could not imagine one person on the Earth who would want to cough up a large sum of money for your release or indeed bail you out of this situation in any shape or form. However, 'wonders' they say, never cease; perhaps at some point in one's history they may even begin!

Once again, your attention leans attentively towards the continuing conversation. You can only guess the replies and statements which are being issued fourth from the other end of the line.

"Yes, I'm still waiting. Yes! What was that?" You hear an excited if not frustrated tapping noise and you imagine the end of a pen or pencil being tapped regimentally on a desktop. No rhythm is distinguishable, just the slow and monotonous sound repeated over and over again. To your ears it is exaggerated and irritating but you are sure that to the person in the next room it is merely a means of passing the seconds - mapping out the slow existence and passage of time.

"Oh, for Christ's sake!" comes the billowing voice from beyond the door. You shudder slightly and a small breeze leaking through the window opposite joins the sun's rays in searching you out, within the hollow room that surrounds you.

"Sometimes I wonder if people like you, speak the same language. Surely, I've made myself perfectly clear! -Now listen! Get me the chap in question, pretty damn quick, because my patience is growing rather thin. Now do you hear me?!" The tapping stops. "Because if you don't, this whole thing will screw up, and I won't be a happy man. There I've given it to you straight. I can't be any fairer than that, now what have you got to say?"

There is silence. You imagine the alarm and confusion that must be ringing in the head of the listener. How would you feel? Frightened? Scared? Or would you be relaxed and think nothing of it - hearing some cheap good for nothing, airing his confidence and impudence? What if that was, what the listener thought? What if they didn't act upon these threats, could they for any reason have understood the seriousness of everything? Perhaps, indeed they couldn't. This could mean a long wait for you, if they were going to continue taking their time over things. Perhaps something would register with them soon and all would be sorted quickly.

"Hello! Hello! Yes, I've got that - Right. So, if I get cut off, I'm to ring this London number … Yes, Good! Yes, I'll continue to hold while you connect me, and no I bloody well don't want to hang-up. THANK YOU!" Seconds tick past. The air of determination in the voice defines without a doubt that there is an alarming frustration borne out of this delay. Patience is non-apparent. Patience is a rude and final word.

The exhaustion of listening is almost indescribable. Your whole mind and body are waiting on the potential outcome of this call. Unbeknown to someone out there, this phone call may bear on the decision of whether you see your way out of this situation, or not, a powerful thought but true. The silence is swallowed up by further conversation.

"Yes! Yes! Y-e-s!"

A moments further delay. As you listen to the quietness, you notice that the room seems to have been eaten up by this silence. It is a hungry, hollow and ill-fated sound, like those lyrics to a song, which had always sounded so ridiculous, when you had listened to them back in the seventies. How did they go? You couldn't remember the words leading up to the significant line, but the memory of that one line had remained with you. You hummed it now in your mind silently to yourself. M-m-m-m- 'Echoes with the sound of silence' Now, you knew exactly what it meant, and how much you wished that you didn't.

You feel ready now to face any consequence as long as the present feeling will be allowed to abate. It was, (and you could only imagine), like being a soldier, during the First World War. Sitting in the trenches waiting for the Germans to advance, waiting for the surge of ammunition fire and worse still, waiting for the grenades to explode. Waiting to have half of your face blasted away, so that finally once and for all you would be comfortably out of it. And be either buried or carted away to be patched up and hopefully be sufficiently mutilated or invalided, so as not to be placed again in the in-human position, of silence.

Your mind wanders and returns to the present in a kaleidoscope of illusionary pictures turning your thoughts from fear to thought again, and again. On the sill under the open window opposite, the small petals of a clematis lie comfortably against the cold stone. Within the petals of one small flower, a busy bee procures his life's repetitive ambition, collecting his endless supply of nectar. The flower is still and without rebuke, she allows nature to take its endearing course within the softness and warmth of her body. The rapture of this moment has been caught by your attentive gaze. Natures' embrace: touching, taking and given in one small moment; a non-conditional exchange, a reciprocal altruism, allowing nature to continue its endearing cycle from one spring to the next, from one season to yet another, so on and so forth. Endless and repetitive, and yet each movement creating a new and different performance spread between the same identifiable and indelible sequence of time. On and on. Forwards, again and again. Over and over. Never slowing never abating, never stopping to check the time. The positive surge of life is moving all around you. Yet you have become an indefinite particle within the existence of all other matter, whether it be breathing or still.

Every murmur of nature now seems to indicate a sensual sense of freedom, beyond your reach. Even the softness of the breeze that draws itself across your ankles like the touch of raw silk natural and new, is no reward for your survival so far, nor is it a helpful promise for tomorrow. The warmth of the sun has gradually begun to deposit its heat within the room, and your arms, still draped in thin linen from the previous evening, now for the first time in some hours, welcome the loss of the previous coolness.

CHAPTER THIRTY-EIGHT

The voice in the other room has now undeniably changed. The distorted and irregular conversation, which was instigated first of all, has now eroded into a very melancholy tone of voice, which intermittently gives way to a pattern of firm staccato words which hold a suggestion of relentless persuasion, determination and periodically a dismal resigned air.

The shadows cast by the sun's light have slowly moved and their new position has caused one long streak to place itself across the toe of your left shoe. This is the closest that this particular shadow has come to you all day and you realise that the day must be drawing well into the afternoon. As your attention reasserts itself to the world beyond the window, you become aware of the absence of sounds beyond the room, other than those performed by the ever-busy performance of nature. The scene is like a camera 'still'. Nothing has happened to cause revelation, or indeed any minutest change to this obscure status quo.

Each occasional chirp from a passing bird; Each tap that the branch of a nearby tree places against the windowpane. Each undressed sound that approaches your ear, offers in turn its welcoming acknowledgement of normality, in a scene procured by chaos and trapped in its own oblivion. The scene stands still. Time moves forward.

The conversation between the caller and the call's receiver continues and is endured at what appears to be more frequent intervals as time progresses. You can only estimate the lapses of time, as your watch was obviously taken or dropped a long while ago.

If only the disappearance of the watch had effected a stationary passage of time, but alas Einstein's theory has not yet been realised.

And so, whether seen or unseen; time ticks on…..And
on……And so on.

PART FOUR

Opening Hearts

CHAPTER THIRTY-NINE

Professor Wayne Burlington sits at his office desk, sipping the contents of a rather hot mug of coffee, his attention following a psychology report that had been handed to him earlier that morning. It is not usual for him to be in the office at this hour on a Saturday; it is only just past nine-thirty; a quiet period of the day. Other members of the office arrive in dribs and drabs, throughout the next eight hours or so, depending on whether they have reports to finish off or preparation for lectures or correspondence to complete, having missed their original Friday night deadlines. Friday night deadlines were seldom met. Some members of the office preferred the tranquillity of a Saturday morning and worked better without the usual manic confusion of a normal weekday. Psychologically they felt better for it, and they were the best to know, after all, being that their combined efforts researched this theory constantly. Mindfulness was the future.

They worked conveniently alongside other research and postgraduates at the London University. Their work closely linked to the research investigations carried out in the many affiliated London units, including University College hospital (UCH) and the Maudsley Psychiatric Hospital. Psychology was becoming a popular choice of degree amongst many of the new entrants to the university, and Wayne Burlington and his team had been kept constantly busy since the last intake of under-graduates had joined the previous September. The lectures, seminars and presentations were daily requirements for these students whose minds begged for new and further information on their chosen subject. Nothing effectively could make them bored or ill determined to continue their studies. They were like hungry suckling youngsters, who required their feed continuously on a daily basis. Satisfaction, competition and successful fuelling of knowledge to a retiring level did not appear to be an option. In some ways it was healthy in other ways it was exhausting, for lecturer and pupil alike; though both continued to survive and indeed thrive.

Wayne was challenging himself with the reviews of two reports, both of which were concerning OCD. He momentarily thought of Didi; then his thoughts returned to the present.

The first case was a young twenty-year old, who had been struck by the illness some thirteen months previously. He was a compulsive hand-washer, and because of the recent intensity of his problem which had evoked constant fears of contamination, he had remained a virtual recluse for the past month. The Community psychiatric nurses from U.C.H. had been responding to his immediate needs, alongside the rest of their team. It was generally hoped that he would not have to be admitted to the psychiatric wing of the hospital. Admissions always seemed to fill the community 'psyche' teams with dread. It was almost a confirmation of their apparent failure. Maintaining and, in some cases, restoring high profile community teamwork was apparently the most important thing on Earth to these dedicated people.

Wayne admired their determination and keenness; but he never viewed any hospital admission as a consequence of failure. You had to understand the importance and indeed the severity of some of these cases, before you could in any way become judgemental of the team themselves and secondly their care or indeed their diagnoses or prognoses. Whilst Wayne had a resolution to always be seen as siding with the patient - they were after all his prime concern; he also had a deep affiliation with the rest of his professional team. Their work would at times have made most people feel humbled. Theirs was often a job which few people would have been keen to take on.

The second report which had come to Wayne's attention that morning was of a similar nature to the first, but this time the subject was a slightly older lady. Wayne felt sure that Didi would be able to help her. The support groups were ideal for people like this. A lady of Forty-two, who had relentlessly struggled through life, despite her chronic OCD, which had shadowed her days and nights, she had managed to lead a relatively normal life, having held down a good job, married and had several children. Wayne admired her for her determination, and the strength and resilience she had shown towards her illness for…

Wayne pulled the paper closer into his field of vision, to confirm what he was reading. There was no mistake … 'Twenty years' … was stated very clearly, on the report in front of him. So why was she seeking help now? … Why not sooner? …He read on. Apparently, some domestic problem had arisen in this woman's life, and as often happens, it was this straw that happened to break the camel's back; or so it appeared. There was only a brief outline of the history surrounding this person, and to Wayne's tactical way of thinking, the domestic problem which had been detailed and outlined quite graphically was indeed quite a simple matter, which for most people would probably have appeared an easy problem to solve. In this patient's case however, it certainly was not.

Wayne directed his eyes across the sheets of paper, which made up the report, before placing them down on the desk in front of him. He felt that he had sufficiently equipped himself with the necessary amount of detail in order to make his own report on the patient and add any subsequent advice or relevant information which might be deemed helpful or necessary for the scheduled Monday morning Seminar.

These seminars were by now routine lectures for the new psychology students. There had been dubious questioning among the undergraduates when the planning of a Monday morning lecture had first been suggested, but the extent of interesting facts and knowledge which these lectures provided had by the end of the first semester, given the event a very positive reputation.

The idea was for each of the psychology lecturers to do a rotation, in which they presented one or two of their immediate cases as a study. Reflecting on the relevant past history, the present psychiatric history, and the current treatments. The progress and prognoses were then carefully catalogued in hope that the case study might be restudied at a later date. This meant any management or subsequent mismanagement could be recognised and recorded and also be witnessed first-hand by the students who so keenly monitored each patient. The piece de la resistance however occurred on the last Monday of each month when one of the senior professor's would take the lectern. It was partially due to the fact that most of their cases were unusual and therefore very interesting, but of course their long-standing practice in the art of lecturing and captivating an audience was by far the more attractive element.

As one student had once described to Professor Wayne in an end of term interview, - 'I don't know what it is you do Sir, nor how it is you do it, but I really do feel as if I've been on a journey through those patients minds.' Professor Wayne was not alone most of his lecturing colleagues could produce performances equally as good as his own; they enjoyed their jobs. In most cases their job was their life, it was hard to visualise any of the university professors actually retiring. Many of them didn't, they couldn't. They just faded into the background and carried on their studies and research in an accepted but unpaid capacity. The knowledge, which they had gained over the years, was almost impossible to perceive. They were talented men and women who dedicated their lives to their research. Some had married, some had children, but it was hard to imagine how they combined these two lives together. Somehow, they were clever enough to do so. And those around them marvelled at their incorrigible resilience.

Wayne was indeed still very much a well-paid member of this professional circle. As he browsed and thought further other his lecture, he knew that he had a clear picture in his mind already, as to how he would present his study on Monday morning. He had decided to use the two cases, which he had been recently observing, as a means of highlighting both the pros and cons of caring for the mentally sick in the community. Some of his contemporaries might question whether these case studies were merely patients with behavioural problems who should not be classed as mentally sick. Wayne hoped that he was not stigmatising these patients by permitting himself to say that any problem north of the 'Foramen Magnum ' should be duly classed as a psychiatric one. Of course, he readily accepted that a tumour of the brain was in no way relative here or indeed alopecia, and he would endeavour to include these observations as a slightly amusing aside to his lecture; whilst remaining sensitive to his subject matter and choosing his moment appropriately.

His lectures were often amusing as well as serious. It helped to cushion the upsetting content of his studies, into a shape or form which might be deemed slightly more tangible.

It was quite obvious that the second case study would be a case for immediate admission. There was no doubt about that in Wayne's mind. There were some patients who reached such a low state of morale that their ways and methods of coping went far beyond the accepted range of normal behaviour. It was in his eyes cruel to let them linger like this. It was by far kinder to allow them the sanctuary of a hospital ward in order that they could be allowed time to readjust their thoughts and be given the therapy they needed. Often these patients were so evidently lacking in sleep and were so ill nourished, that merely providing them with these essential ingredients, was adequate enough to get them back on track. The younger professors often felt that this was highly wrong. Their attitude and reasons suggested that these individuals would be deeply scarred by their hospital experiences and labelled by the stigmatism associated with an admittance, on the grounds of a psychiatric diagnosis. It was the young professors' beliefs that these patients should be held in the community at all costs, whenever possible.

Wayne had seen so many changes in psychiatry in his time. Some made things better others made things a lot worse. It was like many things in life; psychiatry was still in its experimental stage. For Wayne he felt that things were at an evolutionary turn. The work which Didi had been doing with the self-help groups at TOP, showed this. The Psychiatrist who had introduced these new understandings and breakthroughs in the treatment of phobias and OCD cases had caused an unexpected revelation in the use of new treatments, above all else his methods were so simplistic, which in the present world of technological advancement had obviously caused quite a stir. The art of logic, common sense and patience was ideally not as dead as it often appeared to be to the fast-spinning world of today.

He wished it were possible to invite Didi along to Monday's lecture. But alas, as a lay person, there was no facility for a non-graduate to undertake lectures at the university, although it was Wayne's firm belief that DiDi was more than capable and could have probably delivered a performance equal to some of his own contemporaries. However, rules were rules. Maybe there would be a change in the future when this rule would no longer apply; after all they say rules are made to be broken. Wayne smiled to himself. No one was more orthodox than he was! Perhaps at long last he was undergoing some psychological change himself. How frightening!

He began to think about the unpredictability of the human being. No matter how hard we have tried to analyse ourselves and make sense of the mind, someone inevitably comes along and disturbs the results or the conclusions. It was imminent; no matter how sure you were there was indeed always an exception to every rule. The suicidal anecdote was the one that always struck Wayne - When he was in his training, having decided to read psychiatry as his medical option, he remembered at the age of about twenty-seven, feeling that he knew everything that there was to know about the subject, until on one occasion he had been lectured on 'the nature of suicide'. He recalled reading a statement, which included an account stating that 'it was always the quiet ones'. People that jumped up and down, threatening to jump off roofs and slash their wrists were highly unlikely to carry out these threats. In fact, they were not suicidal at all, necessarily' but merely looking for attention.

This was quite possible, but when Wayne had been called to his first suicide, at the age of twenty-eight - A year after he had learnt 'everything that there was to know about this area of psychiatry', he had been unmistakably shocked. The deceased had been a young twenty-year-old, who Wayne had been counselling only two hours previously.

The subject had suffered from manic depression. The young man in question had been in a manic mood that afternoon swearing that he would jump through the ward window if his estranged wife didn't return to him. Unsurprisingly she had left him some weeks previously, unable to cope with the patient's aggressive mood swings. At the time Wayne had given him plenty of attention; the attention that the young man was obviously seeking. He was therefore only markedly surprised when he was alerted by his secretary just a short while later. For when he had first reached the stone concourse at the front of the hospital building, he had not expected to find his young friend sprawled out, in a pool of blood. Having been decapitated on route by the debris of glass created by the window through which he had jumped.

Wayne was always very wary when the word suicide was used. When it was mentioned or even suggested, he would always remain alert to the facts and possibilities, having learnt his lesson the hard way.

CHAPTER FORTY

The shrill ring of the phone wakes Wayne from his reveries. Plucking the receiver from its resting place, he places it against his right ear, and reclines back in his office chair.

"Hello"

"Hello, Wayne?"

"Yes?"

"Oh, thank heavens I've reached you!" The breathless voice of his sister, Colette, sits Wayne upright in his chair in a split second. It took no analyst to recognise the profound traces of worry and concern in her voice.

"Whatever's the matter Colette?"

"Oh Wayne. Someone's trying to get into contact with you, but he's been very impatient, he's already upset Andrew on our switchboard, here. Andrew tried to tell him a number of times that you didn't work at this office. But he just continued to ask for you. He's refused to get off the other line. It was my final hope that I might be able to reach you at the university and thank goodness I have. I really don't know what we would have done otherwise."

"Well don't trouble yourself with that. What's the chaps' name?"

"I've no idea. He doesn't seem to be a very obliging character and so I don't think anybody has actual asked him yet."

"Would it be a good idea, perhaps?"

"Oh Wayne, please don't try to trivialise this. It really does seem quite important, to this man that he speaks to you."

"Of-course!"

"If you wait a moment, I'll just connect you to the other line. Best of luck! Perhaps you'll let me know the outcome of the call later, if you've got time. It all seems a bit unusual if you ask me."

"Yes, sure I'll do that! Now let's have him on the line, shall we?"

A numerous amount of clicks occur as the lines are duly connected. One of which will be Colette cautiously replacing her receiver, in the hope that she has not disconnected the call. Thankfully she hasn't.

"Yes Hello, Professor Burlington here. How can I help you?"

"Hello Professor. Glad to meet you at last. In fact, it's not me who requires your help right now Professor; it is in fact an acquaintance of yours. Someone whom I think you have become quite friendly with recently. A partner in your form of crime so to speak… Let me just say that this person is a thinker like you, someone who thinks they understand the minds of everyone……

"Now just one moment……."

"If you'll just let me finish Professor because what I want you to know is that neither of you can ever read My Mind! and I don't expect you'd truly want to. Let me try to explain. You see sometimes people have peculiar quirks about them, which they know are odd; their definitions are indeed defined in your textbooks – our 'Neurotic' members of society. However, 'I' Professor, befit the alternative member of your society, I am the ever elusive, and essentially sane, Psychotic, by definition of your textbook. I, in theory, don't know or understand my illness; that is to say I do not recognise it. I believe in my delusions and my desires, so you think. But listen to this Professor, I am on a crusade here, and I firmly believe that it is my will, not my delusions, which have placed me in this position."

There is a brief pause as the speaker regains his composure and then hectically continues."This person whom I have here is worth a lot to you I'm sure, but are you willing to pay the price that I've attached to them? Well before you answer that, let's just leave it that we'll wait and see."

He clears his throat before continuing."The only problem is Professor that this being, beside me here, is beginning to get a little frustrating. You see it keeps showing signs of compulsive behaviour. Weird, isn't it? - Well interesting for the likes of you, I'm sure, but for me it's a little different you see, I find all this really irritating. Do you understand what I mean…? Well, it's just that it makes me feel a little out of control myself and I don't like that, at all. So, I'm having difficulty keeping a cap on my emotions here, and I know that this person is shortening my fuse. I don't like it Professor, I don't like it at all, and it's making me feel very uneasy."

"I see!"

"Do you?I'm not sure that you do. This situation is a rather extraordinary one to tell you the truth."

"I'm believing you!"

"Well, you carry on believing me Professor when I tell you that this piece of vermin here deserves all it's getting. I wanted to humiliate and destroy but now the destruction seems a little perverse and unnecessary. But the humiliation, I thought I'd won with that, but now it's 'Me' that feels humiliated, and it's making 'Me' feel bad."

"That's understandable."

"Ahh - Yes understandable, but is it rational?"

"Perhaps?"

"The problem is you see that this person needed a dressing down, after all they've done."

"Would you like to explain?"

"If you're listening?"

"I'm listening!"

"Well firstly there's the persecution."

"Is that your persecution?"

"I'd rather you didn't interrupt. But no, it's my family's persecution that I want to revenge, not mine. The other big issue which really troubles me is why this human being, not only carries out all these cruel incomprehensible acts, but is set on gaining more publicity by becoming a double agent and pretending to understand the minds of others. I think that a revolutionary group is being prepared to intensify and extend the damage that has already begun. These groups are being set up to brainwash people to go out and carry out further attacks. It can't happen, Professor. Do you understand? I must put a stop to it. Unless you back me up, the rest of the world will just think I'm paranoid. But I need you to stand by me here, that is the price that I want you to pay or maybe you will have to live with the fact that your friend here has just signed their suicide note ...!"

The atmosphere becomes increasingly tense as Wayne listens and analyses the words, which he has just heard. It would obviously help to know whose life he is defending he debates whether to ask. There is a 'catch 22' to this scenario. of course. If he believes these acquisitions then this 'friend' may be in jeopardy of imprisonment, and if he refuses, they might die?

His reply must be a serious but simple one. He takes a breath....

"Whom am I defending here the perpetrator or the accused?"

"That's for you to decide. Any other smart questions that you'd like to ask?"

"Only one"

"Go ahead!"

"This person, who are they?"

"I thought you might have already guessed Professor!"

"I wasn't aware that this was a game, sir, I'm trying to be serious."

"So, you really don't have a clue? ...How amazing!" There is a pause, perhaps in order to give Wayne one more final chance at a guess or two, before the voice continues.....

"Whom do you Know Professor who identifies themself by a misleading name so that even their gender is a mystery?"

A sudden dawning engulfs Wayne now and for a second or two he feels completely overwhelmed by a genuine feeling of nausea.

"Who do you know Professor who lives life virtually like a hermit, having extricated themselves from their own family? Who never gets close to anyone, or allows anyone to get close to them?"

Wayne clears his throat ready to speak.

"Surely this mystery person is no mystery to you?"

"No!"

"Davidson's the name on the ticket."

"Yes, I realise who you're talking about."

"So now that we're clear on that, are you prepared to state whether you're with me on this or not?"

"Yes, Yes!…. I mean…No! Let me have some time to think. … This is all a bit of a shock … I don't know what to say."

Wayne thinks quickly, as a spiral of confusing and disorientating thoughts begin to swirl themselves around inside his head.

"Didi…Is Didi safe? Where is Didi?"

"Don't panic Professor. Didi is in safe hands! …the safest hands possible. I am saving the rest of the world from Didi's treacherous undertakings. Believe me Professor we are far more in danger from Didi than Didi is from us. I shall take care of Didi in the best possible way."

"Now hold on there, please! Don't do anything rash, I implore you!"

"Oh, I think that on the contrary it's Didi who's been rash, whatever I do will be seen as understandable retaliation."

"That's a matter of opinion!"

"Maybe so Professor, but I shall prefer to be the better judge. Now I will give you a little time to consider your decision."

The phone goes dead. Wayne replaces the receiver and stares for a moment at the machine. How could such an inert object provide and dictate such news and remain unchanged both emotionally and physically? Perhaps if humans were disguised as machines they would be better placed on this Earth and function more effectively without being distracted or confused by their feelings. As Wayne looks up from his thoughts, he notices that the office clock is showing the time at half-past eleven. Somehow, somewhere someone had stolen hours of Wayne's existence. He still did not know who that person was or indeed his true objectives or reasons for wanting Wayne's attentions. It was hard to believe what he had just heard. He felt certain that he had done the right thing, which was that he had - 'Not confirmed or denied anything', one of the first rules of psychiatry, when working with any kind of delusional or schizophrenic patient. He had effectively played with the unwritten rule, though he wasn't all together sure that he had effectively gained any ground by doing so. He realised that he was nervous too. He had no means of making further contact, all he could do was remain at the office and await another call. There would, he felt sure, be another call; he would just have to remain rooted until it came. Maybe he would have to wait hours - well at least that would give him further time to arrive at his decision - he hoped!

What was there to make of all this? … How had Didi got involved in this scenario? This character must have been watching Didi for weeks! He seemed to know so much about so many things and yet Wayne couldn't help feeling that he had seemingly got the wrong end of the stick or at least put two and two together and unfortunately made six! His delusional mind had overtaken him in this running race, and he was effectively behaving like a loose cannon. But

Wayne could only surmise; nothing at present was clear or concise. It was all just a huge mess. And Wayne really wasn't sure how he was going to mop it all up.

Saturday, Twelve Noon,
The phone on the desk rang. There had been two other business calls during the last half-hour; Wayne had answered them patiently but sparingly, reducing his conversation to the bare minimum. He wanted to keep the line open for that 'all important' call. He had forestalled himself ringing Colette back, although he knew she would be anxious. Finally, it arrived.

"Hello!" Somehow Wayne had forgotten his normal formal tone in addressing his incoming callers. The two former callers, who were regulars and accustomed to their recipient's normal way of answering, had perhaps noted it, but it was doubtful.

"Professor Burlington?"

"Wayne Burlington speaking."

"Good, let us resume shall we - now where did we get to?" Before Wayne can reply the voice continues. "Ah yes! I remember! You were going to give me your decision! I trust you are ready?"

"I have had little time to think. This is difficult for me. I hardly know Ddi; I really feel I can't make a realistic judgement of this without feeling that I knew Didi better. We have only recently been acquainted. We met only last week while I was on a conference. It's hardly as if we're old friends - if you know what I mean. Last night we had a get together, some real old friends and myself, we had invited Didi along because I thought the others would find Didi interesting."

"Oh, Didi's interesting alright professor to the point I am undeniably over- interested, over-confused and definitely over-frustrated. This Didi, this friend, I'm sorry

283

this acquaintance of yours is trying to melt me down. Do you know what I mean Professor?"

"I think so" Internally, he questions his reply; having no clear understanding of what is going on.

"Oh, you can't know Professor. No, you can't it is harrowing beyond belief."

Static comes over the line and the phone held in Wayne's hand goes dead. All he hears is the constant single toned ring, signifying that the line is lost. He holds his breath for a few short seconds and waits, before reluctantly lowering the receiver.

Saturday 6pm
There have been no further calls to Wayne's phone all afternoon. The silence has been death-like.

Finally, it rings! The shrill alarm of its tones jolts Wayne abruptly from his hesitant almost coma-like existence. For the last few hours, he has sat alone, silent, cautiously waiting, wondering. In these lonely few hours, his analysis of the situation has brought him no further to understanding these unfortunate and incomprehensible circumstances, and through some connection that he has formed with his six sense he somehow feels that there is little likely hood of the next phone call helping him, to understand this matter, any better.

He picks up the receiver so certain that it is the caller again.

"Hello! Wayne?"

"Colette?"

"Oh Wayne, I had to ring, I was getting so worried."

"Well thank you!"

"My gut feeling just told me that there was something wrong with this guy who called. He seemed so panicky....so agitated.......so......"

"Colette, you were right to contact me the first time, and I don't mind you calling again, except that I don't really want to keep the line engaged for too long in case he is trying to phone me back."

"I see. Well, what happened after I put him through?

"That Colette is a long story!"

"Too long to explain right now?"

"That's right!"

"I understand."

"Sometimes Sister, you are too understanding! Tell me, what were your first impressions of Didi?"

"Oh, Wayne does this have something to do with Didi….?"

"Colette please don't try to analyse my questions. I don't have time! Your answer is dreadfully important to me."

"Of course! Now let me see. I would say Didi is a well-balanced person, who has gone through a lot of unfortunate psychological trauma in the past. Am I doing alright so far?"

"Please Colette. Carry on."

"Very well. Didi has a seemingly good understanding of the management of people who have undergone similar trauma shown in the mastering work that TOP carries out. Didi is not an expert in the field of psychology, but there is a profound interest there. I wouldn't say it was obsessional. I…. Oh, Wayne I'm sorry I don't think I'm doing very well here."

"Don't worry."

"But you want a broader character outline, don't you?I don't feel I can give you one. Every time I think of Didi I think of what Didi represents, I haven't the foggiest idea what the character below the surface is like."

"Use your imagination, Colette. Just try."

"OK! Quiet but not shy. Self-assured but not arrogant. Well-mannered but not overly so. Well humoured but not trivial. How am I doing…...?"

"Good but carry on."

"Well, I'm running out of compliments."

"Try being more critical, perhaps."

"I'll try! Let me see. It's hard Wayne."

"Don't worry Colette, I don't think I could do any better. In fact, I've been trying for the last few hours, but I just can't make it out."

"You're losing me Wayne."

"I know, I'm sorry. But you have actually helped me in a way. I feel you've reiterated my own feelings."

"Well, I'm glad about that, Wayne. I just wish you didn't have to be so secretive about all this."

"So do I Colette, so do I. Thanks for being so understanding. I better go now, that caller…."

"……Might be trying to get through ... I know"

"Cheerio Colette"

"Yes Wayne. Ring me when you can!"

Wayne replaces the receiver. The clock now shows ten past six.

He watches the slow second hand of the clock moving around the clock face in a mood of trepidation. He wonders how long it will be. What the next call will entail? Whether the next blow will be heavier than the last?

SATURDAY 9pm.

"Hello!" Wayne picks up the phone certain that it had rung, so intent was his need to hear it ring.The line was silent. It was agonising.

"Hello!" He'd done it again. He was glad that he was not being watched. Though so intense was this strange situation that he didn't think that he would have been at all surprised, if somebody did have a pair of binoculars trained on him right now.

"Hello!"

"Hello Professor." Wayne jumps.

"Professor! Are you there?"

"Yes! Yes, I'm here. Wayne could hear the feebleness reflected in his voice. He had not eaten since breakfast, and his mind had been going steadily, since the first phone call this morning - Some twelve hours ago now. He felt restless and irritable and it was difficult not to let it show, but he knew that he had to try. So, he tried very hard. No one was there to tell him how he was doing. All he could do was try to keep up with the caller, which he did his best to do.

"Professor, Didi is not playing the game?"

"I see!"

"But I don't think that you do see professor!"

"I don't?"

"'Professor you have to listen to me."

"I'm listening."

"It's Didi."

"Is Didi all right?"

"Didi is working on me professor. I had this all sorted. All tied up. It was just a simple case of revenge."

"I remember!"

"I wanted to scare Didi; It was retaliation for what Didi had done. That was all. Simple really, or so it seemed, but Didi is breaking me. I need you to back me up professor so we can end this straight away. Do you understand?"

"I do."

"Then will you help me turn Didi in?"

"I don't think that I can. I think there are a lot of misunderstandings here. A lot of grey areas, which are not easily justifiable. A few frantic phone calls are not really enough to sort this situation out, now I must ask you - Do you understand what I am saying?"

"I don't want to listen, professor. I just want to carry out my mission! You are trying to distract me."

"Not distract but make you hthink." Working with what appears to be the upper hand Wayne continues. "What you are doing is irrational. It is easy to jump to conclusions when you are in a confused and vulnerable state. No one is going to harm you if you turn yourself in, providing Didi is safe."

"Didi is safe."

"Of course! And therefore, you have nothing to fear."

"But I almost had Didi professor!"

"Certainly!"

"It was the odd behaviour that did it."

"I'm sure!"

"No, it 'Was' Professor, Didi wouldn't pick things up off the floor. It was frightening. Then there was the repetitive washing. Those hands were getting red raw. The scrubbing backwards and forwards; I had to drag Didi from the sink, kicking and screaming, it was painful. Everything has to be done in an order - it is exhausting - it never stops."

"I understand. Didi has had an illness in the past. I expect the stress of the last few hours has exacerbated the condition. It can be pretty painful to watch if you're unaccustomed to the problem. Now listen, Didi is sick. You must understand that. Let Didi go. This is doing neither of you any good."

"How can I do that?"

"Let's meet - Anywhere you say."

"That would not be wise Professor, let me leave Didi somewhere for you to make the rescue."

"Very well! Name a place."

"Outside 'Jackstraws Castle' in Golders Green."

"That's rather conspicuous, isn't it?"

"Do you want Didi, Professor?"

"Very well. What time?"

"I will leave Didi there in the rear car park at midnight. Give me a few minutes to leave, before you come looking."

"Very well!"

"Goodbye professor, I hope you will think again about taking up my cause and carrying on from where I left off. I was so close to holding Didi, but I realise that you can hold someone physically more easily than you can hold on to their mind. Good luck professor, au revoir."

"Indeed. Goodbye!"

PART FIVE

MINDFUL AWARENESS

CHAPTER FORTY-ONE

You had been pleasantly reassured to see Professor Wayne appear, walking towards you, as he helped you up and began to slowly walk you towards his car, you noticed the face of Colette peering through the open rear window. Her face shared the look of relief that you had seen on the professor's face a few moments earlier. There is silence as you step into the back of the vehicle and try to make yourself comfortable. You are not sure which feels the most uncomfortable your back, your ankles, or your wrists, though the throbbing on the side of your face seems to be delivering its own form of punishment. The blood conveniently dried up has formed a contorted mask down the right-hand side of your face, which pulls excruciatingly every time you try to alter your expression.

"Comfortable?"

You nod to the best of your capabilities.

"Wayne's place, for the night? I'll come too. Add a bit of moral support." Colette smiles. Her face looks different to the first time you watched her, just a week or two ago. She is less aloof and there is a feeling of intense understanding and empathy pouring forth.

You shake your head. Once is enough for your company to register your negative response.

"Very well, your home it is!"

Professor Wayne steps on the accelerator pedal and your journey begins.

Through the dark streets of London, you watch through a hazy head of confusion. A sense of relief and intrigue still attributes itself to you. And it is not until you reach the sanctuary of Kensington, that your emotions suitably lock with the moment, and you feel a tear begin to build in the corner of your eye. A few seconds later you begin to cry.

The parting of companions is soon over, after a gentle hand or two has helped you down the front steps, which seem a lot steeper than usual.

A mindful conversation takes place for a second or two. No questions are asked. No one mentions police, though it is obvious to you that the others are thinking along these lines too. Some situations just don't call for the obvious to happen, and there is not always an explainable reason.

As you shut out the last whispering draft that creeps around the edge of the closing door, your fingers grip the catch for support. Finally with the door closed you stand with your back lent against the solid wood and sigh and then cry a little more.

Then painfully you make your way down into the kitchen to put the kettle on; oblivious of the time it seems the most appropriate thing to do. Grabbing a biscuit from the barrel you retrace your way back up the stairs, clutching that ever-ready glass of wine that you snatched from the fridge as you passed. A strange combination but then who cares.

You make your way to your favourite chair and fall into its welcoming body. The ceiling light is bright at this angle, though, and turning the chair slightly on its castors to avoid the glare, the corner of the previous Sunday's newspaper appears beneath your feet.

Putting down the wine and forcing the last piece of biscuit into your mouth, you brush the crumbs from your fingertips and pick up the paper. It unfolds as you lift it up cautiously to read the headlines.

'English PLO suspect released at Tel Aviv airport.'

And slowly despite the pain of your injuries you begin to flex your facial muscles and with uncertainty you smile. Then as you begin to follow the murmurations of your thoughts, our book closes.

Yet, as you perhaps do, on hearing the final chords of the music play; you return to the beginning in anticipation of hearing the transient notes playing, singing and talking all over again.

THE END ~ *though never forever….*

9 781916 820036